W9-CIE-980

Eblaitica:
Essays on the Ebla Archives and Eblaite Language

Volume 3

Publications of the
Center for Ebla Research at New York University

Eblaitica: Essays on the Ebla Archives and Eblaite Language

Volume 3

Cyrus H. Gordon, EDITOR
Gary A. Rendsburg, ASSOCIATE EDITOR

EISENBRAUNS
WINONA LAKE, INDIANA
1992

Printed in the United States

Library of Congress Cataloging-in-Publication Data

(Revised for vol. 3)

Eblaitica : essays on the Ebla archives and Eblaite language.

(Publications of the Center for Ebla Research at New York University)
Vol. 2– : Cyrus H. Gordon, editor, Gary A. Rendsburg, associate editor.
Includes bibliographical references and indexes.
1. Ebla (Extinct city). 2. Ebla tablets. 3. Eblaite language. I. Gordon, Cyrus Herzl, 1908– . II. Rendsburg, Gary. III. Winter, Nathan H. IV. Series.
DS99.E25E35 1987 939′.4 86-29139
ISBN 0-931464-34-X (v. 1)
ISBN 0-931464-49-8 (v. 2)
ISBN 0-931464-77-3 (v. 3)

The paper used in this publication meets the minimum requirements of the American National Standard for Informaton Sciences—Permanence of Paer for Printed Library Materials, ANSI Z.39.48-1984. ♾

Contents

Abbreviations

AASOR	*Annual of the American Schools of Oriental Research*
AfO	*Archiv für Orientforschung*
AHw	W. von Soden, *Akkadisches Handwörterbuch* (3 vols.; Wiesbaden, 1965–1981)
AIPHOS	*Annuaire de l'Institut de Philologie et d'Histoire Orientales et Slaves*
ARAB	D. D. Luckenbill, *Ancient Records of Assyria and Babylonia*, 2 vols. (Chicago, 1926–27)
ARES	Archivi Reali di Ebla—Studi (Rome)
	1 Alfonso Archi (ed.), *Eblaite Personal Names and Semitic Name-Giving: Papers of a Symposium Held in Rome, July 15–17, 1985*
ARET	Archivi Reali di Ebla—Testi (Rome)
	1 A. Archi, *Testi Amministrativi: Assegnazioni di Tessuti (Archivio L. 2769)* (1985)
	2 D. O. Edzard, *Verwaltungstexte verschiedenen Inhalts aus dem Archiv L. 2769* (1981)
	3 A. Archi and M. G. Biga, *Testi Amministrativi di Vario Contenuto (Archivio L. 2769: TM.75.G.3000–4101)* (1982)
	4 M. G. Biga and L. Milano, *Testi Amministrativi: Assegnazioni di Tessuti (Archivio L. 2769)* (1984)
	5 D. O. Edzard, *Hymnen, Beschwörungen und Verwandtes aus dem Archiv L. 2769* (1984)
	6 A. Archi and P. Fronzaroli, *I Testi Lessicali Bilingui Sumerico-Eblaiti, Parte I: Testo; Parte II: Tavole* (forthcoming)
	7 A. Archi, *Testi Amministrativi: Registrazioni di Mettali e Tessuti (Archivio L. 2769)* (1988)
	8 E. Sollberger, *Administrative Texts Chiefly Concerning Textiles (L. 2752)* (1986)
	9 L. Milano, *Testi Amministrativi: Assegnazioni di Prodotti Alimentari (Archivio L. 2712—Parte I)* (1990)
ARI	A. K. Grayson, *Assyrian Royal Inscriptions*, 2 vols. (Wiesbaden, 1972–76)
ARMT	Archives Royales de Mari—Textes
BA	*Biblical Archaeologist*
BASOR	*Bulletin of the American Schools of Oriental Research*

Bilinguismo	L. Cagni (ed.), *Il Bilinguismo a Ebla* (Naples, 1984)
BIN	Babylonian Inscriptions in the Collection of J. B. Nies
BiOR	*Bibliotheca Orientalis*
CAD	*The Assyrian Dictionary of the Oriental Institute of the University of Chicago* (Chicago, 1956–)
CAH	*Cambridge Ancient History*
Ebla 1975–1985	L. Cagni (ed.), *Ebla 1975–1985* (Naples, 1987)
Eblaitica	C. H. Gordon and G. A. Rendsburg (eds.), *Eblaitica: Essays on the Ebla Archives and Eblaite Language* (Winona Lake, IN), 1: 1987, 2: 1990.
EV	Siglum for "Estratti di Vocabolari" published in MEE 4
JAOS	*Journal of the American Oriental Society*
JCS	*Journal of Cuneiform Studies*
JNES	*Journal of Near Eastern Studies*
KBo	Keilschrifttexte aus Boghazköi
KTU	M. Dietrich, O. Loretz, and J. Sanmartín, *Die keilalphabetischen Texte aus Ugarit* (Alter Orient und Altes Testament 24/1; Kevelaer/Neukirchen-Vluyn, 1976)
KUB	Keilschrifturkunden aus Boghazköi
LAK	A. Deimel, *Die Inschriften von Fara. I: Liste der archäischen Keilschriftzeichen* (Leipzig, 1922)
Lingua	L. Cagni (ed.), *La Lingua di Ebla* (Naples, 1981)
LXX	Septuagint
MAD	Materials for the Assyrian Dictionary
MARI	*Mari—Annales de Recherches Interdisciplinaires*
MDOG	*Mitteilungen der Deutschen Orient-Gesellschaft*
MEE	*Materiali Epigrafici di Ebla (Naples)*
	1 G. Pettinato and A. Alberti, *Catalogo dei Testi Cuneiformi di Tell Mardikh–Ebla* (1979)
	2 G. Pettinato and F. Pomponio, *Testi Amministrativi della Biblioteca L. 2769, Parte I: Testo (1980)*
	2a G. Pettinato, *Testi Amministrativi della Biblioteca L. 2769, Parte I: Tavole* (1981)
	3 G. Pettinato, *Testi Lessicali Monolingui della Biblioteca L. 2769* (1981)
	3a G. Pettinato, *Testi Lessicali Monolingui della Biblioteca L. 2769: Tavole* (1981)
	4 G. Pettinato, E. Arcari, A. Magi-Spinetti, and G. Visicato, *Testi Lessicali Bilingui della Biblioteca L. 2769, Parte I: Traslitterazione dei testi e ricostruzione del VE* (1982)
NABU	*Nouvelles Assyriologiques Brèves et Utilitaires*
OA	*Oriens Antiquus*
OIP	Oriental Institute Publications

Or	*Orientalia*
RA	*Revue d'Assyriologie*
RGTC	Répertoire Géographique des Textes Cunéiformes
RLA	*Reallexikon der Assyriologie*
RS	siglum for texts from Ras Shamra–Ugarit
SAKI	F. Thureau-Dangin, *Die sumerischen und akkadischen-Königsinschriften* (Leipzig, 1907)
SEb	*Studi Eblaiti*
SLE	P. Fronzaroli (ed.), *Studies on the Language of Ebla* (Florence, 1984)
TM	siglum for texts from Tell Mardikh–Ebla
UF	*Ugarit-Forschungen*
UT	C. H. Gordon, *Ugaritic Textbook* (Rome, 1967)
VE	siglum for "Il Vocabolario di Ebla" published in MEE 4
WGE	H. Waetzoldt and H. Hauptmann (eds.), *Wirtschaft und Gesellschaft von Ebla: Akten der Internationalen Tagung Heidelberg 4.–7. November 1986* (Heidelberg, 1988)
ZA	*Zeitschrift für Assyriologie*

INTRODUCTION

A decade has passed since the Center for Ebla Research was established through the generosity of the late David Rose. During those ten years (1982–92) Eblaitology has matured considerably. The fact that Eblaite has important Northwest Semitic features (in addition to the universally recognized East Semitic ones) was not "politically correct" in 1982. By the same token, while Arabic analogues to Eblaite were welcome, Hebrew comparisons were not. In *Eblaitica 1*, it had to be stated that the Center for Ebla Research was not out to prove any special viewpoint but was dedicated to go wherever the sources might lead. In 1992 it is no longer necessary to proclaim or defend the only valid attitude in any rational and honest intellectual pursuit. No scholar need be looked at askance for pointing out a correct or highly plausible Eblaite isogloss in Ethiopic, Arabic, Ugaritic, Aramaic, Hebrew, Phoenician, or Egyptian. Eblaite is Egypto-Semitic and therefore isoglosses may be found in any of the other Egypto-Semitic languages.

The seminars, annual conferences, and publications of the Center have contributed to the progress in, and refinement of, Ebla studies in the ten-year span from 1982 to 1992. It is planned to continue the *Eblaitica* series with contributions from scholars at home and abroad in the interest of advancing our knowledge through essays on the Eblaite language and Ebla archives.

The Center is pleased to present in *Eblaitica 3* an assortment of topics and viewpoints. M. A. Astour's "An Outline of the History of Ebla (Part I)" reflects his command of the history and geography. G. Buccellati's "Ebla and the Amorites" and "The Ebla Electronic Corpus" bring to this series new approaches and new techniques by a member of the official international circle of the Ebla team. W. W. Hallo's "Ebrium at Ebla" is a veteran scholar's analysis of a long-familiar but still challenging problem. C. H. Gordon's "The Ebla Exorcisms" deals with the incantations that shed considerable light on Eblaite linguistics and magic. G. A. Rendsburg's "Eblaite *sa-su-ga-lum* = Hebrew *ss*^{c}*gr*" is an ingenious addition to the evidence for a perceptible degree of linguistic continuity from the third-millennium Ebla archives to the first-millennium literature of the Old Testament.

Cyrus H. Gordon, Director
Center for Ebla Research

An Outline of the History of Ebla (Part 1)

MICHAEL C. ASTOUR

1. Ebla and Third Millennium Northern Syria

Until the discovery of the Ebla archives, northern Syria of the third millennium was virtually a *terra incognita* for the historian. The country has been inhabited since the emergence of modern man; it was one of the regions where the first transition from food-gathering to food-production took place; it is studded with numerous mounds of ancient cities and towns, many of which originated far back in the Neolithic Age; and the ceramic sequence of those mounds that had been excavated or surveyed has been established and synchronized with precision—but the ruins remained mute. While Sumer, followed by Egypt, developed writing around the turn from the fourth to the third millennium, no inscriptions prior to the second quarter of the second millennium were found in any of the north Syrian archeological sites.[1] It looked as though the inhabitants of northern Syria remained illiterate that long. Extraneous information on the region was very scarce for the early period of its history. The earliest mention of the name (and nothing else) of a north Syrian city—which happened to be Ebla—came in a copy of an inscription of Sargon of Akkad (2267–2212).[2] References

Author's note: The chronological system followed in this paper—as in all of my publications—is that of low chronology for Mesopotamia, northern Syria, and Anatolia, and that of "Memphite" chronology for Egypt. My reasons for these options are expounded in the relevant sections of my 1989 book. Since all the events referred to in this paper took place before the conventional year of the birth of Christ, the indication "B.C." has been omitted in all dates. As do Gelb 1977: 16–17, Gelb 1981: 11, Sollberger 1980: 132, and introduction to ARET 8:1, I use "Eblaic" for the language of the Ebla texts, rather than "Eblaite" which sounds well enough in Italian but is a "tongue-twister" (Sollberger) in English. As an adjective for "pertaining to Ebla" in general, I use "Eblean" (cf. "Aramaic" and "Aramean").

[1] Only in 1968 was an inscribed torso of a statue, dated to the beginning of the second millennium, unearthed at Tell Mardikh. It will be considered in §9 below.

[2] Hirsch 1963: 37–39, text Sargon b 2; a poorly preserved copy of the same inscription appears in the same work on pp. 49–50, Sargon b 13. The dates for Sargon have been established by dead reckoning of the figures transmitted in the Sumerian King List (published by Jacobsen 1939, from the last year of the Third Dynasty of Ur which, by synchronisms with the dynasties of Isin and Larsa and of these dynasties with the First Dynasty of Babylon, falls to 1940 (low chronology). (Dates for year 1 of Sargon as arrived at by fifteen scholars have been presented by Boese 1982: 33.) Hallo's proposal (in his article "Gutium," *RLA* 3:714–15, and 1971: 67 fig. 12) to reduce the interval between the dynasties of Akkad and Ur III by assuming that the last kings of

to northern Syria by some of the subsequent south Mesopotamian rulers of the third millennium (Naram-Sin and Gudea) added little to the knowledge of the region's onomastica. In these conditions, any speculation on the remote past of northern Syria could be given credence. One of them, which went back to the turn of the present century, when practically the only documentation on north Syrian toponymy came from Thutmose III's Naharina List, asserted that the place-names of the region were non-Semitic and proved that it was originally, and until relatively late times, inhabited by a population of unknown linguistic affiliation. According to the leading advocate of this theory, I. J. Gelb, the first Semites appeared in northern Syria in the beginning of the second millennium.[3] J. Bottéro, musing about the absence from Sargonic and Ur III records of "one or other of those great and ancient Syrian cities such as Carchemish, Aleppo, or Damascus," ventured as "a fragile hypothesis" the possibility that they may have been concealed by some other names.[4]

The situation changed drastically with the discovery in 1974–1976 of the vast royal archives of Ebla which were recorded in the Early Bronze IVA period and antedated the end of the third millennium by some three centuries.[5] Not only was highly developed cuneiform literacy attested for northern Syria over five hundred years before the earliest previously known evidence of its existence,[6] but the tablets were inscribed in a Semitic language, albeit with a great many Sumerograms. The newly revealed Semitic language (Eblaic), known to us, in the first place, from the non-Sumerian-written words in the tablets and from the Sumero-Eblaic vocabularies,[7] was found to be most closely related to Akkadian and Amorite.[8] E. Sollberger (and, it seems, some other Assyriologists) "would

---

Akkad (after Šar-kali-šarri) ruled concurrently with those of the IV–V Dynasties of Uruk, has not been taken into account because of the agreement between the sum of the duration of the last kings of Akkad and those of Uruk up to, and including, the first year of Utuḫegal (seventy years), and the duration of the contemporaneous "dynasty" of the Gutians from Elulumeš (identified with Elulu, a pretender to the throne of Akkad, by Jacobsen 1939: 207–8) to the defeat of the last Gutian ruler, Tiriqan, in the first year of Utuḫegal.

[3] Gelb 1961 and 1962. I objected to this theory in 1978: 448–51 and 1977a: 124–25, both written before the discovery of the Ebla archives, and examined it in more detail in connection with the toponymy of the Ebla texts in 1988a: 552–55. Gelb 1981: 65–66 retracted, in view of the Ebla evidence, his assertion that there were no Semites in northern Syria before 2000, but continued to claim that the toponymy of the region, including that of the Ebla sources, was non-Semitic.

[4] Bottéro 1965: 561. He added, however, that "our records, not necessarily complete even in their own day, have come down to us only as minute scraps; each new find may amplify them and add to our knowledge of the physical and political geography of ancient Syria," which is exactly what happened.

[5] The chronological position of the period of the Ebla archives will be considered in §7 (planned for part 2 of this article).

[6] Correspondence with the kingdom of Yamḫad in the royal archives of Mari (late eighteenth–early seventeenth century).

[7] Published by G. Pettinato and his collaborators as MEE 4. A fuller edition of the bilingual lexical texts is being prepared by A. Archi and P. Fronzaroli as ARET 6.

[8] Gelb 1977: 25; Gelb 1981: 47.

suggest that it *is* Akkadian."[9] If this were the case, the language of the Ebla texts might be considered a foreign language, adopted by the scribal elite along with the cuneiform script, as this happened indeed with Akkadian in the following millennium among several non-Akkadian and even non-Semitic societies, and the native speech of Early Bronze northern Syria would still remain unknown. But Eblaic, though close to Akkadian, is not identical with it in its grammar and vocabulary, and Sollberger himself recognized that "there is, of course, no denying the existence of West-Semitic elements in Eblaic, but so are there in the Akkadian of Mari and Amarna, but no one, to my knowledge, has ever thought of calling these 'dialects' West-Semitic."[10] From the point of view of linguistics, one may debate whether Eblaic was a separate Semitic language,[11] or Akkadian influenced by West Semitic,[12] or "the Semitic lingua franca used in the cuneiform world during the middle of the Early Bronze Age . . . the mixture of Semitic dialects written by the scribes of Ebla in the twenty-third century."[13] But what matters from the perspective of ethnohistory is the evidence of an indigenous Semitic language, or at least substratum, already in the Early Bronze Age northern Syria.

It follows from the extraordinarily abundant anthroponymy of the Ebla texts[14] that Ebla was not a Semitic enclave in a sea of non-Semitic speech. A. Archi has collected the names of individuals pertaining, according to the Ebla texts, to seventeen cities which were widely spread over northern Syria and the adjacent part of northern Mesopotamia.[15] They all display a common onomastic pattern, many of them recur in several cities, and they are Semitic. No Hurrian names have been found in the Ebla texts. As for the alleged pre-Semitic names of undetermined affiliation, Gelb stated that the onomastics of Ebla comprised "a relatively small number of non-Semitic names,"[16] but he did

[9] Sollberger, introduction to ARET 8:1. Gelb 1981: 52 noted that "some Assyriologists still entertain . . . that Eblaic is not only most closely related to Old Akkadian but that it is a dialect of Old Akkadian," but as for him, he repeated his statement of 1977: 26: "Eblaic cannot be considered an Akkadian dialect simply because an Ebla text reads like nothing comparable in the vast areas of the Ancient Near East where Akkadian writing and language were used."

[10] Sollberger, introduction to ARET 8:1.

[11] As Gelb in his aforementioned studies (but see n. 13 below), von Soden 1981, Archi 1987a, and most other authors on the subject.

[12] Sollberger (see n. 9 above).

[13] Gordon 1987: 3. Significantly, Gelb 1987: 50 (his last, unfinished and posthumously published study) avowed: "To me, personally, one of the most nagging questions is the language and the ultimate origin of the incantations and of the monolingual and bilingual vocabularies, which, while composed and written at Ebla, contain a mixture of features, some uniquely Eblaite, some definitely of foreign, Kishite origin."

[14] It is the subject of the comprehensive study by Krebernik 1988b and of the papers at the Rome symposium, July 1985, published as ARES 1.

[15] Archi 1984b. On the linguistic homogeneousness of Eblean anthroponymy see also Krebernik 1988a: 59–60.

[16] Gelb 1981: 65.

not adduce one single example of such names. He intended to include in his last work a section (§4.8) entitled "Non-Semitic Elements in Ebla Names," but as the editor of the paper, M. Civil, noted, "Sections 4.6–4.8 were blank in the ms. and no materials for them were found."[17] D. O. Edzard, in his search for likely " 'candidates' for non-Semitic PNs" at Ebla, singled out two groups of names "which we are not able, 'without hardship' [*ohne Not*], to explain as Semitic, particularly such names which we can arrange into a series with a specific ending."[18] He chose, first, twenty names (actually sixteen, the other four being insignificant variants) which all end in *-g-* with different preceding and/or following vowels. I have already written, and adduced pertaining comparative material, about the danger of mechanically classifying proper names according to their endings.[19] Edzard correctly recognized that most personal names of this group have full or close correspondences in the considerably longer list of Eblean toponyms with the same ending,[20] and that many of these names, both personal and geographical, are also found without the ending *-g-*. But so strong is the aprioric belief that the ending *-ig* (*vel sim.*) is non-Semitic, and so are, *ipso facto*, the names so suffixed, that no attention was given to their stems.[21] If, however, these names (minus the suffix) are examined without prejudice, a considerable number of them turn out to have good Semitic etymologies; and for the rest of them one must remember that each Semitic language has a number of lexemes without cognates in other languages of the Semitic family, which is especially true for Eblaic, a very early and poorly understood entity. How many Eblaic words in lexical texts and incantations have actually been identified by

[17] *Ap.* Gelb 1987: 65.

[18] Edzard 1988: 29.

[19] Astour 1988a: 552–53 and nn. 67–68. Edzard himself admitted 1988: 29 n. 16 that one of them, *Da-mi-gu*, may be Semitic Dam(i)qu 'the good one'. In four more PNs of Edzard's series (*ʾA$_x$-a-mi-gu*, *A-zi-gu*, *U-mi-gu*, *Zi-ri-ig/gu*) the final *-g-* is probably the third radical Q of the Semitic roots of these names (respectively *ʿmq*, *ʿzq*, *wmq*, and *zrq*).

[20] He counted forty-six such toponyms in sixty-three writings; their actual number is somewhat larger. He noted that he could not find a toponymic homologue for *Ḫu-ba-ri-gu/ga*; but cf. *Ḫu-bar*-NI in ARET 8:538 §8 (not yet published at the time of the Rome symposium), and ^{uru}*Ḫu-bar-mu-u*[*l*]*-li*, apparently near Ursu, in a stray Middle Bronze Syrian tablet published by Wiseman 1953: 108. There is nothing non-Semitic in this name. The Sumero-Eblaic vocabulary has the entry VE 175: KA-dim-dim = *ḫu-ba-ra-*[*um*], *ḫu-ba-lum*, *ḫu-ba-ra*. By comparison with VE 1125 and 1126, as interpreted by Civil 1984: 88, the Sumerian vocable in VE 175 should be ascribed the meaning of 'to complain loudly, to shout', which agrees, for its Eblaic counterpart, with Akkadian *ḫabāru* 'to be noisy'. This may be a plausible etymology for a personal name, but the related toponym is preferably to be derived from ^{dug}*ḫu-bar*, the term for a vessel in ritual texts from Emar (373:18 *et passim*, 458:3′, 462:34′), published by Arnaud 1986, which is a cognate of Akkadian *ḫubūru* 'vat for beer'.

[21] See, e.g., Hecker 1981: 169: "A whole series of [Eblean] place-names evoke a rather un-Semitic impression, as, e.g., those in *-ig*(*u*)"; or Krebernik 1988b: 4: "One finds, besides, names of uncertain origin and such ones that, with some certainty, are neither Sumerian nor Semitic; thus *la-ḫa*-NE-*ig* probably belongs to the same linguistic stratum as the numerous place-names that are characterized by the final morpheme /-ik/." Krebernik's example is discussed later in this paragraph.

their investigators?[22] Within the framework of this study, only one example of a personal name in *-ig* can be considered—the very same *La-ḫa-*NE*-ig* which Krebernik (1988b: 4; see n. 21) thought typical for the assumed non-Sumerian and non-Semitic linguistic stratum and Edzard included in his first group of non-Semitic names. However we read the third sign, the resulting name is Semitic. If it is given its prevailing value at Ebla, *bí*, the name *Laḫabig* should be derived from Eblaic *la-ḫa-bù* which, in VE 1052, translates gá-nu$_{11}$^{mušen}; this word of the very peculiar Sumerian of Ebla is, fortunately, quite intelligible and later served as the ideogram for Akkadian *lurmu* 'ostrich'.[23] If it is read *ne*, *Laḫanig* may be connected with Akkadian *laḫan(n)u* 'bottle' (*CAD*) or 'drinking cup' (*AHw*), written *la-ḫa* in Eblaic and used as a measure of liquids.[24] Since the formative *-ig(u/a)* is found attached to Semitic stems and is attested in Semitic-speaking areas far beyond northern Syria, it should be considered Semitic; and it remains a very productive formative in Arabic lexics, toponymy, and ethnonymy.[25]

Edzard's other group of "candidates for non-Semitic PNs" at Ebla is built on a less formal and more subjective basis than the first. He included in it "such names that display four or more consonants but, even by a possible division into two components, stubbornly evade an interpretation in Semitic."[26] This is exemplified by a selection of seven particularly difficult names. But even in those, the morphological structure and one or both components of each are recognizably Semitic and in some cases specifically Eblaic.[27] Even if some future meticulous scrutiny of Eblean personal names should discover among them a few that

[22] Krebernik 1982/83 (part 2); Fronzaroli 1984a; Fronzaroli 1984b; Edzard, ARET 5; and this despite a very broad leeway in the choice of homophones and in assuming omitted phonemes.

[23] In VE 1370 *la-ḫa-bù* translates buru$_4$^{mušen} 'raven'. These entries have not been considered by Fronzaroli and Krebernik.

[24] Names of vessels are often used as toponyms but very seldom, if at all, as personal names. No place-name corresponding to *La-ḫa-*NE*-ig* has so far appeared in published Ebla texts.

[25] See on it Astour 1988a: 553–54. Arabic topographic terms such as *samāriǧ* 'even or plain tracts of land', *ṣarāhiǧ* 'deep rock crevasses', or *šamrūǧ* 'mountain top' belong to the same pattern as the Eblean toponyms *Ša-ma-du-gú*^{ki}, *Ša-na-ru*$_{12}$*-gú*^{ki}, or *Ša-ra-bí-ig-gú*^{ki}.

[26] Edzard 1988: 33. When, as a young student in Charles Virolleaud's Ugaritic seminar in the mid-1930s, I once used the then-fashionable term *Asianic*, the teacher remarked: "When scholars do not understand a word, they call it Asianic."

[27] Because of the importance of the problem for the ethnohistory of northern Syria, I shall present here a brief analysis of Edzard's seven names. (1) *A-za-ḫa-*ḪAR*-da* and (2) *A-za-ḫa-ma-li-da* (ARET 3 has *A-za-ḫa-li-ma-da*): the element *azaḫa-* may correspond to Akk. *ezēḫu* 'to gird'; cf. PN *A-za-ḫi* (ARET 3). For ḪAR*-da*, cf. PN ḪAR*-da-Ma-lik* (ARET 3). If *-ma-li-da/tá*: *malītu* 'fullness'; if *-li-ma-da/tá*: cf. *Li-ma-du/tù*^{ki} (ARET 3) which, in turn, may have been derived from Ebl. *li-ma* 'bowl', a loanword from Sumerian; see Civil 1987: 154 no. 75. Several PNs, at Ebla and elsewhere, are composed with GNs. (3) *Da-ḫa-la-su-*NI: see VE 522 su-du$_7$ = *da-ḫa-lum*; since su-du$_7$ = Akk. *šuklulu* 'perfect', Ebl. *daḫalum* can be supposed to have a similar meaning (cf. also Arab. *daḫala* 'to be an intimate friend', *daḫḫāla* 'protection granted by request'); *-su-ni* (with the genitival ending of the name as a whole) is *-su-nu* 'their' (m.); see Fronzaroli 1982: 96 §1.1.2); cf. Akk. PNs *Bel*(EN)*-šu-nu*, ^{f}*Be-lit-su-nu*, and *A-ḫu-ši-na*. (4) *Ḫu-wa-sa-ra-du* (misprinted *Ḫa-* in Edzard 1988: 33; cf. ARET 3 and Archi 1984b: 245): *ḫu-wa-* is also found, at Ebla, in

are conspicuously non-Semitic and non-Sumerian, there would be no reason to attribute them to a hypothetical "proto-population" of northern Syria rather than to visitors or migrants from some non-Semitic-speaking region. Moreover, the Eblean onomasticon is not of recent date with regard to the age of the archives. A list of ancestors of the Eblean royal house (which will be discussed in §4 below) includes nineteen names—that is, no doubt, nineteen generations—of rulers who preceded Igriš-Ḫalam, the earliest king mentioned in the administrative texts. All of these names are of the same type as the onomasticon recorded in the archival tablets. Even if one assumes the average length of a generation as only twenty years, the list extends the duration of the Semitic dynasty of Ebla by almost four centuries into the past.

The testimony of the Eblean toponymy is equally instructive. The suspicion that some of the "great and ancient Syrian cities" of the second millennium bore different names back in the third,[28] proved to be unfounded. The archives of Ebla revealed a northern Syrian toponymy that was not much different from that of the records of later centuries. To list only the cities that in the second or first millennium, at one time or another, were royal capitals, one already finds in the Ebla archives the following names:[29] Abatu, Agagališ (Igagališ), Alalaḫu, Aštatu, Bargaʾu (Barga), Baṭinu (Biṭin), Dunanab(u), Ebla, Gargamiš, Ḫalam

---

Ḫu-wa-na-i-um^{ki}; cf. perhaps Ugaritic *ḫu-wa-ú* (or *ḫu-wu-ú*) in the quadrilingual vocabulary, corresponding to Sum. KAR, Akk. *eṭēru* 'to spare, to protect' (Nougayrol 1968: 273 no. 183), which is close to Arab. Bedouin *ḫūwah* 'protection tax paid by a weaker settlement or tribe to a stronger tribe', cf. *ḫawi* 'a companion protecting the traveler from his own fellow tribesmen' (see Hitti 1968: 25; Musil 1928: 59–60, 440). *Sa/ša-ra-tù*, in this and other PNs (on which see the next name), has been recognized by Archi 1984b: 235 as *šarrātu* (here probably a divine epithet). (5) *Lu-wa-ša-ša-du*: *ša-ša-du/tù* is one of the many unexplained Eblaic words, but the first element, *lu-wa-*, is a component of the PNs *Lu-wa-sa-ra-tù*, var. *Lu-ša-ra-tù*, and *Lu-a-Ma-lik* (see Archi 1984b: 235, 250); moreover, see VE 1439 nu-uš = *lu-wu-um*, *a-wu-um*, and EV 0315 nu-uš = *lu-wu-um*, which Krebernik 1982/83: 45 and Civil 1984: 85 explained as the precative particle *lu* provided with a noun ending. (6) *Maš-ga-ša-du*: compare, for the first component, the PNs *Ma-ša-gu*, *Maš-gú-tù* (ARET 8) and the GN *Maš-ga-tù*^{ki} (ARET 8, etc.), most probably from Akk. and W. Sem. *mašqû* 'who gives to drink, watering place', as tentatively proposed by Krebernik 1988b: 97; the second component appears in the GNs *Ša-du-ḫa-lum*^{ki}/*Ša-da-ḫu-lum*^{ki}, *Ša-du-gu-lum*^{ki}, *Ša-da*$_{5}^{ki}$, and in the PNs *Ša-du*, *Sa-du*, and is probably the Akk. *šadû(m)* 'mountain', as envisaged for the latter name by Krebernik 1988b: 105. (7) *Zu-ḫu-wa-ti* has nothing unusual about it; it belongs to the same pattern as the Eblean PNs *A-lu-wa-tù* (cf. *A-lu-a*), *A-la-lu-wa-tù* (cf. *A-la-lu*), *Ga-du-wa-tù* (cf. *Ga-du-um* and the Neo-Assyrian GN ^{uru}*Ga-du-a-ta-a* in northwest Mesopotamia), or the Ebla GNs *Mu-a-tù*^{ki}/*Ma-wa-tù*^{ki}, *Lu*$_{(5)}$*-a-tum*^{ki}, *Ma-nu-wa-at/tù*^{ki} (identical with the Amorite PN *Manuwatum* which Gelb 1980: 25 derived from *mnw* 'to count', 'to love', and which is cognate to Arabic *munuwwat* 'vow, desire' and *manwat* 'object of desire'), and, on the eastern edge of northern Mesopotamia, the GN *Sá-du-a-tim/ti-im* (Old Assyrian), *Sa-an-du-wa-tim*^{ki} (Mari). For the element *zuḫu-*, of undetermined meaning, cf. the Eblean PNs *Zu-ḫu-tù*, *Zu-ḫa-an*, and the second-millennium name of the country *Su-ḫu-um*^{ki}/*Su-ḫi*^{ki} in the purely Semitic region of the lower Middle Euphrates.

[28] See n. 4 above.

[29] They are cited here, for the sake of brevity, in normalized forms, and their second-millennium versions are adduced, in parentheses, only if they present substantial differences.

(Ḫalab),[30] Ḫaran(u), Imar, Iritu, Kulan (Kulanni), Neya/Neʾaʾu (Neya/Niya/Niʾi),[31] Qaṭanu, Ṭub (Ṭuba), Tunepu? (Tunip),[32] Tutulu, Ukulzat, Ursaʾum (Ursu/Uršu). Scores of other Eblean place-names recur in second-millennium records relating to northern Syria, though many do not—in part because of the incompleteness of the documentation, in part because of replacement of some old names by new Hurrian ones, or simply as a result of the archeologically attested decline of the number of inhabited sites compared with the Early Bronze Age. But by and large, one observes a considerable toponymic continuity in northern Syria. And since toponymy is much more conservative than anthroponymy, its linguistic picture provided by the Ebla texts is of great historical importance. With the exception of a limited number of place-names of Sumerian origin (most of them derived from words that had already been adopted into the Semitic speech of the region), the toponymy of Ebla is Semitic—etymologically for intelligible names, at least structurally for those that remain obscure. This means that the cities and towns of the Ebla Empire had borne their names for centuries before they were recorded, probably since their very foundations,

[30] The equation of Ḫalam, the principal shrine city of ᵈʾÀ-da (Haddu), with Ḫalab (Aleppo), which played the same role in the second millennium and later, was proposed by W. von Soden in 1981 (see Astour 1988b: n. 50) and advanced in print in von Soden 1987: 84 and 86 n. 44. Von Soden derived both forms from a presumable **Ḫalamb*. I prefer to see here a case of the very frequent interchange *m/b* in Semitic languages and in Eblaic transcriptions of Sumerian words and names.

[31] This place-name is spelled NE-NIᵏⁱ (ARET 2), in which both signs are polyvalent, and probably also NE-*a-ù*ᵏⁱ (MEE 1, ARET 3), which can be read *Ne/Bí/Pi₅-a-ù*ᵏⁱ. If, nevertheless, I venture the identification of the place so named with the well-known ancient city which is generally, and in my opinion correctly, located at Qalᶜat el-Muḍīq (the citadel of classical Apamea), it is because the excavations of the latter site have disclosed there the remains of an important settlement going back to the Late Chalcolithic Age and populated during the successive phases of Early Bronze, including the time of Ebla IIB1; see Voûte 1972: 94 (after the information of the director of the excavations, J.-C. Balty); Courtois 1973: 69–70; Balty 1981: 18 and bibliography; on the reason why Middle and Late Bronze levels had not yet been excavated see Balty 1972: 63 and n. 8. Moreover, in VE 1155, eden-gi 'plain of reeds' is translated into Eblaic by NE-NI-*um*, which corresponds to NE-NIᵏⁱ and agrees to perfection with the location of Qalᶜat el-Muḍīq overlooking the (recently drained) extensive marshes of el-Ġāb.

[32] This toponym, spelled DU-NE-BÙᵏⁱ, has so far been signaled in only one Ebla text, TM.76.G.222, in the formula quoted by Pettinato, MEE 1:6434, as ᵈ*R*[*a-sa*]*-ap Tu-ne-pù*ᵏⁱ. In this transliteration, the name is close enough to that of Tunip, a major Late Bronze Age city in central Syria which I proposed to identify with the citadel mound of Hama; see Astour 1977b. That important archeological site was inhabited at the time of Ebla IIB1 and may be expected to appear in the Ebla texts, though DU-NE-BÙᵏⁱ can also be read *Du-bí-bù*ᵏⁱ or *Tù-bí-bù*ᵏⁱ. There is also a toponym, rather frequently mentioned in the Ebla texts, which was originally read *Du-bí-tum*ᵏⁱ by all their editors but then changed to *Tù-ne-ép*ᵏⁱ by Pettinato 1979a: 281, followed, nine years later, by Archi in ARET 7. The use of TUM for *íb/éb* in final position at Ebla is dubious; the town is predominantly mentioned in the context of northeastern places. If its name is read *Tù-ne-tum*ᵏⁱ (cf. ᵈ*Ra-sa*⟨*-ap*⟩ *Du*-NI-*tum*ᵏⁱ in ARET 7:10 §8 compared with ᵈ*Ra-sa-ap Du*-NE-*tum*ᵏⁱ in TM.75.G.11045, cited in MEE 1:4985), it reminds one of ᵘʳᵘ*Tu-ni-it*ᵏⁱ in Alalah Tablet 77:4 (level VII). The reasons for distinguishing the Eblean *ʾÀ-ma-at/tù*ᵏⁱ from *ʾÀ-ma*ᵏⁱ and both of them from Hama have been expounded in Astour 1988b: 141 n. 23; see also n. 281 below.

which for some of them went far back into the Chalcolithic and Neolithic Ages. It is a strong argument in favor of viewing the Semites of northern Syria—along with those of the rest of greater Syro-Palestine—as natives, and not intruders, of the region.[33] Thus the Ebla texts not only illuminate their own period but also throw light deep into prehistory.

2. *The Name and the Site of Ebla*

Even before the city of Ebla was discovered at Tell Mardīḫ, the correct pronunciation of its name was an object of controversy. A. Goetze stated that "we should read Ebla and not Ibla; the name is—except by Gudea—spelled with *ib* (i.e., *eb*) and not with '*íb*' (i.e., *ib*)." This distinction in vocalization between the two homophones was unfounded; but his other argument was more to the point: "The unpublished text Bo 409 offers ^{URU}*E-eb-la-a*."[34] I. J. Gelb, conversely, always wrote *Ibla* and, in 1977, affirmed: "I read *Ib-la*^{ki} (and Ibla), and do not feel obliged to transliterate the name as *Eb-la*^{ki} (and Ebla) in conformance with the spelling ^{URU}*E-eb-la-a-pa* which occurs a thousand years later. . . . Furthermore, there is no evidence whether the name should be read *Ib-la*^{ki} (or *Eb-la*^{ki}) with *b*, rather than *Ip-la*^{ki} (or *Ep-la*^{ki}), with *p*."[35] He reiterated a few years later: "In my original article, I wrote 'Ibla' (not 'Ebla'). . . . I have changed the spelling to Ebla in this article not out of persuasion but in deference to the precept that *nec Hercules contra plures*."[36] Gelb was seconded by R. Biggs who spoke of "the name of a city called Ebla—or Ibla—we do not know for sure which it is, or even if we should have a 'p' rather than a 'b',"[37] and E. Sollberger: "There is no shred of evidence for the reading *eb-* of the sign IB. On the contrary, everything points to the reading *ib-*."[38] But is it really so?

Concerning the vowel of the sign, one should not disparage lightly the testimony of the Hurrian spelling in KUB 45 84:15. The same spelling recurs repeatedly in both the Hurrian and the Hittite versions of the much-older bilingual narrative with which I shall deal in §9 below.[39] It is true that the Hurrian ver-

[33] The problems outlined in this paragraph have been discussed in somewhat greater detail in Astour 1988a.

[34] Goetze 1953: 103 n. 1. For the then-unpublished Hurrian text Boğazköy Tablet 409 he referred to A. Ungnad, *Subartu* 1936: 51 n. 2; it has since been published as KUB 45 84. The name in question is actually written there ^{uru}*E-eb-la-a-pa* (line 15), with the Hurrian suffix of dative.

[35] Gelb 1977: 5.

[36] Gelb 1981: 10.

[37] Biggs 1982: 13.

[38] Sollberger, introduction to ARET 8:1.

[39] The narrative, inscribed on six tablets in various states of preservation, is scheduled to be published in KBo 32; its contents are known so far from communications by Otten and Neu, which will be referred to in the relevant notes to §9. Otten speaks of "frequent mentions of ^{URU}*E-eb-la*(-)," and quotes in particular ^{URU}*E-eb-la-am* [KBo 32 11 i 99 (Hurrian) and ^{URU}*E-eb-la-um-na-aš* (Hittite ethnic) KBo 32 16 ii 13.

sion has once *I-ib-la-pa*,[40] but we should be guided by the conclusion reached by E. A. Speiser: "It may be stated as a general rule that [Hurrian] writing with *i* does not preclude the reading *e* whereas even an occasional use of *e* eliminates the reading *i*."[41] Not only in Hurrian or Hittite, but in a juridical text from Emar as well, one finds the spelling LÚ *E-eb-la*.[42] In Thutmose III's Naharina List, no. 306, the name is written *ᵓE-b-rə*, in which the initial group is a very rare one, found again only in Ramesses III's Medinet Habu List, no. 24, *ᵓE-mə-rə* (Emar), and, in the slight graphic variant *ᵓé*, in the Naharina List, no. 192, *ᵓÉ-⌜mə́⌝-[rə?]* (probably Emar), and no. 225, *ᵓÉ-nu* (perhaps Eblean *I-nu*ᵏⁱ/*A-nu*ᵏⁱ).[43] If Hurrians, Hittites, Emariotes, and Egyptians took pains to emphasize that the opening vowel of *Ebla* had to be read /e/, why should we ignore it?[44] As for the closing labial of the sign, the Egyptian transcription of the name is decisive. Egyptian group writing strictly distinguished /b/ and /p/, and since the name is written with *-b-*, its reading is ascertained as /Ebla/ and not /Epla/.[45]

As for the linguistic affiliation of the name *Ebla*, those scholars who dealt with it concurred in seeing it as West Semitic, though they differed in their proposals of its etymology and semantics, none of which is fully convincing.[46] The situation is complicated by the early presence of the very same place-name in two areas far removed from Syria and from each other. One of these, in the

[40] KBo 32 15 iv 7.

[41] Speiser 1941: 21, with the remark in n. 34: "For the same orthographic principle in Hittite cf. Sturtevant, HG 51."

[42] Arnaud 1986: no. 254:1.

[43] Cf. the relevant entries of those lists in W. M. Müller 1906: pls. 44–53 and 64–74, or Simons 1937: lists 1 and 27. My notation of the group writing in the latter list is given in Astour 1968: 751.

[44] Gelb's objection to reading *Eb-la*, quoted above, implied that the spelling ᵘʳᵘ*E-eb-la-a-pa* was late. Fronzaroli 1977: 151–53 hinted at the writing *I-ma-ar*ᵏⁱ in earlier texts and ᵘʳᵘ*E-ma-ar/mar* in later ones as a parallel to the vocalic shift from an earlier *Ibla* to a later *Ebla*. But the analogy with *Imar/Emar* is misleading. The difference in denoting the opening vowel of that name was graphemic and not phonemic. It was written *Ì-mar*ᵏⁱ at Ebla because no personal or geographical name began there with the sign E (which was extremely rare at Ebla outside of Sumerian lexical texts). The Mariote scribes and, a few decades later, the scribe of AT 456 (Alalaḫ VII), followed the traditional spelling *I-ma-ar*ᵏⁱ, but other Old Babylonian scribes, including those of Alalaḫ VII, wrote the name with an initial E, which reflected the actual pronunciation. The same may be assumed for *Ebla*.

[45] Another piece of evidence in the same direction may be provided by the Ugaritic PN *Ibln*, if one could be certain that it—and the similar Amorite *Ib-la-nu-um*—signify indeed 'the man of Ibla', as thought by Buccellati 1966: 135.

[46] J. Lewy 1951: 371 n. 45: a variant of *ᵓābēl* in ancient Palestinian place-names (the vocable is variously explained as 'watercourse' or 'meadow'); taken up by Isserlin 1956: 83. Goetze 1959: 201: related to Amorite personal names beginning with *ibl-*, *ibil-*, *yabil-*, from *ybl* (*wbl*) 'to bring'. Fronzaroli 1977: 158–65: related to Arabic *ᵓablaᶜ* 'a strip of white rocks' (this etymology, without elaboration, is assumed by Matthiae 1981: 220). However, Fronzaroli's principal toponymic parallel, Mount Ebal (*ᶜÊbāl*) at Sichem, does not convince: as evidenced by the Septuagint transcription, *Gaibal*, the name began with an etymological ġayin, which would not have been omitted in Eblaic writing.

Transtigris north of Mount Ebiḫ (Ǧebel Ḥamrīn), is attested in all periods from the Sargonic to the Neo-Assyrian and, because of its importance for the understanding of a crucial episode in the history of its north Syrian namesake, will be considered in §7. From the point of view of comparative toponymy, there is nothing exceptional in this duplication; in fact, a significant number of Eblean place-names have their exact or very close correspondences in the Transtigris.[47] It is more difficult to explain the other recurrence of the name.[48] A Sargonic text mentions gú-Eb-la^{ki} 'shore of Ebla',[49] and two Ur III tablets from Umma refer to i$_7$-Eb-la^{ki} 'the canal of Ebla': one, from year 5 of Amar-Sin, lists a worker (guruš) of ^{d}Nè-iri$_{11}$-gal i$_7$-Eb-la^{ki}, that is, of the shrine of Nergal (at) the canal of Ebla;[50] the other, from year 4 of Šu-Sin, deals with the delivery of thirteen date palms of i$_7$$^{!}$-Eb-la^{ki}.[51] According to Sauren, the canal was located in the province of Umma and led to the shrine of Ebla.[52] Ancient Mesopotamian canals whose nominal elements were written with the determinative ki derived their names from cities or towns located on their banks. The hydronym i$_7$-Eb-la^{ki} presupposes thus the existence of a settlement called Ebla in southern Sumer as early as the Sargonic period. How are we to explain this homonymy? Should we assume that *Ebla* was originally a Sumerian place-name (of uncertain etymology, as many city names of Sumer) and was transferred, through early Sumerian colonial and cultural expansion, to both the Transtigris and northern Syria?[53] A different, and perhaps simpler, hypothesis may also be proposed. Naram-Sin listed Ebla among the cities and regions he conquered, and added that people of these places were made to "carry the basket of his god ^{d}*A-ba$_4$*,"[54] that is, they were used at forced labor, no doubt in the heartland of Naram-Sin's

[47] This phenomenon and its possible historical background require a special paper. At the beginning of Eblean studies, it caused much confusion in reconstructing the international connections of Ebla and, in particular, the arena of military operations between Ebla and Mari, as presented in the relevant sections of Astour 1987: 7–14 (written in 1983). Similar misplacements of Eblean localities were committed by Pettinato 1979a and 1981; Fronzaroli 1980: 48–49; Saporetti 1981; Archi 1985b: 63.

[48] The alleged "tower of Ebla," built near Babylon in year 27 of Samulael (Edzard 1957: 124 and n. 177), is now read AN.ZA.GÀR.UR.ZÍR (*RGTC* 3:18), or An.za.kàr.ur.KU (*CAD* D 145), in which UR.KU can be transliterated UR.GI$_7$ = *kalbu* 'dog', as Kraus 1972: no. 264:6′.

[49] *RGTC* 1:211, with reference to Nikolskij 1915: no. 10:3.

[50] Schneider 1931: no. 88-285-286; *RGTC* 2:260.

[51] Sollberger 1965: 26; *RGTC* 2:260. The readings erín-Ib-la^{ki} in Schneider 1930: no. 32:5 and tir-íd-Ib-la^{ki} no. 382: 35–37 (indexes, pp. 5 and 28) are not confirmed by his own hand copies and have not been included in *RGTC* 2. BIN 3 491:32, which Pettinato (*RLA* 5:10) read d[am!]-gàr eb-la^{ki} and linked it with Syrian Ebla, and Owen and Veenker 1987: 278 read lú$^{!}$-gú$^{!}$-eb-la^{ki} and identified it with "Gu-Ebla in Sumer," should probably be read lú$^{!}$-Dur$^{!}$-Eb-la^{ki}, as in Kang's indexes to BIN 3:23 and 34, and *RGTC* 2:35, a town in the Transtigris.

[52] Sauren 1966: 24 n. 98, 107.

[53] Astour 1988a: 551. Of the other three north Syrian toponyms with doubles in Sumer adduced there, only Apišal can be retained. *Aš-da-ba$_4$*^{ki} and *A-u$_9$-ru$_{12}$*^{ki}, as transliterated in MEE 1 no. 1661, are actually written *Lá-da-ba$_4$*^{ki} and ⌜*Ba*⌝-*u$_9$-ru$_{12}$*^{ki} according to the publication of the text in ARET 7 94.

[54] Hirsch 1963 Naram-Sin b 5; Sollberger and Kupper 1971: IIA4e.

empire. He also stated in the same inscription that Nergal opened for him the path to the conquered areas. The Ebla in the province of Umma, with its shrine of Nergal, could well have been a settlement of Naram-Sin's deportees from the distant city of Ebla.[55] Though the scarce records of the Sargonic period provide no other example of such a practice, one finds an exact parallel to this supposed case in a historical inscription of Šu-Sin,[56] in which that king boasts, among other things, of having defeated the city of Simanum (in the far north of the Transtigris),[57] settled its people, as his war booty (n a m - r a -a š - a g - n i) on the border of Nippur, and built for them a town called Simanum.[58]

Turning now to the site of Tell Mardīḫ, there is nothing in its geographical position that would have predestined it to become, and remain for a few centuries, the dominating city of northern Syria. True, it is a very impressive archeological object: its circumvallation encloses an area of 56 hectares, slightly larger than that of Mari (54 hectares) and exceeded in Ciseuphratean Syria by only three Bronze Age sites: Mišrifeh-Qaṭna (100 hectares), Tell en-Nabī Mend-Qidši (75 hectares), and ᶜAšarneh (60 hectares).[59] But Ebla did not reach this size until the period of its archives, almost a thousand years after its modest beginning.[60] It was claimed that Ebla "was located at the intersection of important trade routes."[61] This is true for Ḫalab, Ebla's successor as the hegemonic city of northern Syria, but not for Ebla which stood on only one road, the north–south artery of inner Syria. Because of Ebla's location between the marshes of el-Maṭḫ and the massif of Ǧebel Zāwiyeh, the intersections of that artery with other major roads took place many miles north and south of the city. It was a long way from Ebla to the Mediterranean Sea, the Euphrates, the cedar forests of Mount Amanus, the silver mines of Mount Taurus, the fertile Plain of Antioch and Quweiq Valley. Ebla stood in a treeless plain of mediocre soil, without a river, perennial stream, or springs—water had to be drawn from wells.[62] The principal asset of the area around and south of Ebla was sheep-breeding and textile industry based on the wool of the extensive flocks.[63] But only after the rulers of Ebla

[55] Which of the two Eblas known to us it was will be considered in §7 below.

[56] Published and commented upon by Civil 1967.

[57] On its probable location see Astour 1987: 42–47.

[58] Quoted inscription, IV:24–V:23. The deportees from Simanum in the area of Nippur appear in several judicial and economic tablets of the Ur III period, summarized with references by Civil 1967: 36 and Gelb 1973: 76–77.

[59] Figures according to van Liere 1963: 136 and map; Weiss 1983: 49.

[60] Matthiae 1981: 53.

[61] Prospectus of *WGE*; also Pinnock 1988: 110 on Ebla "being founded on an important crossroads of routes carrying to Mesopotamia timber from the Syrian coast, and probably silver, and other metals, from the Anatolian plateau." In point of fact, timber from the north Syrian mountains was transported by the shortest land route to the Euphrates and then floated down the river, while silver, gold, and copper from Sophene and Anatolia were brought to Mesopotamia, since the Uruk period, by the road Malatya—Diyarbakir—Tell Brak—Tigris River, later used by the Old Assyrian merchants.

[62] Cf. de Maigret 1978: 83–85; de Maigret 1981; 1984.

[63] Cf. Gelb 1986.

succeeded in gaining control over the grain and cattle of the northern plains, the olive groves and vineyards of the hills, the timber of the mountains, an extraordinarily abundant labor force,[64] and the Euphrates road to the southeast, did the accumulation of wealth in Ebla transform it into the capital of a vast, composite empire. We do not know what events brought about it, but we may recall that the elevations of Paris to the capital of France and of Berlin to that of the German Empire were due not to their geographical positions but to interplays of largely accidental factors of dynastic, political, and military character.

3. The Beginnings of Ebla

Compared with several other ancient cities of northern Syria whose roots reach deep into the Neolithic Age, Ebla is not a very old site. A surface survey of the mounds of the el-Maṭḫ basin found that the earliest pottery there was chaff-faced simple ware, characteristic of ᶜAmuq phase F, which is generally attributed to the period between 3500 and 3000; and even that pottery was present at ten sites only, in the immediate vicinity of the lagoon, and not comprising Tell Mardīḫ.[65] Of course, conclusions drawn from collecting surface sherds are only approximate, and pottery absent from the slopes of the mound may be discovered, by soundings or excavations, deep inside it. This is what happened at Tell Mardīḫ: diggings at the Acropolis did not reach the bedrock, but those in sector B of the Lower City, directly southwest of the Acropolis, did find sherds of chaff-faced simple ware immediately over the rock.[66] This added Tell Mardīḫ to the earliest settlements of the region but did not lower their chronology. Apparently, the colonization of that agriculturally marginal region started relatively late. Perhaps it was stimulated by a growth of population in some better-endowed areas of northern Syria, or by a significant increase of foreign demand for the commodity which the region could best produce—wool.

The latter possibility appears the more plausible of the two in the light of the revolutionary changes in international relations that were taking place in the second half of the fourth millennium. These five hundred years comprise, in southern Mesopotamia, the Early, Middle, and Late Uruk periods and the first half of the Jamdat Nasr period.[67] It was at that time that the Sumerian civilization achieved its full and characteristic expression—when the population of Sumer coalesced around a number of urban centers, when it developed the government system of city-states, deviced a peculiar architecture for its ever larger and taller temples, created a many-faceted representational and applied art, and

[64] Cf. Archi 1988c.

[65] De Maigret 1978: 86–87 and fig. 10. On phase F of the ᶜAmuq sequence cf. Braidwood and Braidwood 1960: 256-58, 513-16; Watson 1965: 73-75. Porada 1965: 176 dated the end of ᶜAmuq F at 3200.

[66] Matthiae 1981: 52.

[67] Certain authors combine Middle and Late Uruk with Jamdat Nasr as the Protoliterate period. On that terminology, see Mallowan 1970: 327–30.

invented a system of writing. The blossoming economy of Sumer now needed more raw materials than ever, all of which, except clay and reed, had to be imported. While Sumer had not been isolated from surrounding countries before the start of the Uruk period, it now reached out vigorously in all directions and established not just trading posts but actual colonies along the principle supply routes.[68] These are identified by massive use of distinctive Uruk pottery and, in several cases, by architecture and urban layout. One line of Sumerian expansion led eastward to Elam, with Susa as a colonial settlement, and northeastward to Media, where the archeological site of Godin played the same role and was possibly founded as a transshipment point of lapis lazuli.[69] Another route led northward to Assyria, where Sumerian colonies of the Uruk Age were established at Nineveh and Tepe Gawra,[70] and to Arbelitis, where such a colony was unearthed at Tell Qalinğ Aġa, a mile south of the great citadel mound of Irbil.[71] A third route led northwestward from the Tigris to Sophene and Melitene and is marked by Urukian colonies at Grai Reš near the southeastern corner of the Sinğar massif,[72] Tell Brak, a major center at the confluence of the Ğaġğaġ with the Ḫabur,[73] Norşuntepe and Tepecik in the Elaziğ province of Turkey (classical Sophene),[74] and the autonomous but Uruk-influenced level VIA settlement at Arslantepe near Malatya.[75] The purpose of this road (which anticipated one of the two principal Old Assyrian roads to Cappadocia) was to provide Sumer with the copper of Ergani-Maden, the gold of the placers near Harput, and the silver of Keban. The fourth line of Urukian colonial penetration is the one that has a direct relation to the topic of this study, but it seems advisable to present it within its historical context.

It led up the Euphrates to northern Syria and connected Sumer, in the first place, with a group of Urukian settlements above the river's great bend, which were excavated as part of the salvage project in the area destined to be flooded by the construction of the Ṭabqa Dam.[76] There were three of them, clustered closely together along the right bank of the Euphrates. Unlike the Uruk levels in

[68] General characteristics of the Uruk/Protoliterate period are given in Frankfort 1951: 52–61; Porada 1965: 158; Roux 1980: 75–85.

[69] Weiss and Young 1975: 14–15; Lambert-Karlovsky 1978: 114–15.

[70] On these sites, and a survey of Uruk period expansion in general, see in the last place Algaze 1986.

[71] Reported by Abu Al-Soof 1966 and 1969 and Abu Al-Soof and Es-Siwwani 1967. Brief summary in Roux 1980: 79; Abu Al-Soof's article in *Sumer* 29 (1973), referred to in Roux 1980: 407 n. 9, does not deal with Tell Qalinğ Aġa.

[72] Lloyd 1938: 140; Porada 1965: 176–77; Mallowan 1970: 404–6.

[73] Mallowan 1947: 1–87; Mallowan 1970: 408–9; Porada 1965: 157–58; Oates 1977: esp. 234–36; Oates 1982: esp. 196; Oates 1983; Oates 1985; Fielden 1981.

[74] Burney 1980: esp. 159.

[75] Palmieri 1981; Mellink 1985: 553; Mellink 1989: 113.

[76] A general survey of the archeological sites of the salvage area was presented by van Loon 1967. Of the numerous reports on excavations of the individual sites, only those pertaining to the three objects discussed in this section will be referred to.

older cities such as Tell Brak, these three sites were built on virgin soil by colonizers from Urukian Age Sumer.[77] The first, coming from the south, was the city formed by the two separately excavated mounds, Ḥabūbah South and Tell Qannās.[78] It stretched for a kilometer along the floodplain and covered an area of eighteen hectares. Six kilometers farther north stood the smaller but still significant site of Tell el-Ḥağğ.[79] High over the Euphrates Valley, on a spur of the Ğebel ᶜArūḍah, four kilometers north-northwest of Tell el-Ḥağğ, rose a complex of temples and houses for their personnel.[80] The inhabitants of Ḥabūbah South–Tell Qannās did not farm for themselves, their city was purely commercial. It is easy to see the reason for its foundation: it stood in the spot where the Euphrates flows closest to the southern part of the Amanus Range, so much valued and praised in ancient times for its forests of cedars and other conifers. The terrain between the mountain and the river is largely even, with a few easy grades, and suitable for transportation of heavy logs. The city's role as the eastern terminal of the Amanus–Euphrates road is confirmed by the discovery of two Uruk-influenced sites along it. One is Tell Abū Danneh, on the present-day highway from Aleppo to the Euphrates, twenty-eight kilometers from Aleppo.[81] In its level VII, Uruk pottery coexists with local ware, which indicates that people of Uruk culture settled there among a native population.[82] The other is Tell Tabara el-Akrad in the ᶜAmuq, two kilometers east of Açana-Alalaḫ.[83] In its levels VI and V there appears a pottery that "shows affinities with,"[84] or "is closely related to,"[85] the Uruk and Jamdat Nasr pottery. The interesting thing is that no such pottery has been found in other excavated mounds of the ᶜAmuq, as though an intrusive element had influenced just this town. It was located near the point where the road from Aleppo and the Euphrates bifurcated, one branch leading, as now, to the mouth of the Orontes, and the other (now only a trail, but much used in ancient and even early modern times) to the Fırnız Pass of the Amanus.[86] It is possible that the name of the southern part of the Amanus, adja-

[77] This point was made by Oates 1982: 196.

[78] Ḥabūbah South, together with Ḥabūbah Kabīrah, was excavated by a German mission, and Tell Qannās by a Belgian one. The results of the exploration were summarized by both directors: Strommenger 1979, 1980; and Finet 1975, 1978, and 1979.

[79] Excavated by a Swiss mission for only two seasons. The results of the second campaign, which reached the bottom level of the mound, were summarized by Stucky 1973.

[80] Excavated by a Dutch mission. See van Driel 1980, 1983; van Driel and van Driel-Murray 1979, 1983.

[81] Excavated by a Belgian mission. See Tefnin 1980.

[82] Algaze 1986: 131 compared this situation with that at contemporary Tepe Gawra.

[83] Excavated within the framework of the British archeological work in the ᶜAmuq. See Hood 1951.

[84] Hood 1951: 119, 127, 132.

[85] Woolley 1953: 35.

[86] I have reasons to believe that this pass and the road leading to (or from) it were used by Ḫattušiliš I in his destructive raid on Alalaḫ VII, by the army of Cyrus the Younger in 401, and that Alexander the Great intended to use them in 333 when the Persian advance forced him to turn northward to Issus.

cent to the ᶜAmuq, which was written KUR *A-dil-úr* and KUR *Di-il-ur* in the Babylonian Lipšur Litanies,[87] was derived from d i - l u - u r, the Sumerian reading of the ideogram MÁ+MUG 'mast' (pointing to trees fit to be made into masts),[88] and that it went back to the time when Sumerians first gained access to its timber.

The new archeological finds also clarify the circumstances of the most spectacular facet of the Sumerian cultural expansion during the Late Uruk and Jamdat Nasr periods, namely the sudden appearance in late Predynastic Egypt of a whole array of Sumerian artistic and technical features, including cylinder seals, brick-making, buildings with recesses and salients, locally made images of Gilgamesh-like figures, fantastic animals, south Mesopotamian boats, and the stimulus diffusion of writing, all of which gave a powerful boost to the hitherto slow development of Egyptian civilization. H. Frankfort, who presented a fine synthesis of the problem,[89] wondered by what way this influence had reached Egypt. Not from the north, he thought, for "in Syria we do not find signs that native culture was deeply affected by contact with Sumer." Even though he admitted that "this may be due to the incompleteness of our evidence," he preferred to hypothesize a sea route from the Persian Gulf to the Red Sea around South Arabia.[90] Nowadays, when Sumerian presence in northern Syria during the Uruk period has been archeologically established, it is understandable that they were able to use the timber of the coastal range for building seaworthy ships on the Mediterranean.

Urukian settlements on the Euphrates have been discovered far upstream from Ḥabūbah South–Tell Qannās and its neighbors. At Carchemish, a pottery similar to the Uruk ware of Sumer suddenly and completely replaced the earlier Chalcolithic material.[91] Şadi Tepe, some eight kilometers north of Carchemish, was found to be full of Uruk pottery and baked clay cones; this "expands significantly our evidence for the activities of Sumerian colonists along the Upper Euphrates in late fourth millennium B.C."[92] Much farther upstream, deep soundings in the great mound of Samsat revealed Lake Uruk pottery in great quantity and diversity.[93] Upstream from Samsat, on the left bank, another Late Uruk settlement was uncovered at Hassek Hüyük,[94] which appears to have served as the bridgehead of a road toward the mining district of Ergani-Maden and Altin Ova. Tell Ḫuwayra, between the headwaters of the Balīḫ and the Ḫabūr, is shown by

[87] Reiner 1956: 132–33, nos. 10 and 12, probably doublets.

[88] Elsewhere (in ḪAR.RA = *ḫubullu* XXII:8′, and in Hittite and Neo-Assyrian records) it is written *Adal(l)ur* or *Atal(l)ur*. Cf. The Eblean phonetic transcriptions of Sumerian d i l i - r u as d a - l i - r u$_{12}$-w u in the bilingual lexical texts VE 228, EV 055, 0161, and the Eblean toponym *Da-lu-rí*^{ki} ARET 8:541 §23.

[89] Frankfort 1951: 121–37.

[90] Frankfort 1951: 136–37.

[91] Woolley in *Carchemish* 3:236.

[92] Algaze 1989a: 7–8; Algaze 1989b: 255.

[93] Mellink 1988: 110; Mellink 1989: 113–14.

[94] Behm-Blancke 1988; Mellink 1988: 101; Mellink 1989: 115.

its pottery[95] to have been a Late Urukian station on the highway from the Ḫabūr Triangle to the Euphrates bend.

Around 3000 the Sumerian establishments in northern Syria ceased to exist. The temple complex at Ǧebel ᶜArūḍah was destroyed by fire. Tell el-Ḥaǧǧ was totally abandoned.[96] The occupation of Ḥabūbah South–Tell Qannās suddenly stopped without any material traces of violence, as though the inhabitants of the city had mounted boats or keleks and floated down to their old country. At Tell Tabara el-Akrad, the Uruk-Jamdat Nasr pottery abruptly ended with its level V and was replaced in level IV with the entirely different Ḫirbet Kerak pottery, which appeared in the ᶜAmuq sites of phase H and elsewhere in Syria.[97] We do not know what caused the end of Sumerian presence in northern Syria, but its timing explains why the Sumero-Egyptian contact was disrupted at the time of Narmer's accession. But if this brief and precarious connection across the eastern Mediterranean made such an impact on Egypt, one can well imagine how much greater was the legacy of the Uruk civilization in northern Syria.

This brings us back to Ebla. The city arose during, or on the eve, of the greatest penetration of northern Syria by Sumerians. Should we guess, as did Matthiae, that Ebla was founded, or developed soon after, by Sumerian colonists who were attracted to the area by the marshes of el-Maṭḫ, which reminded them of the swamps of their native country?[98] Such an assumption can be substantiated only by the presence of a significant quantity of Uruk pottery at the site, and so far none has been found. But Ebla could hardly remain unaffected by the dynamic Sumerian civilization, especially if our hunch about Ebla's export of wool to Sumer as early as the Uruk period is justified.[99] Matthiae plausibly pointed to the use of the Sumerogram en—which was the specifically Urukian title of that city's supreme priest-king—as the designation of the king of Ebla in the period of the archives: it could not have been borrowed in the Early Dynastic period, when Ebla had no contact with Uruk, but "relate[s] to much earlier and apparently close connections between the environment and culture of archaic Uruk and the culture of Ebla."[100] It must be added that the title en was borne not only by the king of imperial Ebla but by his vassal rulers as well: the influence of archaic Uruk was not limited to Ebla.

[95] Moortgat 1960: 21; Moortgat 1962: 11.

[96] The brief report by Stucky 1973 does not mention whether signs of violent destruction have been found at the site.

[97] There was a layer of ashes on top of the excavated building of level V, but according to Hood 1951: 132 it is insufficient as evidence of destruction of the whole town.

[98] Matthiae 1981: 218–19.

[99] Gelb's 1986 comparative study of the relative importance of sheep-breeding and farming in, respectively, southern Mesopotamia and northern Syria is instructive: surplus of grain in the former, surplus of wool in the latter. In fig. 1 on p. 164 Gelb indicated that Lagaš was self-sufficient in wool; but on pp. 158 and 160 he quoted Nikolskij 1980: nos. 85, 214, and 310, "that sheep and wool were imported from Elam in return for grain, indirectly indicating that the Lagash area was not suited for raising sheep." Other city-states of Sumer could not have been much different in this respect.

[100] Matthiae 1981: 217; cf. 215–20.

4. *The Early Third Millennium and the Eblean King List*

The end of Mardīḫ I is conventionally put at 2900, which coincides with the beginning of Early Dynastic I in southern Mesopotamia and of Early Bronze II in Syria. At the beginning of 1980, the final centuries of Mardīḫ I and all of the following Mardīḫ IIA period (which lasted till the construction of the great royal palace G of the archives) could be characterized by the director of the excavations as "obscure."[101] Recently acquired archeological and epigraphic data shed much light on at least the major pat of Mardīḫ IIA. Remains of a large administrative edifice from an early phase of Early Bronze III (i.e., ca. 2700)[102] have been uncovered on the southern slope of the Acropolis below the royal palace G and were designated as building G2.[103] Its eastern wing, which contains numerous jars and pots, suffered from a fire, while the western wing seems to have been emptied and abandoned. At least two construction levels from a latter part of Early Bronze III were identified on top of building G2, as well as a terrace built of bricks of the same dimensions as those of the royal palace G and preparatory to its erection, but belonging to the final phase of Early Bronze III. It is thus clear that throughout that period there went on a constant activity of building, rebuilding, and replacement of royal residences in the same place of the Acropolis, reflecting the growth of wealth and power of their occupants, until it culminated in the vast royal palace G of Early Bronze IVA.[104] It also implies an uninterrupted continuity of political power in Ebla. This explains how a stone vase with the cartouche of King Chephren (middle of the twenty-sixth century) happened to belong to the furnishings of royal palace G which was built almost two centuries after the reign of that pharaoh.[105] It had been brought to one of the earlier palaces and had been transferred to the new one along with other valued heirlooms.

We are very fortunate, for such a remote historical period, to know the number, the sequence, and almost all the names of the kings who ruled Ebla and its domain from these successive palaces. Until 1986, the names of only two rulers explicitly called "king of Ebla" (en-*Eb-la*^ki^) were known, *viz.*, Igriš-Ḫalam and

[101] Matthiae 1981: 209; cf. 52: "Almost nothing is yet known of the occupation of the first half of the third millennium."

[102] The chronotomy and absolute chronology of Syrian Early Bronze period are approximate. Matthiae 1981: 66 synchronized the beginning of Early Bronze III in Syria with that of Early Dynastic II in southern Mesopotamia, about 2700. Porada 1965: 178 dated the beginning of Early Dynastic II at 2750. The pottery found in building G2 is "clearly comparable with the ceramic horizon of ᶜAmuq H and Hama K" (Matthiae 1987: 138). According to Braidwood and Braidwood 1960: 518, "Phase H roughly parallels the range from late Early Dynastic into the first part of Early Dynastic III in Mesopotamia." The corresponding levels of phase K at Hama are placed by Fugmann 1958: 278 between shortly after 2700 and 2400.

[103] This and the following facts on building G2 are based on the brief report in Matthiae 1987: 136–38.

[104] The same excavation campaigns unearthed new extensive areas of palace G (Matthiae 1987: 140).

[105] On this vase and its chronological implications see §7 (planned for Part 2 of this article).

Irkab-Damu.[106] In that year, Archi published a list of sacrifices (one sheep per recipient), divided into two groups.[107] The second group consists of eight deities, defined as "gods of cities who dwell at Daritum,"[108] who do not concern us here. The first group is composed of ten personal names, each of which is preceded, in a separate case, by the divine determinative (d i n g i r); it ends with the formula e n - e n 'kings'. The first two of these ten names are, most significantly, Irkab-Damu and Igriš-⟨Ḫa⟩-lam.[109] It was thus clear to Archi that the document named ten deceased and deified kings of Ebla, listed in reverse chronological order, that is, beginning with the latest of them—the same arrangement as in the Ugaritic list of posthumously deified kings[110] and in the enumeration of Šamši-Adad I's ancestors, inserted into the Assyrian King List,[111] but unlike the normal chronological sequence in the Genealogy of the Ḫammurapi Dynasty.[112] Archi cited an Eblean tablet in which the fifth and sixth kings are named—both with the determinative d i n g i r—among divine recipients of bread offerings,[113] and he noted, in passing, that the nominative list TM.74.G.120, probably a scribal disciple's exercise, contained in its obv.i:2–ii:5 the same ten names, and in the same order, as the sacrificial tablet in question.[114]

Archi entitled his study "the first ten kings of Ebla," but a further investigation of TM.74.G.120 revealed that these were, on the contrary, the last, or almost the last, in the Eblean royal sequence. Biga and Pomponio found that "the ten names of TM.74.G.120 are not the only ones of the lexical text to reappear

[106] Igriš-Ḫalam: TM.75.G.1237 (MEE 1 676), twice; TM.75.G.1371 = MEE 2 45:obv.v:5–rev.i:1. Irkab-Damu: TM.75.G.2342 (MEE 1 1781), published in Pettinato 1977b: 238–40 and Pettinato 1979a: 120–22, obv.iv:6–8, obv.v:7–vi:1.

[107] Archi 1986a. The tablet, TM.75.G.2628, was published again in ARET 7 no. 150.

[108] Archi 1986a: 218 nn. 2–4 transliterated the place name *Da-ri-íb*[ki] instead of his previously used normalization *Da-rí-tum*[ki], identifying it with *Da-rí-bù*[ki], and possibly with *Dar-áb*[ki], which also occur in Ebla texts. I prefer to render the final sign by its usual value in final position, *-tum*, and I must call attention to the circumstance that *Da-rí-bù*[ki] is not found in the often-recurring and characteristic geographical context in which *Da-rí-tum*[ki] appears. On p. 217, furthermore, Archi thought it probable that Darib/Darab was identical with *Tá-ra-b* of Thutmosis III's Naharina List, modern el-Atāreb, and with [uru]*Ta-ri-bu* in the kingdom of Ugarit. Of course, the possessions of Ugarit never reached the area of el-Atāreb, nor is the geographical association of Daritum compatible with a location at el-Atāreb or the Ugaritian Taribu (now Tirbeh, a short distance northeast of Ras Shamra).

[109] The omitted sign in the latter name was restored from the text TM.74.G.120 (see n. 114 below).

[110] RS 24.257 = *KTU* 1.113; cf. Kitchen 1977; Pardee 1988: 164–66.

[111] Gelb 1954; Kraus 1965.

[112] Finkelstein 1966.

[113] TM.75.G.570:rev.ii:18–iv:5 (En[ɔ]ar-Damu and Išar-Malik).

[114] Archi 1986a: 217 n. 26. The text belongs to the very first lot of tablets discovered at Tell Mardīḫ and reported by Pettinato 1975; a hand copy of the obverse appeared in Pettinato 1979a: 50; full transliteration in Archi 1988a: 213. The second half of the text consists of personal names arranged by their initial elements. The import of the first part had not been recognized before the publication of TM.75.G.2628.

in administrative texts preceded by the sign AN [= dingir] as recipients of food offerings," but that this is also true for the entries 16, 17, and 19 of the list,[115] and Archi added the entry 22.[116] Moreover, these scholars agreed that *Iš$_{11}$-ar-Da-mu*, who heads the list of TM.74.G.120 and does not appear in TM.75.G.2628 (ARET 7 150), was Irkab-Damu's successor and either the last or the penultimate king of Ebla in the age of the archives (this depends on whether the king had to be dead in order to be listed with his predecessors, or a purely nominative list without cultic associations could be compiled during his lifetime). Išʾar-Damu is attested as a "king's son," and the fact that he is seldom mentioned does not necessarily imply, as thought by Archi, "that he either ruled for a very short period of time or that he even died before his father did":[117] at Ebla, a reigning king was referred to simply as en.[118]

Here are the names of the twenty-two kings of Ebla as they are listed in TM.74.G.120, normalized and rearranged in straight chronological order, with numbers in parentheses indicating their positions in the original:

1. Rumanu (?)[119] (22)
2. Namanu (21)
3. Da [....] (20)
4. Sagiš(u)[120] (19)
5. Daneʾum (?)[121] (18)
6. Ibbini-Lim (17)
7. Išruṭ-Damu (16)
8. Isidu (15)
9. Išruṭ-Ḫalam (14)
10. Iksud (13)
11. Talda-Lim (12)
12. Abur-Lim (11)
13. Agur-Lim (10)
14. Ibbi-Damu (9)
15. Baga-Damu[122] (8)
16. Enʾar-Damu (7)
17. Išar-Malik (6)
18. Kum-Damu[123] (5)
19. Adub-Damu (4)
20. Igriš-Ḫalam (3)
21. Irkab-Damu (2)
22. Išʾar-Damu (1)

[115] Biga and Pomponio 1987.

[116] Archi 1988a: 214, which see for all references to the administrative texts in question. On the cult of deceased kings at Ebla cf. Fronzaroli 1988, with additions and corrections in Fronzaroli 1989.

[117] Archi 1988a: 215.

[118] As noted by Archi 1988a: 220, the documentation from Ebla has "no royal inscriptions, but administrative documents in which the king is indicated only by his title."

[119] Transliterated EN-*ma-nu* by Archi, Ennuma by Biga and Pomponio 1987. The small sign *nu* is placed on top of the large sign *ma* in this and the following name, which should, in all probability, be read *Na-ma-nu* rather than *Na-nu-ma*. Cf., however, the PN EN-*nu-mu* ARET 4 20 §28.

[120] *Sa*-[. .]-*s*[*u*] in the original; restored by Biga and Pomponio 1987 on the basis of the occurrences of dingir *Sa-gi-iš* and dingir *Sa-gi-su/si* as a recipient of food offerings.

[121] Either *Da-ne-um* or *Da-bi-um* /ṭâbiʾum/.

[122] In TM.75.G.2628 *Ba-Da-mu*; as in the case of [*I*]*g-ri*-[*i*]*š-lam* in the same text (for -*Ḫa-lam*), we should think that the scribe had inadvertently skipped a sign.

[123] In TM.75.G.2286, an inventory of deposits of quantities of silver and gold (published in Pettinato 1986: 401–2), the first one is credited jointly to Kum-Damu and Igriš-Ḫalam, although their reigns were not consecutive; cf. Archi 1988a: 215–16.

The list of kings ends with obv.iii. It is followed by a group of (originally) thirteen names (obv.iv:1–v:4), of which the first two in col. iv are totally destroyed, and of the next one, only the initial *šu*$^{?}$ is extant. Of the remaining ten names—even though none of them is marked with the determinative ki—seven or eight closely resemble known Eblean toponyms, *viz.*, *Zi-a-lu* (cf. *Zi-ʾà-ru*$_{12}$^{ki}, *Zi-ʾà-ar*^{ki}, *Zi-a*-LUM^{ki}), [*Za*]$^{?}$-*mi-ù*[124] (cf. Za-mi-um^{ki}), Kul-ba-nu (cf. Kul-ba-nu^{ki}, Kul-ba-an^{ki}),[125] *Eb-la* (needs no commentary), *Du-mu-dar* (cf. *Du-mu-u*$_{9}$^{ki} with the omissible toponymic suffix *-dar*),[126] *Bir*$_{5}$*-bí-la-nu* (cf. *Bir*$_{5}$*-bí-ra-nu*^{ki}), *La-da-ù* (cf. *La-da*^{ki}, *La-da*$_{5}$^{ki} with the suffix *-aʾu*, often added to Eblean toponyms), and perhaps *Iš*$_{4}$$^{!}$*-sa-nu* (cf. *Ì-ša-núm*^{ki}).[127] The question is, why did the scribe insert this group of names after the list of Eblean kings?[128] Did he, after finishing it, pick up for copying an unrelated list of some towns of the kingdom, omitting, however, their geographical determinatives? Or does the lack of the determinatives indicate that these names were perceived as relating not to the towns as such but to their eponyms who were used to lengthen the royal pedigree beyond the earliest remembered name of an authentic king? This device is found in all of the analogous compositions referred to above—the genealogies of Šamši-Adad I and the Ḫammurabi Dynasty and the Ugaritic texts on the worship of dead kings, all of them of West Semitic background.[129]

But the names of the kings which precede this toponymic group are genuine personal names, most of them of peculiarly Eblean character. We may regard them as authentic names, preserved in memory because of the invocations of the deified royal dead at the commemorative sacrifices in their honor. They may have been committed to writing quite early, for literacy at Ebla could not have

[124] The missing sign was a narrow one, like *a* or *za*.

[125] This correspondence has been noted by Archi 1988a: 214 n. 27, though without a firm conclusion as to its nature.

[126] Cf. *Kul-ba-an-dar*^{ki}, instead of the usual *Kul-ba-an*^{ki}, in one of several lists of towns of a specific district; *ʾA*$_{x}$*-la-la-dar*^{ki}, compared with *A-la-lu*^{ki}; *ʾA-ru-ak-dar*^{ki} and *Ru-bù-ù-dar*^{ki} in the List of Geographical Names (MEE 4 56, of south Mesopotamian origin), compared with Eblean toponyms *ʾA-ru*$_{12}$*-ak*^{ki} and *Ru*$_{12}$*-bù*^{ki}.

[127] The first sign is DIŠ (vertical wedge), rendered by Archi AŠ. It is true that in Old Akkadian script the single wedge could be read *aš*, whether it was traced horizontally, vertically, or aslant. But it could also stand for *eš*$_{4}$/*iš*$_{4}$. For the spelling, cf. the Eblean PN *Iš-sa-mu*.

[128] Among the entries of this group, only *A-bù-gàr* (no. 30 of the list) looks like a true anthroponym, of which both elements, *abu* and *gar*, are frequently met in Eblean and Old Akkadian onomastics, although that particular combination does not appear in either of them. At Ebla, numerous place-names coincide with personal names. The last item of the group, *Sa-kum-e*, is somewhat unusual; the sign *e* is extremely rare in writing of Eblaic words and names. Perhaps it is here the Sumerogram E 'dike'? Cf. *Eb-al*^{ki} lú pa$_{5}$ 'Ebʾal at the canal'.

[129] So as not to deviate from my subject, I only note in general that the early parts of the two former genealogies are composed not only of names of West Semitic tribes (which was duly noted by Finkelstein 1966) but also of names of well-attested Mesopotamian and Transtigridian cities, and that of the five names of the *rpim qdmym* 'ancient shades of dead' in the Ugaritic royal funerary ritual RS 34.126 (its several publications include that by Bordreuil and Pardee 1982), at least three are city names: *Trmn* (Tarmanu in northern Mesopotamia and its homonym in northern Syria), *Sdn* (Eblean *Si-da-nu*^{ki}), and *Rdn* (Eblean *Rad-nu*^{ki}; cf. *Ri-da-(an-)na*^{ki} in MEE 4 56).

started *ex abrupto* with the beginning of the now extant archives. Did the twenty-two kings known to us by name form a dynasty? Archi thought at first that they did not, since "none of these kings bears the same name as one of his predecessors" and this may mean that "kingship was not transferred within the same family."[130] But the use of dynastic names is not a universal feature of dynastic régimes. As a matter of fact, repetitions of royal names did not occur in the historically attested early Mesopotamian dynasties—Lagaš I (with one single exception),[131] Akkad, Ur II, Lagaš II, Ur III, Isin I, Larsa, Babylon I, Pre-Sargonic and Old Babylonian Mari, and Sealand I. It was only after ca. 1800 that the first cases of recurring royal names took place in certain dynasties—Assur and Ešnunna, and later the Kassite Dynasty, in Mesopotamia, Yamḫad and Ugarit in northern Syria. But even in the first millennium, there was not a single repeated name among the twenty-two Davidic kings of Judah who reigned for ca. 425 years. Besides, if not by dynastic succession (which may have included transitions of power to collateral branches of the family or through marriage), how else were the kings of Ebla raised to the throne? Archi himself has several times rejected Pettinato's assertion that Eblean kings were elected for terms of seven years,[132] and has recently used the expression the Ebla dynasty or the Eblaite dynasty.[133] The strongest argument in favor of viewing the Eblean king list as representing a dynasty is the fact that, at the time of the archives, offerings of food and clothes are attested to several of the dead kings, including the very first one of the sequence. This widely attested practice was only an officialized form of ancestor worship which was a strictly familial affair.[134]

What does the figure of twenty-two kings represent in terms of duration? Rowton once calculated the average lengths of reign for the First Dynasty of Babylon, three periods in the history of Assyria, and the Twelfth Dynasty of Egypt: the figures range from 23.1 to 27.3 years.[135] For the dynasty of Akkad, counting the three years of the four pretenders as a single reign, the average is 22.6, without them, 25.4; for the Third Dynasty of Ur, 21.6; for the Eighteenth

[130] Archi 1986a: 215, referring to the ten kings of ARET 7 150.

[131] Enannatum I and II.

[132] Pettinato 1977b: 235; Pettinato 1979b: 78–79; Archi 1979a; Archi 1984a: 26–29; Archi 1988a: 217–18.

[133] Archi 1988a: 212, 215.

[134] On *kispu*, the banquet of the dead, in Babylonia, cf. the example quoted by Dhorme 1949: 231; at Mari and Amorite Babylon, cf. Finkelstein 1966: 113–16. Of special interest are the contemporary (late Pre-Sargonic) tablets on ancestor worship in the royal family of Lagaš collected by Deimel 1920 (cf. also Bauer 1969). They differ from the Eblean testimonies in including female family members, but resemble them in designating the recipients of the offerings as en-en, even though it was not the title of the rulers of Lagaš. Only Lugalanda, Enentarzi, the high priest Dudu (probably Enentarzi's father), their womenfolk, and the remote character Gunidu were honored under UruKAgina, who replaced Lugalanda but was Enentarzi's brother-in-law. Gunidu was the father of Ur-Nanše, the first ruler of the dynasty; his appearance in the ritual tablets indicates that he was considered the ancestor of Dudu's family as well; but none of the rulers of Ur-Nanše's line were included.

[135] Rowton 1952: 20–21.

Dynasty of Egypt up to and including Akhenaten, 23; for Judah up to the fall of Jerusalem, 19.3; with Jehoiachin's nominal reign up to 561, the figure will be 20.4. Let us take twenty years as the minimal probable average, which would give 440 years for the twenty-two kings of Ebla, and let us round it down, to be on the safe side, to 400 years. If these are added to the probable date of the destruction of royal palace G, which I put at ca. 2300,[136] the beginning of the dynasty would go back to ca. 2700, which is also the approximate time of the erection of the first royal palace (building G2) on the southern slope of the Acropolis.

The progress in the understanding of Eblean tablets brought about a radical revision of the number and names of the kings of Ebla at the time of the archives. Until 1985, all scholars engaged in Eblean studies accepted the sequence arrived at by Pettinato,[137] *viz.*, Igriš-Ḫalam, Irkab-Damu, Ar-ennum,[138] Ibrium,[139] Ibbi-Zikir.[140] But in that year, at two separate Ebla symposia, Archi[141] and Pomponio[142] demonstrated that, although the latter three men were very powerful personages at Ebla, they are never mentioned with the title en but are found in juxtaposition to the unnamed bearers of that title, and that their sons and daughters are entirely distinct from persons designated as sons and daughters of en.[143] Ar-ennum, Ibrium, and Ibbi-Zikir, by a meticulous and painstaking prosopographic research, were put in the right chronological setting as the contemporaries and seconds-in-command of the actual last three kings of the period of archives, Igriš-Ḫalam, Irkab-Damu, and Išᵓar-Damu. Synchronisms with other persons, notably with the dynasties of Mari and Emar, confirmed that the period of archives had lasted for three generations, or approximately sixty years.

Relatively little is known of Ar-ennum, and there is no proof that he was the father of Ibrium.[144] But Ibbi-Zikir was a son of Ibrium, and his own son, Dubuḫu-Ada, was a high personage during the tenure of his father. He appears on one level with Irᵓak-Damu, the crown prince,[145] and the way in which he is

[136] This date is substantiated in my contribution to the forthcoming *New Horizons in the Study of Ancient Syria*, edited by Mark W. Chavalas and John Hayes (Malibu: Undena).

[137] Pettinato 1979b: 76–78.

[138] Written AR-EN-LUM. Archi 1988a: 208 prefers the transliteration *Ar-ru*$_{12}$*-lum*. Both readings are onomastically possible. Until a new spelling variant, which could point to the correct values of the second and third signs, is discovered, I will use the conventional form Ar-Ennum.

[139] Pettinato wrote the name *Ebrium*, which makes no real difference.

[140] Pettinato transliterated the final element (which occurs in several personal names) *sí-piš*, proceeding from Ugaritic *špš* 'sun'. Most other scholars transliterate it *zi-kir*, on which cf. Krebernik 1988b: 110–11.

[141] At the symposium held in Rome, July 15–17, 1985; published as Archi 1988a, jointly with Biga 1988 and Milano 1988.

[142] At the meeting held in Naples, October 9–11, 1985; published as Pomponio 1987.

[143] This was also detected by Michalowski 1988: 272–75, originally read at the Heidelberg Symposium, November 4–7, 1986.

[144] For a detailed study of Ibrium, see W. W. Hallo, "Ebrium at Ebla," elsewhere in this volume.

[145] The role of Irᵓak-Damu (or Ilᵓak-Damu) was elucidated by Biga and Pomponio 1987. According to TM.75.G.1764, quoted by Pettinato 1979b: 95 and n. 60, eighty-one bovines were assigned as food for the king, sixteen ovines as food for Irᵓak-Damu, one hundred forty ovines as food for Dubuḫu-Ada, and fifteen ovines as food for the personnel of the palace.

mentioned in the texts indicates that he was regarded as the future successor to his father's high office. The importance of that office can be perceived from evidence such as MEE 1 1 (TM.75.G.1261).[146] This inventory of imposts opens with the section mu-tù *Ib-rí-um* 'contribution of Ibrium', which exceeds beyond comparison the amounts listed in the subsequent sections: mu-tù-mu-tù lugal-lugal 'contributions of governors',[147] mu-tù-mu-tù u_4-u_4 *Ib-rí-um* 'contributions of the time of Ibrium', consisting of entries from twelve cities, most or all of which had their own kings,[148] and níg-ki-za en-en 'dues of kings', additional miscellaneous entries. In the analogous document ARET 8 528,[149] the opening section, entitled mu-tù *I-bí-Zi-kir*, contains even greater amounts of gold and numbers of pieces of clothing than that of Ibrium. Thus the bulk of the royal revenue was collected and delivered to the treasury by the holders of the unnamed office which obviously endowed them with an enormous power. Several of Ibrium's sons and grandsons held in tenure numerous land estates and entire towns scattered over the whole territory of the kingdom.[150] As we learn from TM.75.G.1444, the lands were bestowed by the king, but at the request (or shall we say: demand?) of Ibrium who addressed him in the most informal way, and it was not the sons of Ibrium who swore allegiance to the king but the king who swore by the highest gods that he would not take back their grants.[151]

None of the three known incumbents of this high post is ever mentioned otherwise than by name, and thus we do not know the title of their office. Archi now uses for it the conventional term *vizier.*[152] We see that at Ebla at the time

[146] Commented upon by Archi 1982: 218–19 (without reference to the inventory or publication number) and Astour 1988b: 150. In both articles, Ibrium is still considered a king.

[147] On the meaning of the term lugal at Ebla see Archi 1982: 203–4. In the document in question, the section lists contributions from two judges jointly and from eleven other men, together twelve entries.

[148] In the closely related document TM.75.G.1297, summarized in MEE 1 736, the corresponding section (contributions of twelve cities, nine of them appearing in MEE 2 1) bears the title níg-ba en 'gift (to the) king'. Archi 1982: 219 quotes from another (unspecified) document of the same kind that its corresponding section is entitled "deliveries of the countries (kalam-*tim*-kalam-*tim*)."

[149] Which differs in not having the governors' section.

[150] Astour 1988b: 152. New texts of this kind appeared in ARET 7.

[151] Published by Edzard 1981a. The introductory formula (repeated in §§2, 5, 16, and 22) is *en-ma Ib-ri-um si-in* en 'thus (says) Ibrium to the king', also used by Ibbi-Zikir in addressing the king, and in letters with instructions to his sons, principally Dubuḫu-Ada, and to lower officials; see Pettinato 1980: 233; Biga 1988: 292–93.

[152] Archi 1988a: 220; commentary to ARET 7 21 and elsewhere in the volume. The closest we come, in an Ebla text, to the definition of the function of Ibrium and Ibbi-Zikir is in TM.75.G.1452, published by Fronzaroli 1980. This deed of land grants to sons of Irik-Damu (who was a son of Ibrium) is presented as di-ku_5 en *wa* SA.ZA_x^{ki} di-ku_5 'judgment of the king and judgment of SA.ZA_x^{ki}'. The latter term has been explained as 'treasure room, treasury' by Civil 1983; here it stands for 'prefect of the treasury', as, e.g., in the treaty text TM.75.G.2420, published by Sollberger 1980, passim, *en-ma* en *Eb-la*^{ki} *ì-na* *A*-BAR-SÌL^{ki} means 'thus the king of Ebla to (the king of) *A*-BAR.SÌL^{ki}', or *en-ma* en *ʾA-du*^{ki} *ì-na Ma-rí*^{ki} in TM.75.G.2561, published by Pettinato 1986: 398–400, passim, means 'thus the king of Adu to (the king of) Mari'.

of the archives a dynasty of chief executive officers of the realm was formed beside the royal dynasty, enthroned and consecrated by tradition. What gave them this power? It was suggested that Ibrium's family belonged to a lateral line of the royal house,[153] or that a system of "corporate royalty," in which several families had the right to the crown, existed at Ebla,[154] but there is not a shred of evidence for it, and historical parallels do not corroborate it. Beside the analogies—close ones, but from remote times and places—of the Carolingian majordomos to the last Merovingian kings, and of the Tokugawa dynasty shoguns to the nominal Japanese emperors, one finds a similar development in the Ur III monarchy, where a veritable dynasty of sukkal-maḫs[155] was highly influential for three generations under Šulgi and his successors.[156] An equivalent title, sukkal-gal, is attested in some Ebla texts, but only for Mari, where its bearer stood in the third position after the king and the heir-apparent.[157] It also occurs in a Pre-Sargonic tablet from Mari itself,[158] but nothing is known about the scope of competence of its bearer.

5. *The Wars with Mari*

The texts published up to now tell us practically nothing about the military establishment of Ebla, though they mention quantities of daggers and spearheads. But there is no reason to assume that the growth of the Ebla Empire was peaceful and unchallenged. A remarkable, though difficult, document sheds light on a turbulent chapter of Ebla's history before the start, and in the early years, of the period of archives. It informs us about a long series of wars between Ebla and its allies on one side, and the neighboring and rival empire of Mari on the other, and it enables us better to understand the subsequent relations between them. Incidentally, the document in question, which emanated from a Mariote ruler, helped to establish the internal chronology of Pre-Sargonic Mari.[159] The

[153] Biga and Pomponio 1987.

[154] Michalowski 1988: 271–72.

[155] Literally 'great envoy', translated 'chief minister' by Thureau-Dangin 1907: 149, 'grand vizier' by Jacobsen 1970: 174, 409 n. 8, and Roux 1980: 163–64, and 'grand-regent' by Hinz 1971: 656.

[156] The last of the three, Ir-Nanna, was, according to his inscription (*SAKI* no. 22), the governor-general and supreme commander of the entire Transtigris region of the empire. However, his Eblean counterparts do not seem to have been in charge of any particular part of the domain of Ebla.

[157] MEE 2 13:obv.ii:1–iii:5 (the tablet deals with Enna-Dagan the king and other persons from Mari); ARET 7 6 §4 (attribution to Mari inferred by Archi from the contents of the tablet); the title is written sukkal:gal in both texts. In ARET 7 1 §3, the shorter title sukkal is attributed to a Mariote dignitary for the same reason. In the kingdom of Ebla the term sukkal appears infrequently and designates simply a messenger.

[158] Charpin 1987a: 79, no. 20 §11.

[159] Archi 1985a.

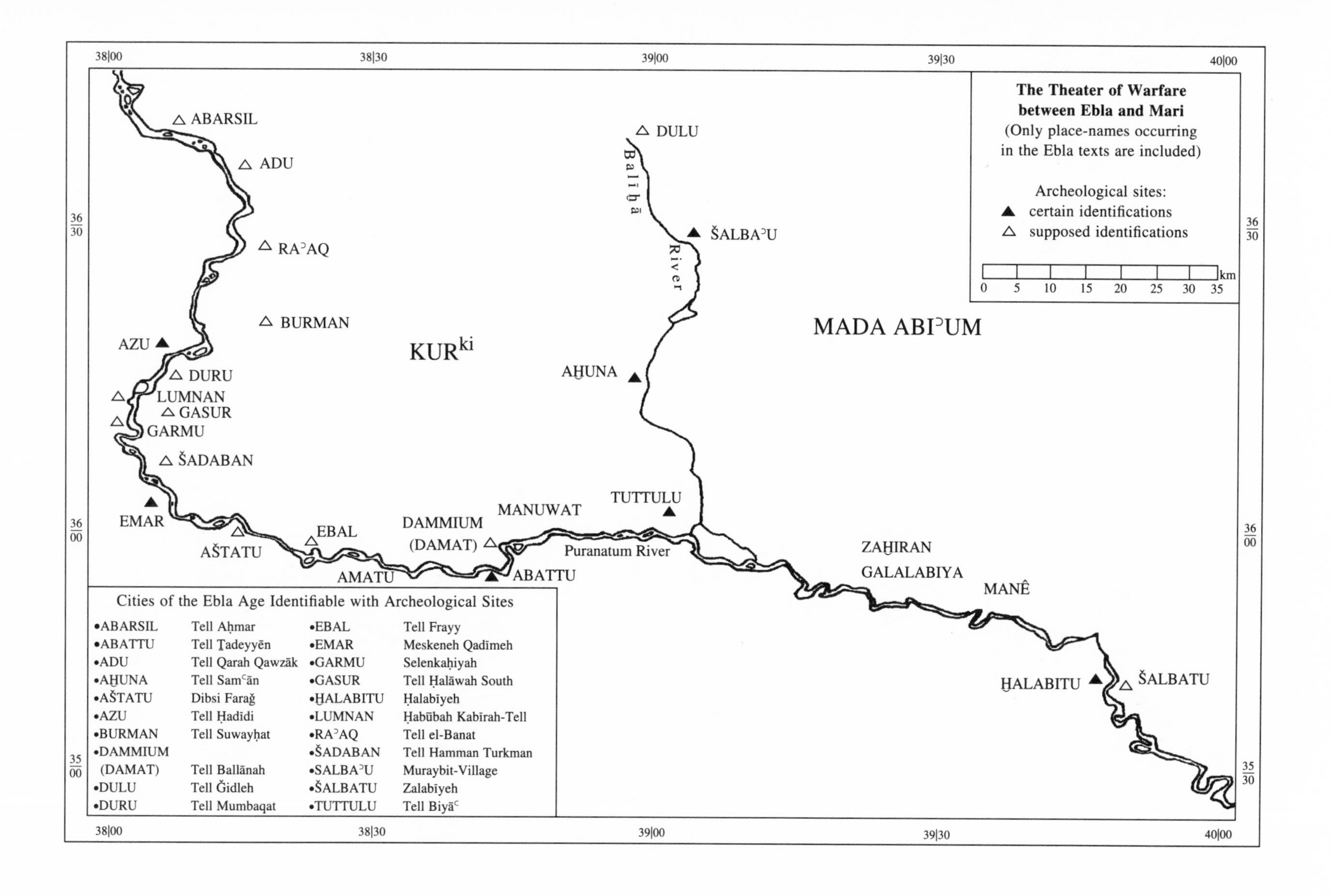
The Theater of Warfare
between Ebla and Mari
(Only place-names occurring
in the Ebla texts are included)
Archeological sites:
certain identifications
supposed identifications
0 5 10 15 20 25 30 35 km
38|00
38|30
39|00
39|30
40|00
36/30
36/00
35/30
35/00
ABARSIL
ADU
RAᵓAQ
BURMAN
AZU
DURU
LUMNAN
GASUR
GARMU
ŠADABAN
EMAR
AŠTATU
EBAL
AMATU
DAMMIUM
(DAMAT)
ABATTU
MANUWAT
TUTTULU
Puranatum River
AḪUNA
ŠALBAᵓU
DULU
Baliḫā River
KURki
MADA ABIᵓUM
ZAḪIRAN
GALALABIYA
MANÊ
ḪALABITU
ŠALBATU
Cities of the Ebla Age Identifiable with Archeological Sites
•ABARSIL Tell Aḥmar
•ABATTU Tell Ṭadeyyēn
•ADU Tell Qarah Qawzāk
•AḪUNA Tell Samᶜān
•AŠTATU Dibsi Farağ
•AZU Tell Ḥadīdi
•BURMAN Tell Suwayḥat
•DAMMIUM (DAMAT) Tell Ballānah
•DULU Tell Ğidleh
•DURU Tell Mumbaqat
•EBAL Tell Frayy
•EMAR Meskeneh Qadīmeh
•GARMU Selenkaḥiyah
•GASUR Tell Ḥalāwah South
•ḪALABITU Ḥalabīyeh
•LUMNAN Ḥabūbah Kabīrah-Tell
•RAᵓAQ Tell el-Banat
•ŠADABAN Tell Hamman Turkman
•SALBAᵓU Muraybit-Village
•ŠALBATU Zalabīyeh
•TUTTULU Tell Biyāᶜ

text, TM.75.G.2367, has been published and studied by Pettinato,[160] who understood it as a "military bulletin of the campaign of Ebla against the city of Mari," commanded by the Eblean general Enna-Dagan, who in one single victorious march traversed all the places mentioned in the text till he entered Mari as a conqueror and proclaimed himself its king. Soon after, Edzard, in a short but incisive analysis, clarified the meaning of the text and showed who did what to whom.[161] Proceeding from there, let us consider the import of TM.75.G.2367 in its broader political and geographical context.

The text begins with en-ma *En-na-Da-gan* en *Ma-rí*^{ki} *ì-na*[162] en *Eb-la*^{ki} 'thus (says) Enna-Dagan, king of Mari, to the king of Ebla'. Unfortunately for us, the king of Mari observed the Eblean formulary of not calling the reigning king by his personal name. Then, without transition, he lists his three predecessors' and his own military exploits against cities and areas, most of which are known as vassal states or direct possessions of Ebla. The letter can thus be called, in modern diplomatic language, an *aide-mémoire*; its purpose was, it seems, to justify Mariote territorial claims during peace negotiations. The three earlier kings of Mari mentioned by Enna-Dagan are Saʾumu, Ištup-Šar, and Iblul-Il; he omitted his immediate predecessor, Nizi,[163] probably because no military actions against Ebla took place in his time. Of these, only Iblul-Il is attested at Mari itself as one of its Pre-Sargonic kings.[164] Enna-Dagan's letter is terse and repetitious. Military actions are described according to the formula: GN_1[165] RN en/lugal[166] *Ma-rí*^{ki} tùn-šè *in* GN_2 dul-sar[167] gar which, by comparison with the analogous recurring formula in the inscriptions of Eannatum and Entemena of Lagaš,[168] should

[160] Preliminary translations and interpretations: Pettinato 1977a; Pettinato 1979a: 103–8 (with a map of the alleged march of Eblean troops to Mari on p. 103), 153; complete edition: Pettinato 1980, reprinted Pettinato 1986: 395–97. Kienast 1984 elaborated on Pettinato's conception of the text.

[161] Edzard 1981b. Kienast 1984 defended Pettinato's view, but Pomponio 1988: 319 and n. 14 adduced new arguments against it. Edzard's reconstruction of events was followed, in agreement with other tablets on the Ebla-Mari relations, by Archi 1981c, 1985a, 1985b.

[162] However this preposition is read—*ì-na*, *lí-na*, or *ʾa*$_x$*-na*—its equivalence with Akkadian *ana* is generally recognized.

[163] Thus normalized by Archi 1985a: 47 n. 2 and in *PRU* 7.

[164] Through inscriptions on votive statuettes found, broken into pieces, in the temple of Ninni-Zaza; Parrot 1953: 208–9; Parrot 1967: 318, 323, 328; Parrot 1974: 28–30; Strommenger 1960: 28–29; Sollberger and Kupper 1971: 88–89; M. Lambert 1970: 169–71.

[165] The number of place-names in each paragraph varies from one to four.

[166] No importance should be attached to the interchange of the titles en and lugal for the rulers of Mari in Enna-Dagan's letter. The Pre-Sargonic kings of Mari bear exclusively the title lugal both in Mariote and Eblean texts. Enna-Dagan's intermittent use of en in a letter addressed to a king of Ebla is simply an inconsistent attempt to follow the Eblean royal formulary.

[167] In one section this expression is preceded by the numeral 2, and in two sections, by the numeral 7.

[168] E.g., Umma^{ki} tùn-šè bé-sig$_{10}$ saḫar-dul-TAG$_4$-bi 20 bí-dub, translated 'he defeated Umma and piled up twenty mounds' in Sollberger and Kupper 1971: 50, 58, and explained on p. 57 n. 6: "The expression saḫar-dul-TAG$_4$ . . . dub 'to pile up earth into a mound' describes the ritual act performed (by the victor) after a battle: the (enemy) corpses are piled up and covered

be understood 'RN, king of Mari, defeated GN_1 at GN_2 (and) piled up earth into (one or more) mounds [*scil.*, over heaps of enemy corpses]'.[169] Here is a summary of the text, divided into paragraphs for separate actions as in Pettinato's edition but differing from it in the demarcation of §§9–12:[170]

1. Saʾumu defeated Aburu and Ilgi, "countries"[171] of Belan, "raised a mound" in the steppe[172] of Labanan.
2. Saʾumu defeated Tibalat and Ilwî, "raised a mound" in the steppe of Angai.
3. Saʾumu defeated the "countries" of Raʾaq, Irum, Ašaltu, Badu in the confines of [. .]an, "raised a mound" at Naḫal.
4. Ištup-Šar defeated Emar, Lalayum, and the emporium? of Ebla,[173] "raised a mound" at Emar and at Lalayum.
5. Iblul-Il captured (šu-dug_8) Galalabî, [. . . .], and the emporium?, and defeated Abarsil at Zaḫiran, and "raised seven mounds."
6. Iblul-Il defeated Šada, AddaliNI, and Arisum, "countries" of Burman, at(!)[174] Sugurum, and "raised a mound."

with earth. A representation of this ceremony is carved on the reverse of [the Vultures'] stele." Thus also rendered by Steiner 1986: 222–23 and Kienast 1980: 259.

[169] Thus translated by Pettinato 1977a *passim*; but in his 1980 edition of Enna-Dagan's letter he accepted instead the interpretation of the phrase by Kienast 1980: 259–60 (suggested by the latter's student G. Selz) as corresponding to the Akkadian formula *ana tīli u karmi târu* 'to reduce (a city) into ruin mounds and debris', with sar (which may stand for $kiri_6$ 'garden') rendering *karmu* in its West Semitic meaning 'vineyard' but standing for *karmu* as Akkadian 'ruin, debris'. It is ingenious but contrived in its presumption of an interlingual pun.

[170] All proper names, except those of the four kings of Mari, are place-names.

[171] Kalam-*tim*-kalam-*tim*. For the concrete meaning of the term, cf. TM.75.G.2136, published by Pettinato 1978: 51–52, a list of cities, most of which are well attested in the Ebla texts, followed by an-šè-gú 17 $kalam^{ki}$-$kalam^{ki}$ *in* šu en *Eb-la*^{ki} 'total: seventeen countries in the hand of the king of Ebla', and the text (without inventory number) quoted by Archi 1982: 219, in which "the third section concerns the deliveries of the 'countries' (kalam-*tim*-kalam-*tim*) (such as Harran, Emar, Tuba) which, though being directed by independent dynasties, were in the circle of Eblaic hegemony."

[172] Kur^{ki}. It may, of course, signify 'mountain country', as translated by Pettinato (perhaps because of his identification of Labanan with Mount Lebanon, which is geographically out of the question). In Ebla texts, however, kur^{ki} appears several times as an area of large-scale sheep-breeding, which does not fit the forested mountains of northern Syria but points rather to the open steppe. Besides *šadû* 'mountain', KUR also stands for *mātu*, one of the meanings of which is 'open, or flat, country'.

[173] *Ga-nu-um Eb-la*^{ki}; *ga-nu-um* also appears by itself in §5 below. The nature of the first sign (*g/k/q*) allows more than one interpretation. Pettinato 1980: 239 translated "canneto" (canebrake); Kienast 1980: 256 and n. 17 took up Pettinato's previous (1977a: 25) translation "commercial colony" and postulated the transformation *kārum* > **kānum*; the former makes little sense *per se*, the latter is phonetically improbable. Geller's (1987: 144 n. 11) identification of *ga-nu-um* as Akkadian *qannu(m)* 'border, environs' makes better sense, and I myself thought so previously; but the context requires a more specific point, suggesting an equation with *kannum* in ARMT 21 93 *et passim*, rendered by the editor "entrepôt."

[174] The text has here lú, the Sumerogram for the relative and determinative pronoun. It does not recur elsewhere in the letter and makes poor sense in this passage, for Burman and Sugur(r)um

7. Iblul-Il defeated Šaran and Dammium and "raised two mounds."
8. Iblul-Il departed from Birat and from Ana of Ḫazuwan[175] and received the tribute of Ebla in the midst of Mane.[176]
9. Iblul-Il plundered (?)[177] Emar, "raised a mound."
10. Iblul-Il defeated Naḫal, Nubat, and Šada, "countries" of Gasur,[178] at Ganane,[179] and "raised seven mounds."
11. Enna-Dagan defeated Barama—twice[180]—and Aburu and Tibalat, "countries" of Belan, "raised [a mound]."
12. Of the concluding paragraph of the letter, only the beginning remains intact: *ma-da-a in* ì-giš kalam-*tim*-kalam-*tim* šu-dug$_8$,[181] which may be tenta-

---

were two separate client kingdoms of Ebla, Burman being the more important of the two. The context requires here, as in other similar passages of the letter, the preposition *in* 'in, at', referring to the site of the battle.

[175] The phrase *ʾà-na Ḫa-zu-wa-an*^{ki} presented a problem to the editor of the text; see Pettinato 1977a: 26 and, differently, Pettinato 1980: 241–42; Edzard 1981b: 94. A simple solution would be to connect *ʾà-na* with the toponym *A-nu*^{ki}, *A-na-*⌜*a*⌝^{ki}, ideographically IGI^{ki}, well attested in several Ebla texts as located in the general area where most of the events outlined in Enna-Dagan's letter took place, and still appearing as *À-na*^{REGIO} in the hieroglyphic Hittite stele Tell Aḥmar 1 §10, published anew by Hawkins 1980. Tell Aḥmar, ancient Til-Barsib, was in the early first millennium the capital of Bit-Adini, a state with possessions on both sides of the Syrian Euphrates. The omission of the determinative ki recurs in §3 (*in* zà [. .]-*an*, *in Na-ḫal*, though *Na-ḫal*^{ki} in §10), and cf. *in* kur^{ki} *La-ba-na-an* (§1), in which one determinative seems to have been deemed sufficient for both linked names. For the construction of è ('depart') with the preposition *in*, cf. *ina bītim ṣia* 'get out of the house' and *ina* GN *nitiṣi* 'we departed from GN', quoted in *CAD* A/2 358b, s.v. *aṣû.*

[176] The toponym is written *Ne-má*^{ki}, but Pettinato 1980: 244 was right in stating that "NE-*má*^{ki} is certainly identical with *má*-NE^{ki} of other texts." It appears in the same spelling in several documents connected with payments of indemnity to Mari, including TM.75.G.2592: obv.v:4 in Archi 1981c: 135–36 and ARET 7 3, 6, and 7, equated by the editor (Archi) with *Má*-NE^{ki}. The reading *Má-ne*^{ki} derives from the probable identity of the town with ^{uru}*Ma-ni-e* of the Chaldaean Chronicle, on which more will be said further in this section.

[177] Instead of the usual tùn-šè 'defeated', the text has here the sign TUM×SAL, on which Pettinato 1980: 244 noted: "Although the reading of the composite sign TUM×SAL is unknown to me, its meaning 'to defeat' has been deduced from the fact that it is attested in MEE 1 959: obv.iv:4 [now MEE 3 44] immediately after tùn-šè and before nam-ra-ak ['booty'], thus in a genuine military context." The question of that sign's identity with LAK 29 and its reading KAM$_x$ does not concern us here, because it does not contribute to understanding its semantics.

[178] The reading of this name and the location of the city so named will be briefly discussed below.

[179] Pettinato's identification of *Ga-na*-NE^{ki} with 'the land of Canaan' hardly needs refutation.

[180] *Ba-ra-a-ma*^{ki} 2. Pettinato rendered the figure 2 "for the second time," but duly noted (1980: 244) that it does not fit the city in question which has not been mentioned earlier in the text, though it does fit Aburu and Tibilat (§§1–2).

[181] Pettinato 1980: 242, 244 tentatively translated these words "I have bound the scepters with the oil of the countries," basing his interpretation of the first word as *ma-ṭa-a* (Hebrew *maṭṭeh*, Ugaritic *mṭ*) on an entry of the bilingual vocabulary which gives *ma-ṭa-um* as the Eblaic equivalent of Sumerian giš-RU (or gis-šub), and on sacrifices offered to the giš-RUs of three divinities in a cultic text, on which see Pettinato 1979b: 112. In point of fact, the relevant entry, VE 413, has giš-RU = *ma-du-um*, *wa-ru*$_{12}$*-um*, and the related EV 0103 has giš-RU = *wa-ru*$_{12}$*-um.* But giš-RU does not mean 'scepter'; it is an ideogram for Akkadian *tilpānu* 'throwing stick, bow' and *qaštu*

> tively translated 'the two lands,[182] with the oil of captured "countries"', the subject and predicative of the sentence having been lost in the destroyed cases which follow.

The two lands, in the present context, are probably Mari and Ebla. Oil, which was widely used in religious and magic rituals throughout the Semitic world, also had a political function in Ebla. Mandatory offerings of oil by client kings of Ebla actually included payments in gold, silver, clothes, and other objects,[183] and this is what Enna-Dagan meant by 'oil of captured "countries"'. A curiously worded item appears in the revenue register MEE 2 1, already discussed in §4 above; the first entry of its final part (rev.i:1–9) is níg-ki-za lugal *Ma-rí*^{ki} *in* u_4 nídba-ì-giš *Eb-la*^{ki} *wa Ma-rí*^{ki} 'dues of the king of Mari (consisting of five pieces of clothing) in the day of oil offering by Ebla and Mari'. This joint 'offering of oil' (or exchange of gifts), apparently on a specific day, may have commemorated the conclusion of peace between the two powers, to which Enna-Dagan seems to allude in the closing paragraph of the Mariote version of the events.[184]

Despite its terseness and one-sidedness, Enna-Dagan's letter contains precious geographical and chronologic data. Not all of the places it mentions are known to us. We find no other occurrences (at Ebla or in other sources) of Aburu, Belan,[185] Tibalat, the steppe of Labanan,[186] or the steppe of Angai[x$^?$]. But the majority of the places do occur in the Ebla archives or in other ancient records, and even though only one of them has been firmly pinpointed in the terrain, it is feasible, by carefully correlating the available data about them, to obtain a general picture of their approximate locations.[187] All of these localities belonged, in different capacities, to the Ebla Empire. Some of them were capitals

---

'bow', which agrees with its Eblaic equivalent *warûm* 'to shoot, to throw' (Old South Arabic and Ethiopic *wrw*, Ugaritic *yry*, Hebrew *yārah*). While šu-du$_8$ (Akkadian *kamû*) can mean 'bind, tie', its association with "countries" suggests here the same meaning 'captured' as in §5.

[182] *Ma-tá-a*, oblique case dual of *mātu* 'land, country', which appears, spelled out, in the divine title ^{d}BE *ma-tum* (see Pettinato 1979a: 103) and in the lexical entries VE 795a: ^{d}BE kalam-*tim* = *ti-lu ma-tim*, and VE 795b: dingir-kalam-*tim* = *be-lu ma-tim.* Cf. also the toponyms *ma-da-* ᵓ*A-bi-um*^{ki} ARET 1 3 §39″, and *ma-da-I-za-an*^{ki} ARET 1 4 §57′, in which the first element represents, as in Old Akkadian, a Sumerianized ideogram of *mātu.*

[183] Cf. Astour 1988b: 149 and n. 69, with references.

[184] Of the sequence, there remain only *Ib-lul-Il* lugal *Ma-rí*^{ki}, perhaps named here in connection with the peace arrangement between Ebla and Mari under him, and *si-na-at* (or *ší-na-at*), unclear in the absence of a context.

[185] Unless it is equated with *Ba*$_4$*-la-nu*^{ki} in the unpublished text TM.75.G.1626 (MEE 1 1064), as transliterated by Pettinato 1986: 243, 356, and normalized Pettinato 1986: 255 (Balanu). But in his longhand transliteration of the text (cf. n. 244 below), the name is clearly written *Ba*$_4$*-la-mu*^{ki}.

[186] As a personal name, *La-ba-na-an* occurs in ARET 1 11 §44.

[187] The statement by Archi 1985b: 63 that "the difficulty . . . consists in the impossibility of identifying almost the totality of the toponyms cited in the letter" is too much on the pessimistic side. Archi's attempts of identifying Gasur and Ḫazuwan (see nn. 190 and 191 below) attest to the difficulties he encountered.

of client kingdoms, *viz*., Emar, Burman, Raᵓaq,[188] Abarsil,[189] Gasur,[190] Ḫazuwan,[191] and Sugurum. Two other client kingdoms involved in the war, as we learn from a related Eblean document,[192] were Ebal and Manuwat. Others belonged to some of those client kingdoms, and thus were under an indirect (but very real) control of Ebla. Several are attested in Eblean administrative texts as Ebla's direct possessions.[193]

The most important and best known of these cities is Emar, the Late Bronze site of which has been excavated from 1972 to 1982 under the direction of Jean Margueron at Meskeneh Qadimeh.[194] Lalayum is linked to Emar in §4 and must

[188] Emar, Burman, and Raᵓaq, along with Garmu and Lum(u)nan, are often mentioned together and in the first places of enumerations, as though they formed a geographically coherent and privileged group of client states.

[189] On the name and the political status of this city see Astour 1988b: 147–48.

[190] Written *Ga-sur*$_x$^{ki}, in which the second sign, ŠÁR×MAŠ, is defined in the Eblean list of sign names (MEE 3 52:rev.i:11–12; Archi 1987c: 96; no. 66 in both editions) as *su-ru*$_{12}$*-um*. The reading *sur*$_x$ for ŠÁR×MAŠ is confirmed by the List of Geographical Names from Abu Salabiḫ and Ebla (MEE 3 56), entry 111, written *Sur*$_x$*-gal* in both versions, which corresponds to *Su-ur-gal*^{ki} (MAD 5 67:ii:10), cf. Steinkeller 1986: 34, and by the occurrence at Ebla of *Ga-su-lu*^{ki}, a graphic "lambdacized" variant of *Ga-sur*$_x$^{ki}. Concerning Edzard's reading of the second sign as KAM rather than *sur*$_x$ (in ARET 2:115), cf. Astour 1987: 7 and nn. 25 and 26. Archi 1981c: 165 reads both forms of the sign, ŠÁR×MAŠ and ŠÁR×BAD (KAM) as *sur*$_x$; in Archi 1985b: 63 he still identified *Ga-sur*$_x$^{ki} with Gasur (later Nuzi) in the Transtigris, but here we are dealing with one of the several uncanny cases of homonymy between north Syrian and Transtigridian places (see n. 47 above). Some references to Gasur in the Ebla texts have been presented in Pettinato 1981.

[191] *Ḫa-zu-wa-an*^{ki} (also *Ḫa-su-wa-an*^{ki}, *Ḫa-zu-wa-nu*^{ki}) has been persistently identified by Archi (ARET 3:323; 1984b: 236–37; 1985b: 63) with Ḫaššum of the Mariote, Ḫaššu/Ḫaššuwa of the Hittite records, which he placed "on the right bank of the Euphrates, and not necessarily further north than Ursaᵓum" (near or at Gaziantep). But according to the Mariote and Hittite records in question, that city was located in the far northwest of Syria, near the border of Anatolia. As I briefly stated in 1971: 14 and 1989: 89 n. 102, it is probably identical with the royal city, excavated by U. Bahadir Alkim at Tilmen Hüyük. In any case, its location does not fit into the theater of military operations as it emerges from TM.75.G.2367.

[192] TM.75.G.2290, which will be discussed further below.

[193] I decided to abstain from bringing in here the references to the occurrences of all of these place-names in the editions of the Ebla texts. This would require too much time and space. In the absence of a comprehensive gazetteer, they may be looked up in the indexes of the individual text collections. The spelling variants are easy to recognize in most cases. Let it be noted that *Íl-gi*^{ki} (§1) is probably a contracted form of *Ì-la-gu*^{ki} (cf. *Ìr-ku*^{ki}/*Ìr-ra-ku*^{ki}/*I-ra-ku*^{ki}, perhaps an /r/ variant of the preceding toponym), and *Dam-mi-um*^{ki} (§7) may represent a differently suffixed variant of *Da-ma-at*^{ki} (cf. *A-bù-la-tù*^{ki} and *A-bù-li-um*^{ki}). *Ad-da-li-ni*^{ki} (§6) may be seen as an /l/ variant of *A-da-rí-in*^{ki}; this, in turn, may be the same as *A-da-ra*^{ki} which is mentioned in the aftermath of the war.

[194] Unfortunately, this final stage in the history of the city was built, in the latter part of the fourteenth century, at a new site to which the population was transferred from its old habitat, probably as a result of its destruction by an elemental catastrophe such as an unusually violent inundation. The old site, which may have contained archives from the Early and Middle Bronze Ages, has not been recovered, and never will be. Even so, the information produced by the numerous cuneiform texts from the Late Bronze city helped to clarify the approximate locations of several towns mentioned in the Ebla archives.

have been located not far from it and on the same bank.[195] Abarsil, as we learn from Ebla's treaty with it,[196] possessed a harbor and ships, evidently on the Euphrates. One clause of the treaty (B12a) warns the king of Abarsil not to delay the messengers from the Eblean king's "brothers" of Kakmium, Ḫazuwan, and Irar. This means that Abarsil stood at the crossing of the Euphrates by an important road—perhaps the one near Tell Aḥmar—though it is not clear on what bank; but it definitely proves that Ḫazuwan was located east of the river.[197]

The way in which Enna-Dagan's letter speaks of Šada and Arisum helps us to visualize the spatial relationship between the kingdoms of Burman, Gasur, and Ebal. In the first place, it should be stated that Šada,[198] a town frequently mentioned in Ebla texts, reappears, along with three other Eblean towns,[199] in the list of thirty-four "countries" conquered by Tukulti-Ninurta I of Assyria.[200] The inclusion of those four cities reflects Tukulti-Ninurta I's annexation of the strip of land on the left bank of the Euphrates north and east of its great bend which, at the time of Šuppiluliumaš I, had been ceded by Šattiwaza of Mitanni to the Hittite appanage kingdom of Carchemish.[201] According to Enna-Dagan's letter (§6), Šada and Arisum belonged to Burman, but in §10 Šada is attributed

[195] In all probability, *La-la-ì-um*[ki] is identical with the locality *Bīt-La-la-im*[ki] or *ša-La-la-im*[ki] of the Mari tablets, which belonged to the district of Ziniyan, the farthest area under the control of Mari up the Euphrates. There is no room here critically to examine the entire pertaining Mariote documentation, but cf. n. 226 below.

[196] TM.75.G.2420, published and tentatively translated by Sollberger 1980. The edition and translation of the same text by Pettinato, which I was kindly permitted to read in manuscript, has not yet been published to the best of my knowledge.

[197] And not very far from Abarsil, since *ʾÀ-na*, attributed to Ḫazuwan in Enna-Dagan's letter (see n. 175 above), is listed as IGI[ki] in the Abarsil treaty among several cities (including Carchemish) which the king of Ebla claimed as being "in his hand" and which must have been of concern to Abarsil. Birat (*Bí-ra-at*[ki]), mentioned in the same section of the letter as Ana Ḫazuwan and otherwise known as a town administered by an Eblean prefect (lugal) (MEE 2 14:rev.i:1) and one of the places with large flocks belonging to the king of Ebla (Archi 1984c: #10, obv.iv:1), must have been located in the same area.

[198] Spelled *Ša-da*$_5$[ki]. The second sign, URUDU, had in Old Akkadian only the syllabic value *da*$_5$, and I agree with those editors of Eblean texts who transliterate it thus and not *dab*$_6$. Cf. the variants in the spellings of toponyms *A-da*$_5$[ki] = *A-da*[ki], *La-da*$_5$[ki] = *La-da*[ki].

[199] These are, in the order of Tukulti-Ninurta I's list: no. 10, [kur]*Šá-a-da* = Eb *Ša-da*$_5$[ki]; no. 13, [kur]*Du-ri* = Eb BÀD[ki]/*Du-ur*[ki]/*Du-úr*[ki]; no. 14, [kur]*Ú-za-mi-ia* = Eb *Ù-za-mu*[ki]; no. 27, [kur]*Šá-da-ap-pa* = Eb *Ša-da-ba-an*[ki] = Emar [uru]*Ša-tap-pa/pí/pi*.

[200] Weidner 1959 no. 16; translations *ARAB* 1: §166; *ARI* 1: §775. It was wrong to provide each of the thirty-four entries of the list with the standard definition "in the border area between Assyria and Babylonia," as done by Nashef in *RGTC* 5. Some of the identifiable places of the list were situated north or east of Assyria, and the four names cited in the previous note find no correspondences except on Assyria's Euphrates border with the Hittite Empire.

[201] As this is stated in KBo 1 1:rev.18–21, 30–34. If Tukulti-Ninurta I did not mention Aḫuna, on the lower Balīḫ, one of the places ceded by Mitanni to the Hittites, it was probably because it had already been taken away by his predecessor Shalmaneser I. Tukulti-Ninurta I's rule over the Transeuphratean zone of the Hittite kingdom of Carchemish is confirmed by the epigraphic finds at Tell Frayy (on which more below), which attest to the replacement of Hittite administration by Assyrian in the latter part of the thirteenth century.

to Gasur, and in certain administrative Ebla tablets Arisum is defined as belonging to Ebal[202] or, more specifically, to Ebal "of the steppe."[203] Changes of sovereignty over border towns constantly appear in the records of Ebla, Mari, and other ancient Near Eastern states. In the present case, they indicate (*a*) that Burman, Gasur, and Ebal were all three located on the left bank of the Euphrates near its great bend, and (*b*) that they formed a triangle in which Burman abutted on Gasur in the south and on the hinterland of Ebal in the east. Can one find a clue to a more precise location of Ebal?

Ebal, a rather extensive territorial state,[204] often appears in the Ebla texts as consisting of two parts: Ebal "of the steppe" (*Eb-al*^{ki} lú Edin^{ki}, or simply Edin^{ki}) and Ebal "of the canal" (*Eb-al*^{ki} lú pa$_5$,[205] or simply *Eb-al*^{ki}). There are traces of three short inland canals of uncertain age, apparently spring fed, on the right bank of the Euphrates,[206] but the remains of only one old canal were significant enough to be noted on geographical maps and in descriptions of the area—the el-Frayy ("Little Euphrates") on the left bank of the river, whose dry bed between high dikes is shown running for ten km from the homonymous tell to its old outlet into the river at Qal^{c}at Ǧābar, but whose original inlet lay another four km further west.[207] Tell Frayy is a major mound[208] which was partially excavated in 1973 by Syrian-American and Syrian-Italian expeditions. What is important for my topic is that the site was occupied in the Early Bronze IV period and that it yielded a small lot of Middle Assyrian tablets from the latter part of the thirteenth century.[209] These tablets, we are told, "show the presence of a

[202] ARET 8 524 §3: ᵓ*À-rí-šu*^{ki} ᵓ*À-rí-ẓu*^{ki} lú *Eb-al*^{ki}.

[203] ARET 4 9 §8: ᵓ*À-rí-ẓú*^{ki} lú *Eb-al*^{ki} lú Edin^{ki}.

[204] As counted by Pomponio 1988: 318, the number of ugulas (overseers of towns) was "at least nineteen" in Ebal, more than in any other state in Ebla's sphere of influence.

[205] Thus in ARET 1 5 §35.

[206] Van Loon 1967: 6; Strommenger 1979: 72.

[207] The canal is shown on the maps *Raqqa* 1:500,000 and *Resafe* 1:200,000; see also Bell 1910: 519; Bell 1911: 48–49; van Loon 1967: 14 no. 532 and map 1; Bounni 1979: 7. It is now submerged by Lake el-Assad.

[208] Its coordinates are 35°54′ N, 38°23′ E; it lay ca. 27.5 km directly to the east-southeast from the site of Emar. Bell 1911: 49 called it "unusually large"; van Loon 1967: 14 gave its diameter as 500 m; Bounni and Matthiae 1980: 32, as 300 m; their plan of the site has no indication of scale.

[209] Bounni 1979; Bounni and Matthiae 1980; Matthiae 1980; Archi 1980a (Hieroglyphic Hittite material). The tablets have not been published as yet, and I do not know to whom they were entrusted. All we know of them comes from the very brief and somewhat inconsistent remarks by Bounni and Matthiae, neither of whom is an epigrapher. "They reveal," according to Bounni 1979: 7, "the name of the city buried at Tell Fray [and] the names of many of the satellite towns." It is regrettable that the latter are still unavailable to the interested scholars; as for the former, Bounni 1979: 6 states that "Yakharisha, mentioned in the Nuzi [actually Boğazköy] tablets . . . was identified with Tell Fray." If this is so, we are dealing with renaming the city for Yaḫrišša in east-central Anatolia (*RGTC* 6:133) under the Hittite rule. Matthiae 1980: 49–50, on the other hand, believes that "the problem of the identification of Tell Fray remains open" and proposes to see its ancient name in "the toponym Shaparu in one of the letters from Fray IV," but for unconvincing reasons. Arnaud 1987: 237 spells the toponym *Iaḫirišša*.

canal which flowed at the foot of the tell"[210] and indicate that the city "was charged with the control of the use of the waters of the Euphrates for irrigation."[211] A tablet in Middle Assyrian script and north Syrian format, probably stolen from Tell Frayy, deals with sending two men from the same town for work on two canals.[212] Thus, whatever name Tell Frayy may have borne in the thirteenth century, there is a strong probability that it was Ebal in Early Bronze IV.

The survey of the Ṭabqa Dam salvage area shows no mounds on the left bank of the Euphrates for the distance of ca. thirty km upstream from Tell Frayy. This means that no sizable fortified settlements fit for the role of city-states existed in that stretch of land. The kingdom of Gasur must therefore have been situated further upstream, above the eastward turn of the Euphrates, and the neighboring kingdom of Burman still further north, with its capital in one of the several walled sites in that sector of the valley.[213] Raᵓaq, which belonged to the same group of client kingdoms as Burman,[214] is mentioned in §3 as having been defeated, along with three other cities,[215] by Saᵓumu at Naḫal. Since Naḫal is attributed to Gasur in §10, one may suppose that Raᵓaq and the other three cities were also located on the left bank and that their joint contingent went down the Euphrates to meet the Mariote troops.

The localization of the city of Ebal at Tell Frayy makes it possible to envisage the relative position of Manuwat. If it had a common border with Ebal,[216] it

[210] Bounni 1979: 7.

[211] Bounni and Matthiae 1980: 33.

[212] Published, with another similar tablet, by Sigrist 1982: 242–46. He guessed (p. 242 n. 3) that they may have come from Emar, but Arnaud 1987: 237 plausibly suggested that they originated at Tell Frayy with its canals and irrigated cultures, unknown further north.

[213] For Burman, a client kingdom of first rank, the tells of Mumbaqat and Suweyḥat may be taken into account. But an epigraphic find at the former site creates the possibility that its ancient name was BÀD^{ki}, cf. Wäfler 1980 and Steinkeller 1984: 83–34, which also appears at Ebla both in this form and syllabically as *Du-ur*^{ki}/*Du-úr*^{ki}/*Dur-rí*^{ki}/*Du-ru*$_{12}$^{ki} etc., and as ^{kur}*Du-ri* in Tukulti-Ninurta I's list quoted above (n. 199). Mayer's claim 1986: 127–28 that URU^{ki} in one of the tablets from Tell Mumbaqat (around 1500) stood for *Uru/i/a* and was the name of the site does not impose itself. A town of that name is mentioned indeed at Ebla and later Emar, but URU^{ki} (as Mayer himself acknowledged) was the widespread designation of the central city of a district in local records. Suweyḥat, excavated by the Ashmolean Museum mission (see Holland 1976, 1977), fifteen km to the northeast of Mumbaqat, is a significant tell, with twice the surface of Ebla's Acropolis mound; its outer earth rampart enclosed an area of ca. forty hectares (less than Ebla's fifty-six hectares but still impressive); it also revealed levels of Early Dynastic, Sargonic, Ur III, and later ages.

[214] See n. 188 above. According to the cultic text no. 2:vi:19–25 in Pettinato 1979b: 158, they jointly delivered a number of sheep for an official sacrifice. This may point to their being direct neighbors.

[215] All three recur in Eblean administrative texts. *Ì-rúm*^{ki} (or *Ì-rìm*^{ki}), in one text mentioning it, delivered ì-giš-sag (an annual ceremonial tribute) to Ebla (MEE 2 39:rev.i:14–19). *Áš-al-tù*^{ki} is the same as *A-ša-lu*^{ki}, ARET 7 155:rev.v:9 (a register of land grants to grandsons of Ibrium). *Ba-du*$_{6}$^{ki} appears as *Ba-da-a* in another land grant, TM.75.G.1766:obv.ii:7, published by Fronzaroli 1979; *Ba-a-du* in a list of localities with large royal flocks, published by Archi 1984c: no. 10: reviii:4; *Ba*$_{4}$*-du*$^{⌜ki⌝}$, a town with an ugula ká in ARET 3 204 (transliterated there *Gá-du*$^{⌜ki⌝}$).

[216] See pp. 42–43.

could have adjoined it only from the east. No archeological survey of the left bank has been conducted below the Ṭabqa Dam, so no greater precision is possible.[217] By coincidence, and via a completely independent analysis, certain Mari texts testify to the location in the very same area of a town with a similar name: *Ma-nu-ḫa-ta-an*ᵏⁱ/*Ma-nu-ḫa-ta-a*ᵏⁱ, in which the ḪA-sign may have had its Old Babylonian value $^{\supset}a_4$.[218] We learn that (*a*) Manuḫatān lay on the left bank of the Euphrates, opposite Dunnum and Utaḫ on the right bank;[219] (*b*) Manuḫatān is paired with Lasqum as an area of Benjaminite encampments;[220] (*c*) a report about an outbreak of plague groups together Tuttul (Tell Bīᶜa near the confluence of the Balīḫ and the Euphrates), Dunnum, and two towns, Mubān and Manuḫatān, "in the surroundings of Dunnum"; the latter lies "below Lasqum" which recurs, a few lines further, as a "mountain" where the inhabitants of Dunnum fled to escape the plague;[221] (*d*) the leader of a Mariote caravan to Ḫalab states that after it has passed Lasqum, it will reach Emar in three days.[222] The last-cited piece of evidence is decisive: knowing the distance covered by ancient caravans and troops in one daily stage, and the actual number of stages made by an Old Babylonian caravan between Abattum and Emar, we must place Lasqum at between seventy-five km and ninety km east of the latter city.[223] A few kilometers southeast of the site of Abattum, the road leaves the Euphrates Valley and ascends the plateau

[217] A place called Tell Bélâni on modern maps, Al Billani on map 3 of Chesney 1850, and Billânî in Bell 1911: 52 (Tell Ballānah, 35°54′ N, 38°44′ E in *Gaz.Syr.*) overlooks the Euphrates thirty km in beeline east of Tell Frayy. One should beware of hastily equating it with *Ba*$_4$*-la-nu*ᵏⁱ (n. 185 above), for toponyms *Ballānah*, *Ballān* appear in other parts of Syria and derive from the Aramaic and Arabic word for 'bath', which, in turn, is a loanword from Greek (*balaneion*). Besides, the name of the old settlement at Tell Ballānah was *Bidama* (i.e., *Bi-Dāmā* 'house of Dāmā') in the Byzantine period, *Dāmān* in medieval Syriac and Arabic literature (see references in Honigmann 1935: 15 n. 5; Musil 1927: 257). My localization of it is based on the information by Yaqūṭ 2:583 that Dāmān lay five farsaḫs (i.e., ca. twenty-five km) from ar-Rāfiqa (part of medieval Raqqa).

[218] Cf., in Mari texts, *Ia-*$^{\supset}a_4$*-il*ᵏⁱ (ARMT 22 464:1) for the usual *Ia-a-il*ᵏⁱ/*Ia-i-il*ᵏⁱ etc.; in Karanā (Tell er-Rimaḥ) texts, *Za-mi-*$^{\supset}a_4$*-tim*ᵏⁱ (Tell er-Rimah no. 244:ii:5, 245:i:33) for *Za-mi-a-tum*ᵏⁱ; also *Mar*-*$^{\supset}a_4$*-ta-an*ᵏⁱ (ARMT 4 32:5, cf. Durand 1987: 226) = *Ma-ar-a-ta-an*ᵏⁱ (Tell er-Rimah no. 139:14).

[219] A.3835, quoted in ARMT 26/1, p. 126 n. 40.

[220] Unnumbered tablet quoted by Dossin 1939: 986 n. 1.

[221] A.675, published by Finet 1957: 128–29, now ARMT 26/1 259. Tuttul frequently appears in the Ebla texts as an Eblean city, and so probably does Dunnum, written *Du-na-um*ᵏⁱ, not to be confused with *Du-nu*ᵏⁱ in TM.75.G.2136:rev.iii:1, published by Pettinato 1978: 51–52, which was situated, along with the other cities of the list, in the far north of Syria.

[222] ARMT 26/1 17:8–14.

[223] Hallo 1964: 63 concluded from the geographically fixed stops in the mutually complementing Urbana and Yale itineraries that "in fact, the figure of 25–30 airline km/day which emerges agrees with what is known of the speed of travel on foot (or upstream by boat) in Old Babylonian times." In particular, the journey from Abattum to Emar (and vice versa) was covered in three days. I have identified Abattum (in Astour 1978: 2) with the large Tell Ṯadeyyēn on the right bank of the Euphrates, an idea taken up by Kohlmayer 1984: 112 and Kohlmayer 1986: 56–57 and nn. 23–24. (It also appears at Ebla as *A-ba-tù*ᵏⁱ, *A-ba-tum*ᵏⁱ.) The distance from there to Emar, by road, equals eighty-three km.

which falls to the river in long and steep escarpments.[224] This part of the plateau, then, is the Mariote area of Lasqum.[225] The Mariote data agree in placing Manuḫatān in the same area of the left bank where Manuwat is to be located according to my interpretation of Eblean data.[226]

Three towns mentioned in Enna-Dagan's letter—Galalabiya and Zaḫirān in §5 and Manê in §8—are to be placed on the left bank of the Euphrates between the confluence of the Balīḫ and the gorge of Ḫalabit which formed the border between Ebla and Mari.[227] Galalabiya/Galalabitu recurs in Ebla texts as a town which provided corvée workers[228] and, over two thousand years later, in Isidorus of Charax's description of the Royal Parthian Road, as Galabatha, a deserted riverside village, six *schoinoi* (twenty-four km) downstream from Nicephorium (Raqqa).[229] Manê is frequently mentioned in Ebla texts, mostly in inventories of fields,[230] and was in part under the direct rule of Ebla. It appears again in the Chaldean

[224] See the description of the relevant segment of the road (which always followed the same track) in Boulanger 1966: 484. The escarpments are shown on the map *Raqqa* 1:500,000.

[225] J.-M. Durand, the editor of the texts and the author of explanatory chapters of ARMT 26/1, identified Lasqum with the little basalt plateau (called Ḥammat eš-Šamīyeh) much further downstream, on the right bank of the Euphrates, where the ruined castle of Ḥalabīyeh rises above the river. (Both Durand, ARMT 26/1, 126, and Astour 1988b: 146 n. 47, have equated Ḥalabīyeh with Ḫalabit of Mariote—and Eblean—texts.) But Durand's localization of Lasqum is physically impossible. The actual distance from Ḥalabīyeh, by road, to Meskeneh Qadīmeh (Emar) is 195 km, i.e., 65 km per day in the three-day journey from Lasqum to Emar. Even Durand's own inexact figure for the distance, 150 km, and his assumption that the speed of 50 km per day could have been achieved and sustained for three days in a row, are unrealistic. Not only the caravan in question, which included children transported on wagons, but even trained and hardened soldiers could not boast of such an exploit. According to Xenophon, a participant in Cyrus the Younger's march from Sardis to Babylonia, the normal stages of the army were five or six *parasangs* (22.7 or 26.7 km), and only when it reached the Euphrates, "Cyrus sometimes made these stages through the desert very long, whenever he wanted to reach water or fresh fodder" (*Anabasis* 1:5:8); and even then the average length of a stage was seven *parasangs* (31.2 km) (*Anabasis* 1:5:1, 5). And what sense would the statement of A.4018 (quoted ARMT 26/1, 126 n. 37) make that "the Haneans have established themselves, separately, from Ḫalab[it] to Lasqum," if Ḫalabit was located in Lasqum itself? And how many clans of seminomadic sheep-breeders could have been accommodated, separately or otherwise, on the little plateau of ten km by seven km?

[226] Incidentally, the Mariote data considered above shed light on the approximate location of Lalayum (cf. n. 195). According to Durand, ARMT 26/1, 125, the tablet ARMT 23 595 indicates that Manuḫatān belonged to the district of Ziniyān, which at times was included into the district of Sagarātum further downstream. ARMT 23 69, a list of fields in towns of the latter district, begins with Ziniyan and ša-Lalaim, and the tablet M.6637, quoted in ARMT 23 69, associates Bīt-Lalayim with Yaḫappil, which was a twin town or an appellation of Ziniyān.

[227] See Astour 1988b: 146 n. 47.

[228] TM.75.G.2170 (MEE 1 1608) and TM.75.G.2012 (MEE 1 1450), according to the index of geographical names in Pettinato 1986. On the latter tablet, cf. Archi's comment to ARET 1 18 (p. 167).

[229] Isidori Characeni *Mansiones Parthicae* 4, in *Geographi Graeci Minores*, collected by Carl Müller (Paris 1882) 247. As is well known, Eblean scribes often rendered double consonants by doubling the syllable, so that *Ga-la-la-bi-ià/tù*[ki] may be normalized **Gallabiya/tù*.

[230] Its temples of Išḫara and [d]BE (Dagan) are also mentioned.

Chronicle for year 10 of Nabopolassar (616).[231] In that year, the king led the Babylonian army up the Euphrates, through the lands of Suḫi and Ḫindanu, and captured the city of Gablini from the Assyrians on the 12th of Abu.[232] During the same month, the Babylonians went upstream and took the cities of Manê, Saḫiri, and Baliḫu.[233] In the next month, Ulūlu, they retreated and returned to Babylon. The duration of the expedition was too short for the Babylonian army to reach the headwaters of the Balīḫ River, where a homonymous city is attested in the Neo-Assyrian Ḫarrān Census;[234] the Baliḫu in question must have stood near the confluence of the Balīḫ with the Euphrates. If Manê is the same place as Eblean Manê, it had to be located on the Euphrates upstream of Ḥalabīyeh. It is about seventy km by road from the northern edge of the gorge to the nearest point on the Baliḫ, or three normal stages. Very roughly, Manê would mark the first third of the road, and Saḫiri, its second third. Saḫiri is the Zaḫiran of Enna-Dagan's letter, and not only onomastically but geographically as well: the Mariote victory at Zaḫiran took place in conjunction with the capture of Galalabiya which, from completely independent evidence, I have placed in the same segment of the left bank, perhaps only a few kilometers from the presumable site of Zaḫiran-Saḫiri.[235]

The geographical findings presented above show that the hostilities between Mari on one side, and Ebla with its client states on the other, took place in various points of a long stretch of the Euphrates Valley, principally on the left (Mesopotamian) bank of the river, and in some areas of the adjacent steppe. We hear nothing about military actions further east, along the Balīḫ and in central Osrhoene, which were also subject to Ebla. The farthest northward advance of the Mariotes was Iblul-Il's occupation of Ana in the territory of Ḫazuwan, a client kingdom hitherto unaffected by Mariote forays. As correctly inferred by Archi, "at that moment . . . Ebla judged it to be more prudent to deliver a tribute

[231] Wiseman 1956: 54; Grayson 1975: 61 (chronicle 3:1–11a).

[232] Gablini, or Gabalini, recurs as Gabalein, center of a hyparchy (district) which included the mouth of the Ḫabūr, in a document from Dura-Europus, A.D. 180 (C. B. Welles, R. O. Fink, and J. F. Gilliam, *The Excavations at Dura-Europos*, Final Report V, Part I: *The Parchments and Papyri* [New Haven: Yale University, 1959] 25). Its probable location was on the left bank of the Euphrates, at a certain distance upstream from the confluence of the Ḫabūr.

[233] *A-na* ᵘʳᵘ*Ma-ni-e* ᵘʳᵘ*Sa-ḫi-ri u* ᵘʳᵘ*Ba-li-ḫu* (chronicle 3:7).

[234] ᵘʳᵘ*Ba-li-ḫi*, C. H. Johns, *An Assyrian Doomsday Book* (Leipzig 1901) nos. 4, 8, 15, or Fales 1973: nos. 4, 9, 15.

[235] Zaḫiran-Saḫiri may also be mentioned in Mari texts as *Sa-aḫ-ri*ᵏⁱ (once *Sa-ḫa-ri*ᵏⁱ), a town of the Sagaratum district, probably in its northern part. A question arises why it was Abarsil that was defeated by Iblul-Il at Zaḫiran: does not the evidence of the texts suggest that it was located very much further upstream? But in the Early Dynastic phraseology, defeating a city meant defeating its army. The troops of Abarsil may have been deployed at Zaḫiran in the course of an Eblean counter-offensive. Archi 1985b: 65 concluded that Mane should be sought in the territory of Emar on the basis of *in Má-ne*ᵏⁱ lú *Ì-mar*ᵏⁱ, ARET 3 323:rev.iv:8–10. This probably reflects the bestowal upon Tiša-Lim, queen of Emar, of a large land estate at Mane (ARET 2 27a:v:1–2), one of several land grants she received from Irkab-Damu, king of Ebla, which will be discussed further on. None of them belonged to the original territory of Emar, some were located at quite a distance from it, and most, if not all, of them later reverted to the royal domain of Ebla.

to the victorious Iblul-Il."[236] The choice of Manê as the place of delivery was not accidental: if my location of it is right, it lay almost on the southernmost end of the territory claimed by Ebla. The tribute, or war indemnity, was the price paid for the evacuation of Mariote troops. Enna-Dagan's proud reminder is confirmed by a series of Eblean records of payments, in silver, gold, and artifacts, to kings, high officials, and elders of Mari, spread over five Mariote reigns (Iblul-Il, Nizi, Enna-Dagan, Iku-(I)šar, and Ḫidar).[237] Manê[238] was the most frequent place of delivery of these payments, and the largest quantities of precious metals from Ebla were received by Mari under Iblul-Il.[239]

But things did not go smoothly after the indemnity-for-evacuation agreement. Hostilities were renewed soon after, still under Iblul-Il, who, as stated in §§9–10 of Enna-Dagan's letter, again attacked Emar and inflicted a defeat upon three cities of Gasur. It was perhaps as a result of this invasion that the same Eblean dignitaries who had started paying the indemnity to Iblul-Il now dated some of the further installments paid to him[240] as ì-giš sag lugal in u_4 TIL.TIL *Ga-sur*$_x$^{ki} 'the "oil-tribute" (to) the king [*scil.*, of Mari] when he arrived at Gasur'[241] (§7); *in* u_4 kas$_4$-kas$_4$ *Ga-sur*$_x$^{ki} 'when messengers (went to) Gasur' (§14). Iblul-Il's victory in the land of Gasur was the last one in his career, for the document just quoted contains the entry (§16) šu mu-DÚB (or šu mu-"taka$_4$") *Ib-lul-Il* lugal DIŠ mu TIL É×PAP 'assignment for Iblul-Il the king, year when he arrived at the cemetery' (a polite way of saying "died").[242] Thereafter the payments continued through the reign of Nizi, but his successor, Enna-Dagan, broke the peace once again. But the Eblean lands he invaded were the same that had been, many years before, the targets of Saᵓumu's first actions and were presumably located nearest Mari. Anyway, the raid had no sequel. Military luck was not only on the Mariote side. A notice has been preserved that King Irkab-Damu of Ebla presented objects of gold as gifts to the god Ada "in the year when Mari was defeated near Atini."[243] There are also scattered pieces

[236] Archi 1985b: 63. Cf. n. 191 above on Archi's identification of Ḫazuwan.

[237] Nine of these texts have been published by Archi 1981c, one in Archi 1987b: 67–72. A summary of all pertinent documents, with some amendments to the former publication, was given by Archi 1985b. There is therefore no need to consider them here in detail.

[238] Always spelled, in this context, *Má:ne*^{ki} (see n. 176 above).

[239] Cf. the breakdown of receipts for the three reigns beginning with that of Iblul-Il in Archi 1985b: 64.

[240] They are recorded, for the period of four years, in ARET 2 4. The recipient is designated throughout simply lugal and only in §16: *Ib-lul-Il* lugal; but this is customary in records of payments to kings of Mari.

[241] The ideogram TIL in Ebla texts is often considered to stand, at least in many cases, including the present one, for ug$_7$ 'to die', interpreted, when referring to cities, as 'to be destroyed' or 'to perish'. See n. 264 below for a different explanation.

[242] É×PAP was recognized to mean 'cemetery, burial site' by Pettinato 1988: 239, 312–13, with a list of occurrences on pp. 315–16.

[243] *In* mu *Ma-rí*^{ki} TÙN.ŠÈ *áš-ti* *ᵓÀ-ti-ni*^{ki}, ARET 7 115:rev.ii. This is the only unambiguous reference to a defeat of Mari in the hitherto published Ebla texts. There is another date formula which could be understood in the same sense: DIŠ mu šu-ra lugal *Ma-rí*^{ki} in TM.74.G.101, quoted by

of evidence about Eblean reconquests of cities and towns and measures taken in their wake.

Of the pertaining documents reported as of this writing, the most interesting seems to be the unpublished text TM.75.G.2290. Its contents have been related by Pettinato and by Archi only in general terms, but I was able to consult its transliteration thanks to the courtesy of Professors Pettinato and Owen.[244] It begins with the words: dub *ù-su-rí Eb-al*ki DIŠ mu TIL en *Ìr-kab-Da-mu* 'document of the *edict*[245] (concerning) Ebal, year of King Irkab-Samu's arrival [*scil.*, to Ebal]'. This is followed by dispositions concerning holdings of palace land in the town of Išla by the son of Iga-Lim (known from other Ebla texts as a prominent citizen of Ebal) and other persons, with the obligation of delivering "oil offerings," that is, tribute. There is no question of a king of Ebal either in this text or in the related text TM.75.G.1626; however, the statehood of Ebal was not abolished but put under the administration of four men, apparently local ones, with the modest titles of ugula 'overseers'.[246] This political change must be seen in the context of the ongoing war with Mari. Many passages of the text point to a state of war. There are references to en lú tùn-šè *Íl-wu-um*ki (obv.iv:3–5) 'the king who has defeated Ilwum', one of the cities previously defeated by Mari (Enna-Dagan's letter, §2), and to a delivery of spearheads (obv.vi:4–6). The city of Abzu had to provide arrows, spearheads, daggers, and jars of wine (rev.v:3–8), and another town (perhaps Garaman), jars and grain and men (rev.iv:2–6). The son of Iga-Lim and his brothers had to prepare 'a

Pettinato 1975: 367, who translated it 'year in which Šura became king of Mari' and took back his first interpretation "'year of the defeat of the king of Mari,' based on the correspondence šu-ra = *maḫāṣum*." Pomponio 1988: 319 and n. 14, in his refutation of Pettinato's construction of Mari-Ebla relations, pointed out that šu-ra "is not a personal name but a widely attested administrative term" (with references). From the occurrences of šu-ra (literally 'to strike') in Ebla texts it appears that it was used in the transferred meaning of 'to pledge, to guarantee', like the later idioms *pūta maḫāṣu* and *qaqqāda maḫāṣu*, on which cf. *CAD* M/1 80, and Veenhof 1972: 160–61 and n. 274. The date formula could still mean 'year when the king of Mari was smitten', if it were not for the circumstance that the tablet lot discovered in 1974 (room L.2586) was written in the reign of the last king of Ebla, when relations with Mari were peaceful; on the dating cf. Biga 1988: 285–86 and the fact that the king list in TM.74.G.120 (considered in §4 above) includes the name of Išʾar-Damu. As for the date formula DIŠ mu TIL *Ma-rí*ki, allegedly 'year in which Mari perished', and other occurrences of TIL, see n. 264 below.

[244] Pettinato 1986: 255–56 (without mentioning the number of the tablet); Archi 1988a: 216–17. As David I. Owen informed me in the note accompanying the copies of transliterations of three Ebla texts (TM.75.G.1626, TM.75.G.2268, and TM.75.G.2290), "Pettinato left me with many . . . transliterations of these texts, along with permission to quote or otherwise share the information," for which I am grateful to both of them.

[245] The tentative translation of *ù-su-rí* by 'edict', without elaboration, belongs to Archi. Cf. *ù-šu-rí* in a similar phrase in TM.75.G.2268:obv.i:1–3, rendered by Archi 1985b: 67, also tentatively, 'convention' (see p. 59 and n. 373 below).

[246] The four ugula-ugula in question were Bugadu (or Zugadu), Iga-Lim, Abani, and Zuzu, quoted text, obv.iv:8–13; cf. ARET 1 17 §19: Bugadu, Abanu, Iga-Lim, and the son of Nazu of Ebal. The composition of the board of ugulas of Ebal frequently changed, no doubt by their Eblean overlord.

journey to Mari' (níg-kas$_4$ *Ma-rí*[ki], obv.iii:2–8), but the figure of three hundred níg-kas$_4$ (obv.v:3) shows that we are dealing with a contingent of soldiers for an offensive against Mari. Mari is mentioned five times: once in an incomprehensible conjunction with Ebla (*Eb-la*[ki] *wa Ma-rí*[ki] KU.NI.A, obv.vi:2–5), followed by the incomplete sentence *ap an-tá-nu si-in Ma-rí* maškim:e-gi-maškim:e-gi [. . . . .] (obv.vi:6–[11]), which may be tentatively understood 'and therefore, you [*should not send*] ambassadors to Mari';[247] the other mentions are in broken contexts.

King Irkab-Damu's edict was not limited to Ebal. He also entrusted its ugulas with installing a headman (igi-du) in Busa (rev.ii:6–12) and two judges (two *ba-da-ga*)[248] in Abzu (rev.iv:7–11). Other items deal with the ownership of Ḫurbatum (obv.v:9–14), with the garrison (*maš-bí-tum*)[249] at KUR[ki] (obv.vi:10–13), and with other matters at Damat (obv.iii:14) and Šadaban (obv.iii:11, v:1). There is also a mention of some kind of consignment by the cities of Irar, Manuwat, and *Ga-kam$_4$*[ki] 'to thee' or 'with thee' (*áš-tá-kà*) (rev.i:8–ii:5). Most of the places mentioned in TM.75.G.2290 recur, often frequently and in geographically meaningful contexts, in other Ebla texts; their joint occurrence in a territorially coherent text confirms, or establishes for the first time, their general location.[250] Išla and Šadaban appear only here, but Išla was a dependency of Ebal, and Šadaban reemerges, a thousand years later, in the Emar tablets as Šatappa/Šatappi, one of the vassal kingdoms of the Hittite appanage kingdom of Carchemish, intimately connected with Emar economically, judicially, and religiously.[251] It also appears in the list of localities conquered and annexed by Tukulti-Ninurta I as [kur]*Šá-da-ap-pa*, and in other Middle Assyrian records as [uru]*Ša-da-ba-ia-ú* and the ethnic *Ša-da-pa-a-ia-ú*.[252] Since Tukulti-Ninurta I's conquests stopped at the Euphrates, the city must have been situated on its left bank. It may be tentatively

[247] For the conjunction *ap* see Fronzaroli 1981. Maškim:e-gi/gi$_4$ (maškim-gi/gi$_4$ at Fara, maškim:gi/gi$_4$ in the Eblean treaty with Abarsil, see Sollberger 1980: 142) "carried out important functions in relations between states," Archi, ARET 7: p. 227.

[248] Cf. VE 1327: di-ku$_5$ = *ba-da-gu da-ne-um* 'the decider of the trial'; see Krebernik 1982/83: 43 and Fronzaroli 1984a: 137. Judges (di-ku$_5$) at Ebla proper also served in pairs.

[249] Cf. VE 140b: erén ki-gar = *maš-bí-tum, ù-ma-núm, maš-ba-tum*. Erén = Akk. *ummānu* 'troop'; ki-gar = *šikittu* 'foundation, wall, place'.

[250] Busa, Damat, Garaman, and Ḫurbatum are found in lists of fields and land grants. On KUR[ki] as an Eblean district see nn. 172, 264, 334, and 360. The political status of Abzu and Ilwum after the war is not clear. Irar was one of the client kingdoms of Ebla.

[251] Since the edition of Emar tablets by Arnaud 1986 lacks indexes, here is the list of the occurrences of Šatappa/Šatappi (in various spellings); 105:1; 217:1; 218:4; 219:3; 220:[1]; 251:1; 257:4; 261:22; 361:11; 369:56, 58; 381:1, 2, 11, 16; 388:5. Especially instructive for the proximity of Šatappi to Emar are tablets 257 (a verdict of the king and the great ones of Šatappi in the case of a man from Ḫalulazi, which was deposed in the archive of a temple in Emar) and 369, in which high priestesses of Emar and Šumi and the kings of Emar and Šatappi jointly participate in the rite of enthronement of a new high priestess.

[252] For the occurrences in Tukulti-Ninurta I's list see nn. 199 and 200 above; for the other Middle Assyrian occurrences, see Weidner 1936: nos. 72:7, 12; 97:7, in which *ša* was assumed to be the relative particle; but Nashef, *RGTC* 5:240 recognized it as an integral part of the toponym.

placed at the site of Muraybiṭ-village, seven-and-a-half km north and across the river from Meskeneh Qadīmeh-Emar, where a surface survey disclosed material from Early and Late Bronze.[253]

TM.75.G.1626 is topically related to TM.75.G.2290, but the tablet is more damaged and the style is more elliptic. It is a brief of the exchange of messages between Ebal and an unnamed king of Manuwatu and between Abiᵓasu, ambassador of the king of Manuwatu, and Enšedu, u g u l a of Balamu.[254] Ebal is still without a king of its own and is still governed by four men, two of whom (Iga-Lim and Aban) belonged to the tetrarchy listed in TM.75.G.2290. Ebal's letter mentions "the king of Ebla, the king of Irar [here, as often, spelled *Ì-la-*[*ar*^{ki}]], the king of *Ga-kam*$_4$^{ki}," followed by a syntactically convoluted statement to the effect that Ebal and the king of *Ga-kam*$_4$^{ki} gave a food offering (n i d b a$_x$) and that " 'our food' (KUR$_6$-*ni*) in the town of Šulanu (had been taken?) by the ambassador (of the king of Ebla?)." This sounds more like an extraordinary requisition than like normal food supply to a traveling messenger. The middle part of the tablet is too damaged and fragmentary to figure out its meaning. Then something is said about the reception of the ambassador of the king of Manuwatu by the king of Ebla, and the text continues: *en-ma A-bí-a-su* m a š k i m : e - g i$_4$ e n *Ma-nu-wa-tù*^{ki} *ì-na En-še-du* u g u l a *Ba*$_4$*-la-mu*^{ki} n a m - k u$_5$ e n [*Eb*]*-la*$^{[ki]}$ (here one or two lines may be missing), 'Thus (says) Abiᵓasu, ambassador of the king of Manuwatu, to Enšedu, u g u l a of Balamu: The oath (to) the king of [Eb]la [*you should swear*]' (rev.v:3–14). To which Enšedu gave the defiant answer: *en-ma En-še-du nu-na-a an-tá ba tá-šu-mu Eb-al*^{ki} *an-tá* EME-*nu A-bí-a-su an-na* e n 'Thus (says) Enšedu: You are a . . . in the property of Ebal; you are Abiᵓasu the spokesman, I am a king. . . . '[255] Pettinato thought that the text dealt with a contest between Ebal and Manuwat for the administration of "the little town of Balanu [sic]."[256] It looks more likely that we are dealing here with a joint action of Ebal and Manuwat(u) to persuade the recalcitrant u g u l a of Balamu to swear allegiance to Ebla. There is nothing unusual in an u g u l a claiming to be the king of his city. After a certain time, the four u g u l as in charge of Ebal were promoted, or promoted themselves,

[253] Muraybiṭ-village was explored by J. Cauvin (France), but no report seems to have been published. I took my information from Dornemann 1985: 52.

[254] In the first lines of the text, *Eb-*⌜*al*⌝$^{[ki]}$ is followed by *la-ba-*[ ]*-na*, as though it was an epithet of the city. Could it be completed *La-ba-*[*na*?]*-na* and connected with KUR *La-ba-na-an* of Enna-Dagan's letter §1? On the discrepancy between Pettinato's transliterations of the name of Enšedu's city see n. 185 above. If *Ba*$_4$*-la-mu*^{ki} is the correct form, it may be a typically Eblean graphic variant of *Ba-ra-mu*^{ki} (ARET 8 533 §3, no doubt the same as *Ba-ra-a-ma*^{ki} in Enna-Dagan's letter §11.

[255] *Nu-na-a* can hardly mean 'fish' in the present context. For *ba* as a preposition (as in West Semitic) see Edzard, ARET 2: p. 50. *Da-šu-mu*, or rather *tá-šu-mu*, may be related to Hebrew *t*^{e}*šumet* (Lev. 5:21), variously translated 'deposit', 'joint property', or 'security'; cf. VE 72: n í g - g u r$_8$ = *da-šu-mu* and VE 1023: g u r$_8$ = *ma-sa-gàr-tù-um*, *maš-gàr-tum*, which may be related to Hebrew *misgeret* 'rampart, stronghold' and *masgēr* 'prison', from West Semitic *sgr* 'to close' (Akkadian *sekēru*). EME-*nu* probably renders Eblaic *lisānu* (with a phonetic complement) 'tongue', in the sense of 'speech', 'spokesman'.

[256] Pettinato 1986: 255.

to the rank of joint kings[257] and remained loyal to Ebla. But we do not hear about a king of Balamu/Baramu which, as suggested by the pertaining passage of TM.75.G.1626, must have been a neighbor of Ebal and Manuwat.

One may, besides, rectify some guesses concerning Ebla's war practices. Among the extant Eblean dating formulas, two certainly refer to (re)capture of cities: DIŠ mu šu ba$_4$-ti *Ḫa-za-nu-ma*^{ki} 'year when Ḫazanuma was taken',[258] and DIŠ mu šu ba$_4$-ti *Da-ra-šum*^{ki} 'year when Darašum was taken'.[259] Pettinato linked the latter event with "an economic text of only four lines but of horrifying contents: '3,600 dead persons at Darašum' . . . Ebla must have waged war on the city of Darašum with ensuing conquest which cost the life of 3,600 persons.[260] Nor is it the only piece of information about those fallen in war; another document, which registers 3,200 dead of two little towns belonging to the kingdom of Ebal, confirms how bloody the wars in the third millennium must have been."[261] He quoted the latter document elsewhere in the same book as saying "3,200 dead persons of Badanu and Masanu which belong to Ebal," which "presupposes a bloody war between Ebla and Ebal which ended with the defeat of the latter . . . [and] a total destruction of the two centers in question."[262] The key word for this interpretation is the polyphonous and polysemous sign no. 69 of Labat's numeration, which can indeed stand for ug$_7$ = *mâtu* 'to die' and til = *qatû* in its secondary sense 'to finish a life, destroy, perish', but also simply 'to achieve, finish', and *gamāru* 'to be completed'.[263] But the contexts of a great many passages in Ebla texts require still another meaning for this ideogram, and Pomponio correctly concluded that, in these cases, it "indicates a particular position or movement of laborers, animals, and goods, and should not be rendered by ug$_7$ 'dead', as, e.g., . . . in the brief texts that speak of 3,600 *na-si*$_{11}$ TIL of Darašum or of 3,200 *na-si*$_{11}$ TIL of Badanu and Masanu of Ebal . . . : these improbable massacres . . . are most likely movements of labor personnel."[264] The contingents seem to be unusually large, but labor teams over

[257] Archi 1987d: 42 quotes from unpublished texts: *I-ga-Li-im En-bù-uš-Da-mu Ìr-péš-Li-im Bu*$_x$*/Zú-ga-du* 4 en *Eb-al*^{ki} (TM.75.G.1701:obv.i); *I-ti-Il* en *Eb-al*^{ki} (TM.75.G.1701:obv.ix); *Ma-za-a-tù ma-lik-tum Eb-al*^{ki} (TM.75.G.10077:obv.vii); *I-ga-Li-im* en *Eb-al*^{ki} (TM.75.G.10077:rev.vi); *Du-bù-uš-Damu I-ga-Li-im Bu*$_x$*/Zú-ga-du Ì-lum-a-rí-ḫu* 4 en *Eb-al*^{ki} (TM.75.G.10077:rev.xiii).

[258] ARET 1 41:iii:3–5. The place in question recurs, in the shorter form *Ḫa-za-an*^{ki}, in ARET 3 940:ii:3, after the payments of the ì-giš-sag tribute by the kings or representatives of several subject cities of Ebla.

[259] ARET 1 35:ii:1–3.

[260] Pettinato refers to MEE 1 1822, i.e., TM.75.G.2383:obv.i:1–ii:2, which Archi, commentary to ARET 1 35:ii:1–3, quotes as 3,620 (sic) *na-se*$_{11}$ TIL *Da-ra-šum*^{ki}.

[261] Pettinato 1986: 171–72. The document in question is not identified by number either there or at the occasion of its repeated mention on p. 255 of the same book.

[262] Pettinato 1986: 255.

[263] Archi 1980b: 14, commenting on this sign in TM.75.1669, where it systematically stands between place-names and terms for labor teams and their supervisors, thought that it "might be interpreted as til 'finished', meaning 'finished operation'."

[264] Pomponio 1988: 320 and n. 18. Following Pomponio's line of thought, one may narrow down the meaning of til as 'arrived'. Cf., e.g., ARET 8 522 §15: *wa* 1 *mi-at* 20 *na-se*$_{11}$ *Ar-mi*^{ki} *wa*

a thousand strong are not exceptional, and in one known case, "TM.75.G.10250 lists farm workers by 'labor units' é, the sum total šu nigín is 4,580 *na-se*$_{11}$ dub ká *A-ru*$_{12}$*-lu*^{ki}."[265]

It seems possible to discern certain repercussions of the Eblean reconquest of lost territories in documents from the reign of Irkab-Damu. One of them is the apparent dismantling of the kingdom of Gasur. In Enna-Dagan's letter (§10), Gasur is a territorial entity which included, in addition to the capital, the cities of Naḫal, Nubat, and Šada; and a king of Gasur appears in TM.75.G.1626. But in the only subsequent mention of Naḫal,[266] its 'oil tribute' (ì-giš sag) is delivered by *Ḫal-ra-Il*, evidently a variant spelling of *Ḫa-ra-Il*, also known as *Ḫa-ra-ià*, a well-known and very active Eblean prefect (lugal) from the time of the "vizierate" of Ibrium.[267] Nubat (*Nu-ba-ti-um*^{ki}) participated independently, along with several other cities, in the collection of silver to be paid to Enna-Dagan at the time of Ar-Ennum;[268] it delivered two oxen, probably as symbolic tribute to Ebla.[269] Gasur itself frequently appears in administrative texts (lists

---

1 *mi-at* 80 *na-se*$_{11}$ *A-ba-tum*^{ki} til *in* uru^{ki} *Gú-da-da-núm*^{ki} 'and 120 men from Armi and 180 men from Abatum arrived to the towns of Gudadanum'. In the collection of ten passages with til (including the just quoted one) in Pettinato 1988: 313–14, every occurrence of the ideogram can be translated 'arrived' with a better sense that his 'died, dead' which makes the list sound like a bulletin from a plague-ridden city. In Pettinato's entry no. 5, why should a quantity of wool be delivered to two dead persons? The same is true for such dating formulas as DIŠ mu lugal *Ma-rí*^{ki} til (TM.75.G.1574) 'year when the king of Mari arrived' (to Ebla with a visit), rather than ug$_7$ 'died', or DIŠ mu til *Ma-rí*^{ki} (TM.75.G.1452), abbreviation of the same formula rather than 'year in which Mari perished', as thought by Archi 1979b: 111 (incidentally, Mari "perished" several years after the end of the Ebla archives). One more example: the entry (three pieces of clothing) *Rí-ià-Ma-lik Ì-mar*^{ki} níg-AN.AN.AN.AN en *Ì-mar*^{ki} *Mar-tu*^{ki} til *in* Kur^{ki} (ARET 8 524 §14) does not mean that the king of Emar destroyed the Amorites in the steppe (Fronzaroli 1980: 48) or in the mountain (Pettinato 1986: 239) but that Riya-Malik of Emar arrived at the city Martu in the steppe region with three pieces of clothing as a gift to the (local) gods from the king of Imar. On Martu, see pp. 53–54 below.

[265] Archi 1988c: 138. Dub ká means 'document of the "gate"' (subdivision of an administrative district). The attribution of the text dealing with 3,200 men from Ebal to the period of Mariote wars is dubious. One cannot be certain that Badanu and Masanu mentioned there are names of towns and not of persons (a few cases of this kind do occur in Pettinato's readings of Ebla texts). No towns so named have been found in published Ebla texts; conversely, *Ba-da-nu/Ba-da-an* is a personal name that appears in ARET 2 28:i:8, ARET 4 14 §13, ARET 8 522 §18, and ARET 8 525 §9 (in the latter two passages he is a maškim, or agent, of Irʾaq-Damu, crown prince of the last Eblean king of the period of archives); and *Ma-sa-nu* is the name of a man who is mentioned in ARET 8 524 §3 in one paragraph with Ebal and two of its subordinated towns. In the unpublished text, Badanu and Masanu were probably the officials responsible for the labor contingents from Ebal at the very end of the period of archives.

[266] ARET 3 549:vi.

[267] See, e.g., MEE 2 1:obv.v:9 (*Ḫa-ra-ià*) and the analogous text TM.75.G.1297 (MEE 1 736) (*Ḫa-ra-Il*); for the spellings, cf. Kebernik 1988b: 194, 196.

[268] MEE 2 35:rev.v:9; vii:9. It paid altogether seventeen shekels of silver (out of the total of ninety-five minas fifty-four shekels of silver and one mina of gold).

[269] ARET 2 24 §6 (2 gù$_4$ lú *Nu-ba-tù*^{ki}). The city was also known at Mari, cf. ^{d}*Eš*$_4$*-tár ša Nu-ub-tim*, ARMT 23 46:6. On deliveries of single heads of cattle as tribute, cf. Astour 1988b: 148 n. 56.

of tribute, corvée personnel, etc.). As for Šada, it was fully integrated into the royal sector of Ebla's economy. There was a royal estate (é en) there,[270] and Šada is listed in at least four registers of fields and deeds of land grants,[271] one of which, for 1700 *gána-ki* = 100 hectares,[272] has Queen Tiša-Lim of Emar as beneficiary and can thus be assigned to the time of King Irkab-Damu of Ebla. We shall return to this queen presently.

It seems that the fate deduced for Gasur also befell the client city of Adu (*ʾÀ-du*[ki]). But in Adu's case we know more about its antecedents thanks to the intriguing text TM.75.G.2561, published by Pettinato, with an imaginative translation, under the heading "A Document of Political Espionage."[273] It is rather an *aide-mémoire* dealing with diplomatic negotiations and comparable, in this respect, to TM.75.G.1626 discussed above. Adu, from what is known of it, was a city on the Euphrates, perhaps on its left bank. It is mentioned, among other texts, in the preamble to Ebla's treaty with Abarsil as one of several cities (some of them known as royal ones) which are declared to be *in* šu en *Eb-la*[ki] 'under the jurisdiction of the king of Ebla.' TM.75.G.2561 is difficult to understand in many places, but the general gist is clear. A Mariote official came to three towns of the kingdom of Adu and requested bread, beer, oxen, and sheep. The local headmen referred him to the king of Adu. The latter protested that he had a treaty with Ebla, sworn before the gods Kura and Ada. Finally, after an exchange of four more messages, the king of Adu conceded: "The brotherhood with Ebla is not good, but the brotherhood with Mari is good for both of us" (I consider NE-*si-in* /nêšin/, the last word of the text, to be the dative of the first-person dual pronoun; cf. Old Babylonian Mari *-nêšim* 'to us').

The situation reflects war conditions. The demand of food and drink from three towns amounts to requisitions for invading troops. Eblean troops, according to the text, had reaped the barley and taken the oxen and sheep of one of the three towns (*Il-la*-NI[ki]), and the king of Adu declared to the representative of Mari that he was not responsible for it. The shift of Adu from Eblean to Mariote allegiance was no doubt committed under the threat of armed force; the penultimate, barely intelligible passage seems to hint at just that.

After the war, Adu remained a royal city. Of its three dependent towns mentioned in TM.75.G.2561, *Ḫu-ba-tù*[ki] does not appear in other texts. The second, *Sa-ra-bù* (written here without the determinative ki, but certainly a locality, because it had an ugula), recurs as *Sar-ra-bù*[ki] in TM.75.G.1669,[274] a list

[270] ARET 3 740:ii; ARET 4 11 §18. It was the "house" not of the local king but of the king of Ebla, one of his several estates scattered over the empire, like the 1 *li* gána-ki *wa* 1 é en *in Sa-du-úr*[ki] 'one thousand field units and a royal estate at Sadur', ARET 7 154:obv.6–11.

[271] TM.75.G.1724:obv.ii:5–iii:2 (Archi 1980b: 9); ARET 2 27a:i:1–2; ARET 3 111:obv. iii:1–3; ARET 7 155:obv.i:5–6.

[272] As calculated by Milano 1987b: 186–87, the Eblean unit of area measure, gána-ki (or gána-kešda), was equivalent to one sixth of the Babylonian *ikû*, i.e., to 588 sq m (it thus corresponded to the *kumānu* of second-millennium Assyria, Alalaḫ, and Ugarit).

[273] Pettinato 1986: 398–400. The tentative translation by Heimpel 1989: 122 does not make the meaning of the text any clearer.

[274] Published by Archi 1980b: 11–14.

of over forty towns that provided teams of corvée workers and/or daggers and vessels. *Sar-ra-bù*[ki] formed a corvée unit jointly with three other towns (rev.v:4–14). It also occurs elsewhere as *Sar-ra-ab*[ki], *Sa-ra-ab*[ki], *Sa-ra-bu*$_y$[ki], always as a direct dependency of Ebla. The third town, *Il-la*-NI[ki], is mentioned twice in the lengthy list ARET 4 1, as *Il-la*-NE[ki] in §97 and *I-la*-NE[ki] in §116. The list includes both royal and nonroyal cities, but the last-mentioned locality is not associated in any way with Adu. One may infer, as for Gasur, that Adu was deprived of its dependent town as retribution for its disloyalty to Ebla.

Of those rulers who gained from the territorial changes in the wake of the Ebla-Mari war, we know first and foremost of Queen Tiša-Lim. This woman, whose name is found in Ebla texts more often than that of any other client ruler, is titled *ma-lik-tum Ì-mar*[ki] and seems to have been not just a royal consort but a ruler in her own right,[275] or rather a joint ruler of Emar in the pattern of dual or multiple kingship which is attested in several states of the Ebla Empire,[276] for Enzi-Damu,[277] known from other texts as a king of Emar, is named apart from her in one of the land grant documents.[278] The towns assigned to Tiša-Lim by Irkab-Damu are defined as the purchase prices (níg-sa$_{10}$-níg-sa$_{10}$) for the cities of Irpaš[279] and Gurarakul.[280] Irpaš formed a joint tribute and corvée unit with Uduban and Amatu;[281] the approximate location of the latter is known from several Mari texts which put it on the uppermost reaches of the Mariote-controlled sector of the Eu-

[275] As recognized by Pettinato 1986: 271. In ARET 3 772:ii, Tiša-Lim is called ama-gal-*sù* 'his (whose?) great mother', i.e., queen mother, a highly respected position at Ebla. Should one suppose that Tiša-Lim had exercised the power of a reigning queen as a regent for her minor son, and became queen mother after he effectively took over the reins of government?

[276] Archi 1987d: 42 has cited, with references, the evidence on dual or multiple kingship in five states: Armi, Azu, Dugurasu, Ebal, and Manuwat. To those, I may add ARET 1 11 §37: en tur *Du-ub*[ki] 'junior king of Ṭub', and, significantly, ARET 3 584:viii:11–13: en en *Ì-mar*[ki].

[277] Certain authors (Fronzaroli, Pettinato, van Huyssteen) read the first element of this and similar names *Ru*$_{12}$*-ṣí-* rather than *En-zi-*, mainly for etymological reasons. It should be remembered, however, that in VE 799a ^{d}En-zi appears as a variant of ^{d}En-zu VE 799b, and both are rendered by *Su-i-nu* (Old Akkadian *Suʾen*, later dialects *Sîn*, the moon god).

[278] Two deeds concerning Tiša-Lim have been published and commented upon by Fronzaroli 1984c. One, TM.75.G.2396, was issued by King Irkab-Damu; in the other, TM.75.G.1986+3221+4544, that royal name was plausibly restored in a broken passage by the publisher. The latter is supplemented by ARET 2 27a which includes some of the same place names.

[279] This toponym was at first transliterated *Ìr*-ḪUŠ[ki], but after Edzard identified the second sign as PÉŠ in ARET 2 14 §37 and the sign list ARET 2: p. 160, it was changed to *Ìr*-PÉŠ. Krecher 1988: 177–78 noted that the sign in question "is found mostly where parallels favor a reading *baš*$_x$ (*paš*$_x$, *baz*$_x$) or even shorter *ba*$_x$ (*pa*$_x$)."

[280] Spelled *Gú-ra-kul*[ki] in TM.75.G.2396 §1, but *Gú-ra-ra-kul*[ki] which is the more frequent form, in TM.75.G.1986+ §1. It is also found in the Ebla texts in the variants *Gú-la-kul*[ki], *Gú-la-la-kul*[ki], *Gú-ra-la-la*[ki], and *Gú-ra-ra-ab*[ki]. There is no doubt that all of them designate the same place.

[281] TM.75.G.1669 §11, published by Archi 1980b: 11–14. Instead of *Ù-du-ba-an*[ki], ARET 4 8 §23 transliterates another occurrence of that name *Ù-rá-ba-an*[ki] because of *Ù-ra-ba-nu*[ki] ARET 3 310:obv.ii. The fact that Amatu provided corvée teams jointly with a city that used to belong to Emar is a decisive argument (among many) against the widespread but uncritical belief that Eblean Amat(u) was Hamath (Ḥamāh) on the Orontes (cf. n. 32 above).

phrates.[282] Gurarakul, also known as Gurarab, recurs in a thirteenth-century business text from Emar as ^{uru}*Ku-ra-ra-ba*, a town in the vicinity of Emar,[283] though one cannot tell in what direction.[284] The exchange of the towns included the assumption of jurisdiction over them by their new owners: "Moreover, from the towns of Tiša-Lim the king's commissioner (and?) the supervisor of commerce will depart; moreover, from the towns of the king the commissioner of Tiša-Lim (and?) supervisor of commerce will depart."[285] TM.75.G.1986+ confirms that the lands received by Tiša-Lim in exchange for Irpaš and Gurarakul are in her "two hands," that is, under her sovereignty; makes stipulations about the status of their inhabitants, Emariotes, the king's men in his estates, and the subjects of Enzi-Damu who reside in Tiša-Lim's towns; and lists seven of these, but only three names are preserved in full: TÚL-*tù*^{ki} (**Būrtu*), DU$_6$^{ki} lú ⸢*Ḫu*⸣*-ra-zu*^{ki}, and *A-bí-ḫa-tù*^{ki}.[286] A third pertaining document, ARET 2 27a, is a register of land estates in seven towns, partially coinciding with those in TM.75.G.1986+. These are listed in two sections: (*a*) *Ša-da*$_5$^{ki}, *Ḫu-ra-zu*^{ki} together with a man called Damarum, to whom Tiša-Lim gave a grain assignment (še-ba),[287] and (*b*) *Dar-da-ù*^{ki},[288] *Šu-na-ù*^{ki}, *A-bí-ḫa-tù*^{ki},

[282] In particular, ARMT 23 464, which speaks about the fields of *muškēnum*-people between Ziniyān and Amatum (*iš-tu Zi-ni-ia-an*^{ki} *Ia-ḫa-ap-pí-li-im a-di A-ma-tim*^{ki}). On Ziniyān, cf. n. 226 above. Amatum was probably located upstream from Ziniyān, roughly halfway between Imar and the Balīḫ confluence.

[283] Arnaud 1986: no. 119:5, 13. The tablet deals with a loan of fifteen *parīsu* of grain from the town authority of Kuraraba by an Emariote businessman and his associates.

[284] Gurarakul was administered, after it passed under the jurisdiction of Ebla, first by Ibrium's brother Bumaya (ARET 1 2 §31″), then by Ibrium's son Napḫa-Il/Napḫaya (ARET 7 152:iii:4; TM.75.G.1444:ix:15–16, published by Edzard 1981a) as one of his several towns. Both Gurarakul and Irpaš, at least temporarily, had their own kings (ARET 3 232:iv:1′–2′; for the former, see ARET 4 16 §13; ARET 4 17 §7 for the latter), but we do not know their names. On the often purely formal character of promoting a dependent town to royal status see Astour 1988b: 152.

[285] TM.75.G.2396 §§5–6: *ap mi-nu* uru^{ki}-uru^{ki} *Ti-ša-Li-im* maškim en lú-kar è; *ap* [*mi*]-*nu* uru^{ki}-uru^{ki} en maškim *Ti-ša-Li-im* lú-kar è. My translation of this passage, which differs from that of Fronzaroli, is based on the commonly attested meaning of the Sumerogram è at Ebla and on the interpretation of *mi-nu* as 'from' by Krecher 1984 and Biga and Milano, *ARET* 4: p. 133. Lú-kar can mean 'merchant'; but in some texts this title clearly designates an important official charged with the supervision of commerce; see Waetzoldt 1984: 416–19, to whose examples should be added ARET 3 470:obv.ii:9–12: *En-zi-Da-mu* dumu-nita en *Ma-nu-wa-at*^{ki} lú-kar, according to which the function of lú-kar was exercised by a king's son. The query after the putative "and" points to the possibility that maškim and lú-kar may have been one and the same person.

[286] TÚL-*tù*^{ki}, also appearing as TÚL^{ki} (four times in ARET 8, once in ARET 3), should probably be read **Būrtu* and be equated with *Bù-ur-tin*^{ki} TM.75.G.1558:obv. iv:3 (Archi 1984c: no. 10, a register of sheep flocks). DU$_6$^{ki} (Akk. *tillu*) may mean 'mound, hill', but it is attested elsewhere at Ebla as a definite toponym (once spelled out *Ti-la*^{ki}). DU$_6$^{ki} lú ⸢*Ḫu*⸣*-ra-zu*^{ki} may point to its proximity to Ḫuraṣu, which later recurs in the Mariote list of slaves ARMT 22 15:i′:10′ in the ethnic form [*Ḫ*]*u-ra-ṣa-yu*^{ki}. At Ebla, Ḫuraṣu and Abiḫatu are found only in connection with Tiša-Lim.

[287] The custom of "giving" a certain person to the new assignee of a town recurs in other Eblean land grants, e.g., TM.75.G.1444 (referred to on p. 23 and n. 151 above) §§12–14, 39. These men, sometimes bearing the titles ur$_4$ or ugula, were local administrators.

[288] The damaged toponym x̣-*da*-x̣^{ki} in TM.75.G.1986+ §6 may be a vestige of [*Dar*]-*da*-[*ù*]^{ki}. In the form *Dar-du*^{ki} (or *Dar-tù*^{ki}), it occurs in TM.75.G.1340, summarized in MEE 1 778, among cities located on, or near, the Euphrates.

Má-ne^{ki}, *Sá-a-nu*^{ki}.[289] The document ends, without explanation, in two personal names, *En-[n]a-Da-mu* and *A-ti-ir*. The former may have been the king of Manuwat of the same name,[290] and the latter is attested as an official in two records of tribute collection.[291] They may have been witnesses or supervisors of the transfers.

This transaction between Irkab-Damu and Tiša-Lim is very similar to the deal between Abbān, king of Yamḫad in the seventeenth century, and his younger brother Yarim-Lim, as described in the Alalaḫ VII tablets 1 and 456. Yarim-Lim, who remained loyal to Abbān during a civil war, received the city of Alalaḫ in exchange for his previous city, Irridi, which had been destroyed during the hostilities. Besides, other towns were exchanged between Yarim-Lim and Abbān. All told, Yarim-Lim gave away six towns and received eleven (including, incidentally, Emar). From a juridical point of view, the dossier of Tiša-Lim, which antedates the Abbān–Yarim-Lim deal by some seven centuries, is of considerable interest. The question arises: Why was Irkab-Damu so generous with regard to a client queen as to give her at least seven towns in exchange for two? Years ago, Pettinato included Tiša-Lim among the daughters of Ibrium and asserted: "Another princess, Tiša-Lim, was married off to the friendly king of Emar, becoming 'queen of Emar.'"[292] If this were so, one could construe the bestowal of towns upon Tiša-Lim as a munificent dowry. But there is no shred of evidence that Tiša-Lim was a daughter of Ibrium, or of Irkab-Damu, or of any Eblean personage,[293] and Pettinato himself, in his more recent book, no longer claims it.[294]

Notice, however, that two of the towns transferred to Tiša-Lim—Šada and Mane—appear in Enna-Dagan's letter as having been defeated or occupied by Mariote troops. A third, *Sá-a-nu*^{ki}, recurs in a later land-grant record[295] as *Sá-a-⌜nu⌝*^{ki} 1 u r u^{ki} E d i n, that is, it is attributed to the steppe portion of the kingdom of Ebal (see p. 34 above). A fourth, *Dar-da-ù*^{ki}/*Dar-du*^{ki}, or rather *Dar-tá-ù*^{ki}/*Dar-tù*^{ki}, possibly reappears in the Roman period as Derta/Dertha in the 'swamps' (*paludes*) of the Euphrates, that is, the marshy delta of the Balīḫ.[296] These two

[289] In §3, the total of Tiša-Lim's lands (only for the five towns listed under *b*) is given as 9000 g á n a - k e š d a (529.2 hectares). For some reason, the scribe used the ideogram g á n a - k i for the estates in the two towns of group *a* (respectively, 1700 and 900 units), though g á n a - k e š d a, g á n a - k i, and g á n a - k e š d a - k i were identical (cf. n. 273 above).

[290] ARET 1 11 §21.

[291] ARET 2 1 §2; ARET 2 41 §2 (in the latter, along with Uti, known as a son of Ibrium).

[292] Pettinato 1979a: 90–91, 93, 125 n. 48.

[293] The carefully compiled prosopographical lists by Archi, Biga, and Milano, published in 1988, do not include Tiša-Lim. Of the two texts referred to by Pettinato in support of his claim, one (MEE 1 874 = TM.75.G.1436) remains unpublished and Pettinato no longer mentions it in his 1986 book (p. 378) among texts relating to Tiša-Lim; the other (MEE 1 1532 = TM.75.G.2094) deals, according to his own summary, with the marriage not of Tiša-Lim but of Tia-barzu, who was indeed a daughter of Ibrium; cf. Archi 1988a: 242.

[294] Pettinato 1986 mentions Tiša-Lim three times (pp. 144, 271, 284) without referring to her filiation. But on p. 169, vestigially, only her name was removed from the statement "Another princess was given in marriage to the sovereign of Emar."

[295] ARET 7 156:rev.v:1–3.

[296] Tabula Peutengeriana places Derta at the southern tip of a circular island, surrounded by an equally circular body of water, which is connected with the Euphrates through two channels.

towns were also located on the routes of Mariote invasions. Since the donor of all these places, Irkab-Damu, was the king who had reconquered them and concluded the war with Mari, their transfer to the queen of Emar is best seen as a reward for Emar's staunch support of Ebla in the long war in which it bore the brunt of two major Mariote onslaughts. The connection of the grants with the reconquest of the Euphrates Valley is corroborated by an entry in a list of personnel: 30 *na-se*$_{11}$ ⌜šu⌝-⌜du$_8$⌝ *Bù-zu-ga*^{ki} *wa A-da-ra*^{ki} 2 šu *Ti-ša-Li-im*[297] 'thirty men "taken" (from) Buzuqa and Adara (in)[298] the two hands of Tiša-Lim'. The expression šu-du$_8$ is never applied to regular teams of corvée workers, and in the very few cases where it qualifies persons, it should be understood as "taken prisoner."[299] It is hardly accidental that in several records of grain supply for the palace personnel at Ebla one finds a group of eighty women from Buzuqa (dam *Bù-zu-ga*^{ki}), distinct from other categories of women in the palace, and the only one designated by the place of their provenience.[300] One should think that they had been brought into servitude at the palace in the wake of the (re)capture of their home town by Eblean troops.[301] Buzuqa, which appears in at least nine other Eblean texts, recurs in Late Bronze Emar as *Bu-uz-qa* in epithets of gods[302] and as $^{uru.ki}$*Bu-uz-qa* in the description of the enthronement of the priestess *maš*ᵓ*artu* at Emar, in which Buzqa participated with seven men along with delegations from some other towns.[303] It must have belonged to the kingdom of

This is a stylized and enlarged representation of the swampy area (the only one on the Syrian stretch of the Euphrates) formed by the two branches of the Balīḫ at its confluence with the Euphrates. The Ravennate Geographer, 54:3, lists Dertha as the easternmost of six towns on the right bank of the Euphrates below its bend; the westernmost is Barbalissus, the successor of Emar.

[297] ARET 3 460:rev.v.

[298] The preposition *in* 'in' has been omitted in this entry, but is present in the next entry, rev.vi: (persons) *in* 2 šu *Ti-ša-Li-im.*

[299] Thus far, only one document in which šu-du$_8$ is applied to persons and not goods has been published (by Pettinato 1979a: 145–46 and Archi 1979b: 111–12), *viz.*, TM.75.G.309, dealing with *na-se*$_{11}$ from the cities of Ebal, Ḫarran, and Martu. According to the summary of TM.75.540 in MEE 1 208, the same is true for *na-se*$_{11}$ of Martu and Atinu, but the quotation from that tablet in Archi 1988b: 11 no. 6, shows that the term šu-du$_8$ is not used in connection with Martu.

[300] The pertaining records have been published and commented upon by Milano 1987c. One text, TM.75.G.273 (MEE 1 90) ii:11–iii:5, quoted by Waetzoldt 1987: 373, subdivides the "eighty women of Buzuqa" into fifty-five weavers and twenty-five grinders.

[301] At Ebla, the Sumerogram dam stood for 'woman' in general, not only 'wife'. In ARET 2 19:i:3–5 rations for dam are paired with rations for ir$_{11}$ 'slaves'. In ARET 2 17:ii:1–2 one finds 15 dam *sa-bar-tum*, explained by Edzard *ad loc.* as Akkadian *šapartum* 'female slave held as a pledge'. There was also a category dam *a-si-ra-tum* (ARET 3 366:ii:3, ARET 3 971:iv:4), which Archi, ARET 3: p. 237 rendered by "donna di corte" (lady courtier); but these women received for their clothing half of the wool allocation of female weavers, which points to their very low social position. We have here the Akkadian *asirtu*, fem. of *asīru* 'prisoner of war used as worker'. As noted in *CAD* A/2 332: "The word occurs mainly in early OB adm. documents and in texts from the West . . . [a word of] a foreign, West Semitic, provenience."

[302] Arnaud 1986: nos. 373:107, 121; 383:9′.

[303] Arnaud 1986: no. 370:56′.

Emar which controlled a wider territory than its Early Bronze Age predecessor.[304] As for Adara (also attested as Adarin), it probably appears in Enna-Dagan's letter (§6), as Addalini,[305] defeated by him along with Šada, hence located on the left bank of the Euphrates upstream of Emar.

All in all, the outcome of the war was a clear victory for Ebla. To be sure, Ebla continued the remittance of the previously agreed indemnity to Mari. But the border between Ebla and Mari was fixed at the southern outlet from the Euphrates gorge at Ḫalabit (modern Ḥalabīyeh), leaving that fortress on the Eblean side.[306] This follows from the inclusion of Ḫalabit in two largely identical groups of twelve tributary cities of Ebla[307] and from the fact that several points upstream of Ḫalabit figure in Eblean records of tribute, land estates, cattle, cult, etc., while no point downstream of Ḫalabit all the way to Mari is ever mentioned in Ebla texts, except Terqa—but only as a place of purchase of Eblean clothing by merchants from Kiš.[308] The assertion that, after the war with Mari, "Ebla exercised its hegemony from the plain of Antioch up to Emar," while "the territory controlled by Mari began in the west with Tuttul at the Baliḫ"[309] (leaving thus a no-man's-land some 115 km long between the two cities) contradicts the data of the Ebla texts.[310] The southeastern extent of Ebla's rule is especially striking when compared with the situation that obtained in the age of the Mari archives when the entire left bank of the Euphrates and its right bank almost up to Emar belonged to Mari.[311]

The period of wars between Mari and Ebla covered four reigns and part of a fifth at Mari (Saᵓumu, Ištup-Šar, Iblul-Il, Nizi, and Enna-Dagan). Since, for Ebla, the hostilities ended under Irkab-Damu, they must have started, at the latest, in the reign of Kum-Damu. This amounts to from eighty to a hundred years. Like the Hundred Years' War between England and France, the long conflict be-

[304] Buzuqa is not mentioned in Enna-Dagan's letter, but it is listed, with Burman and Nubatium, which are mentioned there, among cities which had contributed gold and silver for payment to the same Enna-Dagan (MEE 2 35:rev.viii:4).

[305] See n. 193 above.

[306] On the location of Ḫalabit see n. 225 above.

[307] These groupings appear in two lengthy records of tribute: (*a*) MEE 2 1:obv.viii:13–rev.i:14: Zaburrum, Utigu, Inibu, Ursaᵓum, Iritum, Ḫarran, Tisum, Ḫutimu, Kablul, Ṭub, Abulium, Ḫalabitu); (*b*) TM.75.G.1297 (MEE 1 736): Ḫarran, Zašaginu, Iritum, Ḫutimu, Ṭub, Utig, Inibu, Kablul, Tisum, Dulu, Šarḫu, Ḫalabî; see pp. 22–23 above. Ḫalabitu is also mentioned in ARET 4 23 §36.

[308] Archi 1987e: 138, documents 7 and 9.

[309] Archi 1988b: 5 and Archi 1985c: 220.

[310] In particular, there is no indication in any published or quoted Ebla text mentioning Tuttul or dealing with relations between Mari and Ebla that Tuttul was controlled by Mari. To be sure, merchants from Mari are frequently attested in Tuttul—but they also visited other cities of Ebla's sphere of domination. The very fact that the activities at Tuttul of people from Mari, Kiš, Nagar, and other cities were recorded in Eblean administrative texts proves that Tuttul was under the jurisdiction of Ebla.

[311] However, if Ebla regained its territory, Mari—as will be seen in the next section—retained the control of the Lower Euphrates trade route.

tween Ebla and Mari consisted of separate raids and battles, divided by periods of inactivity, truces and treaties, their violations, renewed military actions, reprisals against disloyal vassals, and final pacification. The section devoted to this conflict here is a rather long one. But we are dealing with pieces of evidence from which a chapter of real history emerges—a sequence of events, the sites where they took place, the names of the leaders and their aides, and other realia. A historian has here the rare opportunity of reconstructing a coherent picture of the events and their arena. If the historian is faithful to the craft and expects the conclusions drawn to be credible, each step of the deductions has to be substantiated to the best of available knowledge.

6. The Ebla Empire and Its Foreign Relations

What picture of the state and society of Ebla emerges from its archival texts? In a paper read in 1986 at the Heidelberg symposium on Ebla, I showed, to the best of my ability, that the term *empire* applied to the political formation headed by Ebla is indeed fully appropriate and that its structure and institutions conform to the generally accepted definitions of an empire.[312] I shall therefore dispense with repeating the details of my argumentation and its supporting evidence and limit myself, before passing to problems which were not discussed in that paper, to a short glimpse of the geographical and political structure of Ebla in the age of the archives. Ebla dominated at that time a territory of about 85,000 sq km (32,800 sq mi) in northern Syria and northwestern Mesopotamia. Approximately half of it was controlled and exploited directly by the state apparatus of Ebla through territorial governors (lugal), from twelve to sixteen in number, numerous local overseers (ugula), and still more numerous agents (maškim) of various dignitaries.[313] The other half (mainly in the north, on the Euphrates, and in Osrhoene, but interspersed with direct Eblean possessions) was ruled by a great number of client kings, all of whom carried the same title (en) as their Eblean overlord but markedly differed among themselves as to their actual standing.[314] The client kings had to swear allegiance to the king of

[312] Astour 1988b. Except for a few changes on the map (some of them stated in the addenda) and, of course, the then prevailing belief that Ar-ennum, Ibrium, and Ibbi-Zikir were kings of Ebla, I consider that the evidence adduced and the conclusions reached in that paper are still valid.

[313] Cf., on the lugal, Archi 1987d; on the ugula, Pomponio 1988; on the maškim, Waetzoldt 1984: 406–9.

[314] Pettinato 1986: 226–28, 373–85 and Pettinato 1987: 22–24 presented lists of kingdoms attested in the Ebla texts. Their number in the last mentioned of these amounts to 83. Archi, *s.v.* en in the indexes of ARET 1, 3, 7, and in 1982: 203, added four more cities which, in his opinion, had their own kings. However, after elimination of duplicates and careful scrutiny of the documentation (which cannot be expounded here), the number of kingdoms should be reduced by twenty. Of the remaining, Ebla, Mari, Kiš, and Nagar were independent states. This leaves sixty-three royal cities in various degrees of dependence from Ebla. On the other hand, some cities for which no kings are attested in the records, may have had them in fact, for Eblean scribes often registered well-known royal cities simply by their names.

Ebla, to pay him a fixed amount of tribute in precious metals, cattle, cloths, and artifacts, and to deliver, when required, teams of corvée workers.[315] Now we can pass to Ebla's internal institutions.

The society of Ebla was highly bureaucratized. Besides the territorial lugals and ugulas, there were persons with the same titles charged with specific branches of the economy (equines, bovines, ovines, plowmen, smiths, carpenters, corvée teams, male and female slaves, singers, storehouses, grain, vessels, estates of the king and of the "vizier," etc.). There were officials called ur_4/ur_x, perhaps 'collectors',[316] some of whom were assigned, in the king's name, as aides to the sons of Ibrium who were endowed with several towns each.[317] Some others had specialized functions: a-ur_4/a-ur_x, who were perhaps in charge of water for irrigation,[318] and udu-ur_4, who supervised the shearing of sheep and deliveries of wool.[319] There was also a category of officials designated by the ideogram NE.DI or, rarely, by its Eblaic equivalent *mayālum*,[320] some of whom were attached to the queen or certain dignitaries, or were serving in several towns of the realm.[321] Numerous messengers (kas_4, ḫúb/ḫúb-ki) maintained the connections between the capital and its provinces, client kingdoms, and foreign states. In addi-

[315] Bona fide client kingdoms which, at times, supplied labor force to Ebla, were Emar (TM.75.G.2012, see Archi, note to ARET 1 18 on p. 167), Ebal (see p. 41 above), Ebal, Ḫarran, and Martu (TM.75.G.309, published by Archi 1979b: 111–12), Adu (TM.75.G.2561:rev.i:12–iii:11, published by Pettinato 1986: 398–400), Armi (ARET 8 522 §15). A peculiar case is that of 100 dam-III and 70 guruš-III (i.e., female and male workers paid three shekels of silver apiece) from Nagar, distributed among three Eblean labor teams (ARET 1 44 §§3–4, 6). Nagar, a kingdom friendly to Ebla, does not seem to have been under any obligation to it. Perhaps we are dealing with hiring foreign workers for a purpose that is not stated in the record.

[316] The exact functions of these officials are not known. The word ur_4 is listed in the Eblean lexical texts as VE 1307, but without its Eblaic equivalent. Sollberger, ARET 8: p. 68, rendered it by 'shearer', probably from a meaning 'to pluck and gather' of one of the Akkadian values of the sign, *ḫamāmu* (not used for the plucking of wool), but the office was more responsible than that. Perhaps the wider meaning of *ḫamāmu* 'to gather, to collect' would be more appropriate. Ur_x is a variant of ur_4.

[317] TM.75.G.1444 (referred to on p. 23 above) v:18, vi:2, ix:1; ARET 7 153:rev.i:1.

[318] A-ur_4 appears as VE 631, again without its Eblaic equivalent, among terms connected with water. It is perhaps not accidental that some a-ur_x-a-ur_x were given "into the hands of Tiša-Lim," the queen of Emar, whose domain lay on the Euphrates (ARET 3 460:rev.vi).

[319] ARET 8 533 §§62 (five times), 63 (four times); the paragraphs in question deal with quantities of wool by weight.

[320] VE 845: NE.DI = *ma*-NI-*lu-um*, *ma*-NI-*lum*, *ma-ʾà-lum*; 846: ki-NE.DI = *ba-šè ma*-NI-*li-im*, *bu-šè ma*-NI-*lum*. In administrative texts, the term *ma*-NI-*lum* has been found, so far, only twice: in ARET 4 18 §20, and in a date formula quoted in n. 321 below. The duties of the NE.DI cannot be deduced from the texts in which they appear; see for the time being Fales 1988: 208 and n. 43. L. Milano, according to ARET 4: p. 310, has written on *ma*-NI-*lum* in a paper scheduled to appear in *SEb* 6.

[321] The office was important enough for a year to be named DIŠ mu *Eb-la*^{ki} *ma*-NI-*lum al-tuš* [*i*]*n* ZA-BU-LUM^{ki} 'year in which Ebla has installed a *ma*-NI-*lum* in the town of Z.', TM.75.G.1632, quoted by Pettinato in MEE 1 1080 and MEE 1: p. xxxii. He transliterated it *ṣa-pù-núm*^{ki}, which is perfectly possible (cf. Ugaritic *Ṣpn* 'Mount Casius'), but not certain in view of the polyphonic character of all three of its signs.

tion to the royal palace (é-en) with its staff, the capital housed the central economic departments: sa-za$_x$^{ki} (treasury and management of state property all over the kingdom), é-am (storage and distribution of metals), é-siki (storage of wool, textiles, and clothes, as well as of certain quantities of precious metals, probably received in payment for exported pieces of apparel), é-gigir (chariots, wagons, and draft animals), é-maḫ ('Great House', of unknown area of competence), and other specialized "houses." Three categories of officials, ú-a ('providers'), a-am, and ib, were employed in the royal palace and some other departments of the capital city.[322] Religion (temples in the capital and in provincial cities, their personnel, the performance of the cult) was part of the economic and administrative state establishment.[323] Like Sargon, Naram-Sin, and Šulgi later on, the kings of Ebla could install their daughters as high priestesses (dam-dingir, literally 'god's spouse') in subordinated cities.[324] Urban craftsmen were controlled by the state (we hear of é-nagar 'house of carpenters', é-simug 'house of smiths', managed by officials with the rank of the ib). There were slaves, male (ir$_{11}$) and female (géme), some of whom belonged to the king, the queen-mother, the eldest son of the "vizier" Ibbi-Zikir, and to other high-ranking dignitaries, while others were owned by the state administration at large. Their numbers were small in comparison with the principal labor force, the semi-free lower-class population of towns and villages, the male members of which were called guruš (in Eblaic *na-se*$_{11}$) and the female, dam.[325] The numerous cadasters, grain-delivery registers, and census lists of people and cattles from all

[322] On the central administrative bodies of Ebla see Archi 1982: esp. 209–13. Pettinato's presentation, in Pettinato and Matthiae 1976: 1–14, made right after the discovery of the Ebla texts, has been somewhat updated by Arcari 1988. A thorough examination of the palace staff and other departments of the capital was given by Milano 1987c.

[323] Four lengthy documents on the official cult of the kingdom of Ebla have been published by Pettinato 1979b. The same author's 1977c article contains several pieces of evidence on the role of the royal establishment in the performance of the cult. Other data of this kind are scattered in the published administrative texts.

[324] The appointment of Princess Sanib-dulum by her father, King Irkab-Damu, as high priestess at Luban, and her magnificent dowry, are described in TM.75.G.2022, published and commented upon by Archi 1987f. Another such case is in all likelihood reflected in ARET 1 1 §78″, where Da-um-Da-mu dam dingir dumu-mí en Ḫu-za-an^{ki} is to be understood not as 'daughter of the king of Ḫuzan' but rather 'daughter of the king [*scil.*, of Ebla] at Ḫuzan' (which, according to Eblean cadasters, belonged directly to Ebla). Cf. ARET 8 532 §23, in which "fifteen shekels of silver, three *bu-sá*-jewels Irᵓaq-Damu gave to dumu-mí en *Ḫu-za-an*^{ki}." Irᵓaq-Damu was the son and heir apparent of King Išᵓar-Damu, so his gift to the king's daughter at Ḫuzan is easily explainable if she was his sister.

[325] Guruš, in Sumerian, had the basic meaning of 'man', as Eblaic plural *na-se*$_{11}$ meant 'men, people' and the Sumerogram dam stood in Ebla not only for 'wife' but also for 'woman' in general. But very soon guruš came to mean, in Sumer, the class of serfs, "employed mainly in agriculture and derivative, processing industry on public households of the crown, temple, and nobles. They are *glebae adscripti* and owe service to the public household during part of the year," as formulated by Gelb 1972: 88. The social position of the guruš/*na-se*$_{11}$ at Ebla conforms to the same pattern. See Davidović 1988 and Milano 1987c: 539–46.

over the kingdom are rightly seen by Archi as "another element which show[s] how centralized was Ebla's economy."[326] The apparatus of skilled scribes at the royal chancery, who meticulously recorded the smallest transactions in every corner of the empire, adds to the anticipatory resemblance of the economy and society of Ebla to those of the overcentralized and overbureaucratized empire of the Third Dynasty of Ur some three centuries later.[327]

Even this thumbnail sketch of Ebla's governmental organization makes one wonder how Klengel could pigeonhole Ebla under the "early statehood" phase of a postulated schedule of social evolution and seriously explain: "'Early statehood' [*Frühstaatlich*] means that neither the political power of coercion [*Gewalt*] in the form of a monarchic rule [*Herrschaft*] nor the state structure had already been fully shaped [*ausgeprägt*], while institutions and traditions, which had originated in pre-state time, still survived."[328] "Monarchic rule," as we have seen, had existed at Ebla for at least four hundred years—enough time to become "fully shaped"; and as for the "power of coercion," was the tremendous apparatus of regimentation and exploitation merely for show?[329] Of the alleged survivals of "pre-state time," Klengel cited only one, the AB×ÁŠ 'elders/advisers' of the kings of Ebla, Mari, and several client states of Ebla, found even in some cities for which no kings are attested: "As an institution, this body goes back to the tribal structure of the pre-state time, but [an important concession!] under early statehood conditions it could assume a different character."[330] Of course, royal advisers and city elders existed in all times and under all kinds of regimes.

Despite Ebla's proximity to, and partial control of, the semideserts of Syria and northern Mesopotamia, its texts contain no references whatever to neighboring or intrusive nomadic tribes. They certainly existed at that time but did not relate to the social fabric of Ebla. To be sure, the rather frequently mentioned place-name, mostly written *Mar-tu*^{ki}, has been assumed to represent the Sumerian ethnonym Mar-tu = Akkadian *Amurrû* 'Amorite'.[331] The place has

[326] Archi 1982: 213.

[327] See Diakonoff 1959: 253–54 for a characteristic of "the despotic state under the Third Dynasty of Ur": "Such, so to speak, 'premature latifundium' required for its normal functioning an enormous apparatus of overseers, superintendents, bookkeepers, controllers, inspectors, and so on. And we see indeed the rise of an extraordinarily complicated and pedantic system of accountancy with all kind of controls, checking and double-checking of every economic act, a most complex system of reporting and so on."

[328] Klengel 1988: 246 and n. 11.

[329] For instance, TM.75.G.1655 (MEE 1 1093), published by Pettinato 1979a: 154-55 and again 1986: 400-401, records the stationing near *Ti-in*^{ki} of 7,000 guruš-guruš brought there, in one month, by fourteen dignitaries (most of them known as lugals), in detachments from 300 to 800 men, plus 4,700 guruš-guruš Sa-za$_{x}^{ki}$, or the central management, 11,700 men in total. Pettinato thought that these men were soldiers brought to *Ti-in*^{ki} to fight against Mari, but the text does not reveal the pupose of that concentration. Whatever its reason, an operation of that kind demanded a great deal of authority, discipline, coordination, and logistics, which does not indicate a primitive state organization.

[330] Klengel 1988: 250 n. 42.

[331] Neither Mar-tu nor the much rarer *Amurru*(*m*) is written with the geographical determinative ki in Sargonic and Ur III texts.

been identified with Ǧebel Bišri, west of the Middle Euphrates, associated with the Amorites in some cuneiform sources.[332] But Pettinato, while adhering to that identification and location, nevertheless correctly deduced from the textual evidence that it was "a sedentary center, not a nomadic one." Indeed, it was a perfectly ordinary client city of the Ebla Empire, with its king, elders, a renowned temple, and it duly fulfilled its obligations of vassalage with regard to Ebla by paying the ceremonial "oil tribute" and swearing allegiance. At times (perhaps in the aftermath of the Mariote war) it was ruled by an Eblean lugal.[333] One text places Martu in Kur^{ki}, which could signify 'steppe' in general, but designated at Ebla a specific administrative district between the Euphrates and the Balīḫ.[334] As a cultic center, Martu was especially honored by persons from Emar,[335] which may point to its relative proximity to that city. The fact that the toponym was written not only *Mar-tu*^{ki} but also *Mar-tù*^{ki} and, more often, *Mar-tum*^{ki} shows that it was not a Sumerogram but a phonetic rendering of a Semitic name.[336] But what about gír mar-tu, a very common artifact in Eblean registers, which Pettinato understood as 'Amorite sword (or dagger)'[337]

[332] Archi 1985d: 7–11 (introduction to a full list of occurrences of Martu(m) in Ebla texts; Pettinato 1986: 259–61. On Gebal Bišri cf. Kupper 1957: 136–37, 149–50. Sollberger, ARET 8: p. 45, *s.v. Ì-mar*^{ki}, also identified the Eblean *Mar-tu*^{ki} with Amurru, and mistakenly asserted that ARET 8 524 §14 "explicitly placed Imar in Amurru"; on that passage, see n. 264 above.

[333] His name was *A-mu-ti* and he may well have been identical with a brother of Ibrium of the same name.

[334] See the passage from ARET 8 524 §14, quoted and interpreted in n. 264 above. Kur^{ki} appears in some texts listing the numbers of sheep (in Archi 1984c) as a specific unit along with other places. In a text dealing with clothes deliveries, TM.75.G.10022 (MEE 1 4925), one finds the characteristic sequence *Ša-da*$_5$^{ki}, Kur^{ki}, *Ḫa-ra-an*^{ki}. Another cultic center in Kur^{ki} was *A-li-*NI^{ki} (ARET 3 419:iii), also a sheep-breeding area, associated with two places mentioned in Enna-Dagan's letter (Archi 1984c: no. 10). See also n. 360 below.

[335] In n. 264 above I have already explained that ARET 8 524 §14 dealt not with the destruction of the Amorites by the king of Emar but with an offering to the gods of Martu by an envoy of that king. In the same way, the passage quoted as entry 9 in Archi 1985d—(three pieces of clothing) *Ar-šum Ì-mar*^{ki} níg-AN.AN.AN.AN *Mar-tu*^{ki} TIL *wa* udu-sù tùn-šè (three pieces of clothing) *Ba-lu-zú Ì-mar*^{ki} *in* u$_4$ *Mar-tu*^{ki} TIL—does not refer to the destruction of Martu and the victory of the king of Emar, as thought by Archi 1985d: 7–8, but means that Aršum of Emar arrived with gifts for the gods of Martu and slaughtered his sheep (as a sacrifice), and Baluzu of Emar, with similar gifts of clothing, arrived to Martu in the same day. Cf. MEE 2 41:obv.v:12–vi:4: (three pieces of clothing) *Nap-ḫa-Il* níg-AN.AN.AN.AN tùn-šè udu-udu maškim *En-mar*, which records gifts and sacrificial slaughtering of sheep to gods, without any mention of an enemy.

[336] The question whether Sumerian Mar-tu was pronounced /martu/ or /mardu/ is irrelevant here; it suffices to know that the Sumerian term was never written Mar-tum and only once each Mar-du$_8$ and Mar-du, cf. Lieberman 1969: 55 (mar-du at the beginning of the entry "Mardu" in *RGTC* 2:118 is a typing error for mar-dú, i.e., *-tu*). In Eblaic vocables, /tu/ was normally transcribed by *tù* (DU), but the sign *tu* is found in the personal names *Ku-tu* (borne by several men) and *Tu-an* (the same man is listed in another text as *Du-an*) and in the place names *ᵓÀ-tu-du*^{ki} (TM.75.G.1330 = MEE 1 768) and *Na-pa-ku-tu*^{ki} (TM.75.G.1452:obv.iii:13, published by Fronzaroli 1980; the transliteration is confirmed by the photograph of the tablet). *Martu(m)*, like many Eblean and north Syrian places, may have been named for a plant: cf. *CAD* M/1 300, *s.v. martû* B2.

[337] Pettinato, MEE 2: p. 9, *ad* text 1:obv.i:2. Pettinato 1986: 260 assumed that daggers of that type were actually produced by Amorites whose know-how made these daggers "famous in

and was followed by other editors of Ebla texts, though sometimes hesitatingly?[338] It is more probable, however, that mar-tu refers not to the provenience or local style of the dagger but to its form. In the Ebla administrative texts, there are two types of dagger: gír kun and gír mar-tu. The former, literally 'dagger with a tail', is understood by the editors as 'curved dagger' (cf. also Akkadian *patar zibbatu*, same meaning). Then gír mar-tu must have stood for 'straight dagger', corresponding to Akkadian *patru zaqpu* 'straight dagger/sword' and *ziqpu* 'stake, pole, shaft, blade of a weapon', all of them expressing the idea of straightness. Now the Akkadian *martû* (*mertû* and variants) has the meaning of 'stick, pole, shaft (of a chariot)', and also of 'a tree that grows straight and whose wood is very hard, used for making sticks'.[339] We have here a good semantic correspondence. Whether mar-tu was an early Sumerian vocable which later went out of use (like many other Sumerian words in the lexical texts of Ebla), but not before being borrowed into Akkadian, or it was an early Semitism in Sumerian, I do not undertake to decide. Other attempts to detect tribal units at Ebla are even less plausible.[340]

To some scholars, the purely political notion of an empire is associated with an advanced, and therefore late, stage of human society (but, one may ask, did the empire of Genghis Khan represent a very high level of socioeconomic evolution?). Grégoire and Renger have recently tried to present "a more restrained view" of Ebla.[341] One of their favored views is "Ebla as the principal

---

the entire area of the Fertile Crescent." Gír mar-tu is found in the Sumerian word list MEE 3 45–46:obv.viii:1 and its parallel from Fara, and in the bilingual glossary VE 1127, but without its Eblaic equivalent which might have clarified for us its meaning. Cf. the variant gír *mar-ti-in*, ARET 8 524 §50, which pleads against mar-tu being a Sumerogram.

[338] Thus Archi, ARET 1: p. 283, indicated his doubt by italicizing *amorreo*, and Sollberger, ARET 8: p. 62, by putting (?) after "Amorite."

[339] Definition of *CAD* M/1 300, s.v. *martû*. According to this description, it was probably the cornel.

[340] One was advanced by Archi, ARET 1: p. 221: "There is a unique personage, recorded by name and without any reference to an urban center, in this list of cities: a certain Šura-garru, with whom are associated . . . his brothers (seven in ARET 1, no. 4 and four in no. 8), one single elder, and twenty guruš. It seems evident that this personage was the chief of a tribal group." Davidović 1988: 200 noted, in a different connection, that since he is listed among city kings, "Šuragarru had to be a king himself, or at least a high rank person." One may add to it that, first, kings and governors are sometimes listed simply by name, without their cities, and, second, that in ARET 8 524 §32 one actually finds that personage linked to a definite city: *Šu-ra-gàr-ru*$_{12}$ *Si-da-mu*^{ki}. Another assumption of this kind was made by Pettinato 1986: 260. He saw in *Da-da-nu*^{ki} (a city with an en, mentioned only in ARET 8 531 §31) a kingdom of Tidnum, "a famous Amorite tribe of the third millennium," located, like Martu, in Ǧebel Bišri and also "revealed as a sedentary and not a nomadic center." Thus the equation with the Tidnum tribe (Semitic *Ditanu* or *Didanu*) rests only on an assonance of names with different etymologies (*ditānu* 'aurochs', *dadānu* a plant, or a derivation of *dād* 'love', or of *tadānu* 'to give, sell'; cf. the Old Babylonian mention of ^{uru}*Ta-da-an-ne*^{ki} ŠÀ *m*[*a-a*]*t Bi-ri-ti* 'in the midst of the land Between(-the-Rivers), i.e., North Mesopotamia; cf. Finkelstein 1962: 75).

[341] Grégoire and Renger 1988: 214–15.

site of a kind of a 'federated state' [*Bundesstaat*]."[342] But if in such a federation one member state is disproportionately larger and stronger than any of the other ones and is permanently in command—as were Ebla, Athens, and Prussia—we call it an empire.[343] They also favorably noted that "Pettinato speaks of Ebla as a commercial empire" and themselves used the expression "a mere commercial empire." While the first part of Pettinato's 1986 book is entitled "Ebla: un impero commerciale," it seems that Grégoire and Renger paid no attention to his warning: "But whoever thinks that the *pax Eblaica* was only the fruit of peaceful agreements and the consequence of family connections and lengthy negotiations, is wrong. As I stressed earlier, speaking of the term 'empire' to designate the kingdom of Ebla, I am still convinced that Ebla also struck terror militarily."[344] There is no such thing in history as a "mere commercial empire." Such typical "commercial empires" as Carthage, Venice, or Holland acquired and exploited their far-flung possessions and trade routes by naval and military might; and we have seen in the preceding section how Ebla had to fight Mari for four generations to retain its share of the Euphrates Valley.

Commerce certainly played a role in the economic life of Ebla, but not in a greater degree than in the contemporary states of Mesopotamia, and probably in a lesser one, because, unlike them, Ebla was self-sufficient not only in grain but also in wool, meat, olive oil, wine, timber, and stone. In point of fact, we know little about Ebla's commercial activities. Most of the lists of deliveries or acquisitions of small quantities of textiles, clothes, pieces of jewelry, decorative daggers, precious metals, etc., do not represent commercial transactions. They rather record (*a*) imposts to the central authority of Ebla from client kings, governors, and agents, (*b*) diplomatic gifts from and to foreign rulers and dignitaries, (*c*) gifts to members of the king's and the "vizier's" families, (*d*) offerings to gods and temples, (*e*) part of wages of state officials, and (*f*) clothes for craftsmen and workers. Archi, having established that gifts from Ebla to the king of Kiš and his surrounding always consisted of two or three garments, concluded: "Therefore, Ebla did not export clothing to Mesopotamia; instead of documents recording exports, these texts must be concerned with gifts, which leads one to presume an exchange on a reciprocal basis."[345] There is, however, a certain number of instances (duly noted in Archi's summaries of

[342] The authors ascribe this view to von Soden in his Heidelberg paper, but its published text (von Soden 1988) does not contain this term. Von Soden 1980: 326 correctly noted that "the idea of an empire [*Grossreich*] extending about as far as Gaza is probably no longer held" (having in mind Pettinato's exaggerated geographical picture); but the extent and the political structure of the zone of Ebla's supremacy, even reduced to its true dimensions, still satisfy the definition of an empire.

[343] One may recall here the dictionary definitions of "empire" quoted in Astour 1988b:140: "a state uniting many territories and peoples under one ruler"; "a group of nations and states under a single sovereign power"; "an aggregate of nations and peoples ruled by an emperor or another powerful sovereign or government, usually a territory of a greater extent than a kingdom."

[344] Pettinato 1986: 170.

[345] Archi 1987e: 126.

evidence)[346] of actual wholesale export transactions, mainly of clothing sold to Mari, often with the indication of the quantity of silver paid for them. The figures of the pieces of apparel (of several kinds and quality) vary from 120 to 780 per sale. There are only nine instances of such relatively large sales. Besides clothing, there is a very limited number of mentions of other goods exported to Mari in quantities above mere token amounts: grain, wine, wool, aromatic essences, oil, copper axes, wooden containers, sheep, and, in one case, five kg of bronze. Despite Mari being the most frequently mentioned city in Eblean texts, we know for certain about only one merchandise imported from Mari to Ebla: lapis-lazuli, the direct provenience of which is noted in most recordings of its purchases.[347] Ebla brought from Mari a group of about twenty-seven singers who served in the palace along with an equal number of native singers,[348] but this can hardly be considered a commercial transaction.

The only Mesopotamian city south of Mari with which Ebla maintained steady relations was Kiš, the famous metropolis which played a prominent role in the Early Dynastic period and to which, according to Gelb, Ebla owed most of its literate culture.[349] But from the quantitative point of view, the exchange of goods between Ebla and Kiš conforms to Archi's conclusion quoted above. With the single exception of a shipment of 1,153 *gú-bar* (ca. 75.6 metric tons) of barley from Ebla to Kiš,[350] the records deal with courtesy gifts of no economic significance. In addition, there are two mentions of UD.NUN^{ki} (Adab),[351] ca. sixty km southeast of Kiš, and two mentions (in the same text) of *Ak-sa-gú*^{ki},[352] that is, Akšak on the Tigris, ca. forty-five km north of Kiš.[353] Three of them concern gifts of silver (one mina in each case) to the gods of Adab and Akšak through the intermediary of Mariote agents, and the fourth deals with a woman from Adab (for) the queen-mother (of Ebla) along with a son of a singer from Mari.

346 Archi 1985b for Mari; Archi 1981b and 1987e for Kiš, based on a survey of the total written evidence; many of the entries are excerpts from still-unpublished texts.

347 This indicates that lapis-lazuli from Afghanistan did not reach Syria via the difficult passes in the northern Zagros, Transtigris, and Upper Mesopotamia, but by the easier, immemorially old Khorasan road and the Diyala Valley, whence it was carried to Mari and to the south of Mesopotamia.

348 The material on both groups of singers (or, as Archi prefers to designate them, musicians) has been collected by Archi 1988a: 271-84.

349 Gelb 1977: 13-15 and especially Gelb 1981.

350 Archi 1987e: 139, document 28. According to Milano 1987b: 179-80, one Eblean *gú-bar* equaled twenty Eblean sìla, or 120 Mesopotamian *sìla* of 0.85 liter; thus one *gú-bar* corresponded to 102 liters. The U.S. standard weight of a bushel of barley being 48 pounds, and computing bushels to liters and pounds to kilograms, I have obtained the figure of 75.6 metric tons for the shipment, assuming that the specific weight of Eblean barley was not very significantly different from American barley.

351 Archi 1985b: documents 62 and 110.

352 Archi 1985b: document 100.

353 Akšak faced Upi (Opis) on the other bank of the river and, because of the wrong identification of Opis with Seleucia, is often placed much too far downstream. My own investigation suggests for both cities a location on the southern outskirts of modern Baghdad.

Whatever the actual volume of goods moved, in both directions, on the Euphrates route, it is clear from the sheer number of textual references that it was the principal axis of Ebla's foreign relations. Two of the most frequently mentioned client states of Ebla, Manuwat and Ebal (both of them homes of numerous merchants), were situated on that route.[354] Individuals of other client states (Ḫazuwan, Adu, Armi, Kablul) are noted as traveling to, or residing in, Mari or (Abarsil, Kablul) Kiš.[355] If any city emerges from the Eblean documentation as a commercial city *par excellence*, it is certainly Mari. Only a small number of direct or indirect subjects of Ebla, no more than a dozen, are recorded as residing (lú:tuš) in Mari. A somewhat larger number of Ebleans visited Mari with their goods or for other reasons. But in both cases they were restricted to the city of Mari itself; they never set foot in any of the inhabited points strung along the Euphrates between the Eblean border and Kiš. In sharp contrast, the territory of Ebla teemed with Mariote merchants. Their favorite place of residence and business was Dubitum.[356] Sometimes they made their purchases directly from sa-za_x^{ki} and "the house of Ibbi-Zikir," that is, in the capital city itself, but their presence and activity are also attested in thirty other cities and towns of Ebla.[357] Besides, I have counted, in the published texts alone, fifty-four mentions of Mariote merchants (lú-kar *Ma-rí*^{ki}) not connected with specific Eblean localities. In Archi's list of persons from Mari who are mentioned by name in Ebla texts,[358] 150 are designated as merchants;[359] but several of the Mariotes not so designated were also engaged in trade. Their actual number throughout the empire as a whole must have been considerably greater, because among the thirty-two places of their activity only five royal cities (Adu, Ḫalsum, Ḫarran, Kakmium, Manuwat) are recorded, and even these rather casually. What about the other sixty or so client kingdoms of Ebla, including important Euphratean sites such as Ebal, Emar, Burman, Raᵓaq, Abarsil, and so forth? The answer is that these cities were autonomous and their internal doings were outside the scope of the Eblean chancery.

[354] Note in particular Archi 1985b document 17 on the journey to Mari by Enna-Damu, king of Manuwat.

[355] See for references Archi's articles cited in n. 346 above. It is interesting that a Sargonic text from Adab (OIP 14 81:2) contains the ethnic *Kab-lu*$_5$*-li-um*, which Steinkeller 1984: 88 correctly derived from the Eblean *Kab-lu*$_5$*/lu-ul*^{ki}.

[356] On that town and the possible readings of its name see n. 32 above. Its identification with Tunip is further impaired by its role as a headquarters of Mariote merchants; they would not have chosen for it a place that was farther from Mari and the Euphrates than almost any other point within the Ebla Empire.

[357] These are (not counting Dubitu and Ebla mentioned above): Adani, Adu, Azamu, Banayum, Bibitu, Dudulu (Tuttul), Dur (BÀD^{ki}), Gananaᵓum, Guduman, GUNEšum, Ḫaᵓabitu, Ḫalsum, Ḫarran, Kakmium, Mabartu, Manuwat, Mašᵓa, Mašgatu, Mur(u), Neᵓaᵓu, Nubatu, Sabartin, Sabu, Šada, Šalbatu, Šarabik, Šašaranu, Tin, Unubu.

[358] Archi 1985e: 55–58.

[359] 149 lú-kar and one ga:raš.

Thus the prevailing pattern of trade between Ebla and Mari consisted in Mariote merchants being active all over the territory of Ebla, while the government of Mari severely limited the activities of Ebleans in the areas under its own control. Mariote traders acquired in Eblean lands not only commodities but also the boats needed for shipping them to Mari. We know of two such deals. One, ARET 2 29, records, among other items, the sale of 260 sheep "to Mari from Ḫarran" by the Eblean administrator Gida-Naʾim (§1),[360] and by the same man, also to Mari, of unidentified goods from DU^{ki} and Ḫarran, *ḫa-mi-zu in ʾÀdu*^{ki}, and *me-se*$_{11}$ KUR^{ki} (§8), followed by "one mina of silver, the price of one boat [1 GIŠ má]" (§9) and "four shekels of silver, the mast (or salt)[361] which is in the boat that arrived [TIL] to Mari" (§10). *Me-se*$_{11}$ represents the Eblaic and Akkadian *mēsu*(*m*) or *mēšu*, a Near Eastern tree and its valuable wood,[362] thus a typical north Syrian export item. *Ḫa-mi-zu* is a derivative of the Eblaic and Akkadian root *ḫamāṣu* 'to strip by force, despoil, tear off, skin';[363] as a commodity, it probably meant 'rawhide'. If this interpretation is justified, it may provide a clue to the type of boat mentioned in the next entry: one of the round cargo vessels, constructed of hides stretched upon a frame of wood and wicker, as described by Herodotus 1:194 and represented on Assyrian reliefs.[364]

The other occurrence is ARET 7 11 §2: "13 minas of silver in exchange for 90 jars[365] of oil; the price of 417 fabrics, 12 [+3?] headbands, nine triple white

[360] This man (also known from other Ebla texts) is shown in the same record to have sold sheep of Irritum to Nabralatum (location unknown), oxen to Tuttul, and an assortment of goods from DU^{ki} (Alaga), Adu, Harran, and KUR^{ki} to Mari. This arena of his activities confirms the location of the KUR^{ki} district as stated on p. 53 and n. 334 above.

[361] The sign is MUN, but Edzard (ARET 2: p. 150) considered it a "gunated DIM," transliterated it dim$_x$, and rendered it by "mast" (ARET 2: p. 121). The sign appears in the same text, §2, without being connected to a boat. It is dubious whether a river boat, especially if it was of the *quffa* type, needed a mast; salt, on the other hand, has been extracted since ancient times from the salt lake of Ǧabbūl (see Tefnin 1978) in the middle of the Eblean territory.

[362] Ideogram in Akkadian texts: ^{giš}MES; cf. VE 473: giš-mes = *me-šum, mi-šum*. Because the *mēsu*-wood was used for furniture, and by comparison with Syriac *mayšā* and Arabic *mays*-, the tree is usually identified with *Celtis australis* which grows in the Mediterranean region. It is called *micocoulier* in French, *Zürgelbaum* in German, and *nettle-tree* in English. *Me-se*$_{11}$ is mentioned again in ARET 3 859:rev.iii as being bought from the "king's house" for a quantity of wool; the same procedure is attested for other kinds of valuable wood: ARET 1 1 §87 (giš-šim); ARET 1 13 §89 (giš-ád). If the provenience of nettle-tree wood from the semidesert district of KUR^{ki} may appear dubious, one should recall the opinion of paleobotanists that, as summarized by Wirth 1971: 121–22, cf. 130, "about 2500 years ago the largest part of the Syrian Desert was covered with thick vegetation, which consisted not only of grasses, weeds, and dwarf shrubs, but was interspersed in ecologically somewhat more favorable places with woody plants and trees."

[363] Cf. VE 712: igi-du$_8$-du$_8$ = *ḫu-ma-zu a-na-a*, *ḫu-mu-zu* 2 IGI (the second Eblaic entry, omitted in MEE 4, was adduced by Krebernik 1982/83: 236, 27, as 'tearing out the eyes'; compare [lu igi x x] = *ša i-na-šu ḫu-mu-ṣa* in an Old Babylonian lexical text, qouted in *CAD* H 60.

[364] On such boats, called *quffa* in Iraq, see De Graeve 1981: 85–89.

[365] La-ḫa, equated by Archi, ARET 3: p. 365, with Sumerian la-ḫa-an. This may be true etymologically, but la-ḫa-an, Akkadian *laḫannu*, was a drinking cup, used for retail sale of liquor,

belts, 120 na$_4$[366] of high quality wool; one mina of silver and a half:[367] the price of a large boat [má-gal] acquired[368] on behalf of [iš$_{11}$-ki] Mari by Zubalum the ur$_x$." Here again we have a typical assortment of Eblean goods: oil, textiles, pieces of apparel, and wool, bought for export to Mari along with the carrier boat, which was of a larger size than the simple GIŠ má purchased for Mari from Gida-Naʾim, and therefore half again as expensive.

Of course, the Ebleans had boats not only for sale to Mariotes,[369] but those in their own use are not mentioned in the published business texts. We hear of a boatman (*ma-la-ḫu*) from the client city of Irar,[370] and another client city, Abarsil, was obliged by treaty to provide Ebla with, among other items, cargo boats (GIŠ má-NE).[371] The general impression is, however, that for most of the period covered by the archives, Ebleans did not sail to Mari and Kiš in their own boats but used Mariote ones. The gifts in silver, not over one mina each, to the gods of Kiš, Adab, and Akšak, and some other Eblean sendings to

---

while in this case we are dealing with large containers for storing and shipping liquids. The capacity of a la-ḫa is unknown.

366 Na$_4$ ('stone') is the lowest of the three units used at Ebla specifically for weighing wool, see Zaccagnini 1984; it was also used, for the same exclusive purpose, by Old Assyrian merchants: *áb-ni(-im)*. In *CAD* A/1 59, it is rendered by 'talent', which, at least for Ebla, seems to be too high an estimate.

367 1 ma-na bar$_6$:kù / DILMUN-ku$_5$ in the publication, the latter expression left untranslated. However, the sign transliterated DILMUN, which normally follows gín 'shekel' at Ebla, has been recognized by Archi 1987g to simply signify 'weighed, standard', and ku$_5$ (usually transliterated tar in Ebla texts, but ku$_5$ in Pomponio 1980) is the sign for half a mina (thirty shekels).

368 The word is níg-sa$_{10}$, literally 'price', and so translated elsewhere in the quoted passage, but in this and similar contexts rendered 'acquired' by Archi, ARET 7 *ad loc.*, and 'purchased' by Sollberger, ARET 8: p. 64 *s.v.*

369 It may be characteristic for the Eblean acquaintance with navigation that in their bilingual glossary the Sumerian terms má-gal 'large boat' and má-gur$_8$ 'deep-going boat' are translated, respectively, NI-*ša*-NI-*um* (VE 1400) and *zi-ti-gi-du-um*, *zi-gi-tum* (VE 964)—unfamiliar to us but certainly Semitic—rather than by the Sumerianisms *magallu* and *makurru*, as in Akkadian.

370 ARET 8 524 §32. Cf. VE 962: má-laḫ$_4$ = *ma-la-ḫu-um*.

371 TM.75.G.2420, published by Sollberger 1980, lines 140–49, 161–82; translated 'boats', with -ne tentatively considered a mark of plural in Eblaic "heterodox" Sumerian. The vocable má-NE appears in VE 962 (unfortunately without its Eblaic equivalent) among other terms relating to boats. Steinkeller 1987 identified the word which precedes GIŠ má-NE in both passages as "battering ram," but it does not follow that GIŠ má-NE must also designate a siege engine. The general meaning of má-NE can be glimpsed from a comparison with VE 1169: íl-NE = *bí-il-tum*. Neither of the two Sumerian entries recur in standard Sumerian, but Akkadian *biltu*(*m*) means 'load, pack, baggage, burden', from (*w*)*abālu* 'to bring, transport (staples, materials, etc.) to their destination' while íl is the Sumerian counterpart of Akkadian *našû* 'to transport goods, to carry, to bring', and was used in this sense in Ebla texts. Thus NE seems to convey the notion of 'load, (heavy) weight', to which one may compare two other Sumero-Eblaic entries: VE 243: NE:sag, NE-sag=*ba-ga-lu*(-*um*) /bakarum/ 'first-born', the Sumerian equivalent meaning literally 'first in "weight" (importance)'; and VE 388: ì-NE=*a-ba-tu*(-*um*) 'thick oil' (cf. Akkadian *ebû*, Hebrew *ʿabāh*, and, from the semantic point of view, Akkadian *kabtu* 'heavy, dense; honored, important').

Kiš were delivered by Mariote agents. That Mari effectively controlled the Euphratean trade route between Ebla and Kiš follows from the interesting text TM.75.G.2268, from the time of Ibbi-Zikir.[372] It begins (obv.i:1–ii:19): "Document of the *convention* with Mari.[373] The Eblean merchant (may) travel from Mari to Ebla, and he (may) also travel to Kiš from Mari, and he (may) receive [. . .]; and (when) the Eblean merchant goes out to 'the front of the land,' he will pay a 'travel toll.'"[374] Another quoted passage (obv.vii:4–18) relates that after an exchange of communications between *Bíl-za-ià*[375] (an Eblean) and the *ga-raš* of *Šu*-BE, the servant of the (Mariote) king (lugal), the (Eblean) merchant (dam-gàr) *I-si-lum* could buy (níg-sa$_{10}$) wool at [. . .].[376] It is also specified (rev.vi:3) that the transportation is done by deep-going boats (má-gur$_8$). The text implies that before the agreement in question, Eblean merchants did not have the right of sailing by themselves to Mari and, through Mariote territory, to Kiš. It was perhaps as a result of this agreement that the city of Terqa, ca. sixty km upstream from Mari, was opened as an intermediate place of commercial contact between Ebleans and Kišites.[377]

The other known axis of Ebla's international relations, diplomatic as well as economic, traversed Upper Mesopotamia and reached the royal city of Nagar (*Na-gàr*^{ki}). There is a general agreement that Nagar of the Ebla texts is identical with the city whose name (written NAGAR^{ki}) appears in a votive inscription on a statuette from the temple of Ninni-Zaza, bearing the name of King Iblul-Il of Mari,[378] and (in the epithet ^{d}NIN *Na-gàr*^{ki}) in the archaic Hurrian inscription of

[372] Quoted in Archi 1985b: 67. After having written these lines, I was privileged to read the full transliteration of the text (see n. 244 above), but the additional material added little of importance to the crucial passages adduced in Archi's quoted article.

[373] Dub *ù-šu-rí Ma-rí*^{ki}; cf. n. 245 above.

[374] The last clause of the passage is *wa* è dam-gar *Eb-la*^{ki} *al* igi-ki 1 níg-nigín (LAGAB) ì-na-sum The preposition *al* usually means at Ebla 'upon' (somebody, as debt or other responsibility), but with a verb of movement it can mean 'to', cf. ARET 8 534 §52 and p. 51 *s.v.* Igi-ki (also in ARET 4 11 §10: igi-ki è) may be understood literally as 'front of the land' (cf. Akk. *pān māt* GN) = 'boundary', and níg-nigín (cf. Akk. NIGIN, NIGÍN, ideogram for *lamû, ṣâdu, saḫāru, târu*, and VE 509, 629 with remarks by H.-P. Müller 1988: 282–83), as 'payment for the right of business travel'.

[375] As quoted by Archi: GIBIL-*a*-NI (GIBIL = *bíl*); but no such name is known at Ebla, and it is likely that it should be read *Bíl-za-ià*(NI), also found in its fuller form *Bíl-za-Il/Bíl-zi-Il*, borne by an Eblean official.

[376] In the published parts of the texts, Eblean merchants are called dam-gàr (Akkadian *tamkārum*). Ga-raš (or ga-eš$_8$) is rendered 'traveling merchant' in *CAD* K 35, and 'purchaser' (*acheteur*) by Archi 1985b. It is regrettable that the name of the place where the Eblean merchant was allowed to trade has not been preserved.

[377] Terqa appears in Archi 1987e: 138, document 7 (twice), written *Tir*$_x$(BAN)-*ga*^{ki}, and document 9, written *Ti-rí-ga*^{ki}. The value *tir*$_x$/*ter*$_5$ for BAN in Eblean and Old Akkadian writing has been established, apparently independently, by W. Lambert 1985: 531 n. 14, Milano 1987a, and Archi 1987e: 136–37. Archeologists who dug at Mari and at Terqa agree that about the middle of the third millennium Terqa was under the control of Mari; cf. Margueron 1982: 125 and Buccellati 1983: 72*.

[378] Published by Dossin in Parrot 1967: 318 no. 11; improved readings in M. Lambert 1970: 169–70. NAGAR^{ki} is also mentioned in three Sargonic texts (see *RGTC* 1:125), but it seems from

Tiš-atal, *endan* of Urkiš in Upper Mesopotamia, from the late third millennium.[379] Later, *Na-ga-ar*ki occurs in a few tablets of the royal archives of Mari,[380] from which it is possible to establish its approximate location: it stood between Kaḫat (Tell Barri) and Ṭâbātum (one of the mounds on the left bank of the Ḫabūr ca. fifteen km south-southeast of Ḥasekeh).[381] In general terms, Nagar was located to the east of the southern apex of the Ḫabūr Triangle.[382] This time, unlike the cases of misleading Transtigridian homonyms that we have met and that we are going to meet, the probability is that we are dealing indeed with the city in central Upper Mesopotamia. It is not the only city in that area to be mentioned in Ebla texts. A city *Ga-ga-ba-an*ki appears there in three complete and two fragmentary tablets. In one of the former,[383] its elders (and probably its king as well in the preceding damaged paragraph) are listed almost immediately after entries relating to the king of Nagar and before the city of Šanapsugum (near Ḫarran). In another,[384] its mention is preceded by the names of seven cities, of which six were located in northwestern Mesopotamia.[385] *Ga-ga-ba-an*ki can therefore be identified with the city which appears, in identical spelling, in a Sargonic tablet from Tell Brak, a large archeological site near the bend of the Ǧaġǧag River, thus very near the presumed location of Nagar; the toponym is generally normalized Kakkāban.[386] The tablet in question[387] enumerates labor contingents from seven cities, all of which but Kakkabān recur in Old Assyrian, Mariote, Old Babylonian, Hittite, and Middle Assyrian sources which place them

their character and especially from NAGARki being mentioned next to Sippar in one of them that we are dealing there with some insignificant place in Akkad.

[379] Published by Parrot and Nougayrol 1948.

[380] See ARMT 16/1 24; and ARMT 21 426:8′.

[381] The location of Ṭâbātum (Neo-Assyrian Ṭâbēte, Roman Thubida on the Tabula Peutengeriana) follows from its position in Neo-Assyrian and Roman itineraries and geographical associations in Mariote sources. An object which satisfies both the geographical and stratigraphic requirements would be Tell Bdēri (Montchambert 1984: no. 43). It is true that according to Pfälzner 1988 the site was inhabited only in the Early and Late Bronze Ages, but the discrepancies between the reports of the two archeologists are so great that one wonders whether they refer to the same mound.

[382] The map *Deir ez Zor* 1:500,000 shows a sizable mound, Tell Kaukab, on the trail leading from the bend of the Ǧaġǧag River to the Ḫabūr River, almost exactly halfway between Tell Barri and Tell Bdēri. But in the absence of a surface survey and a sounding of the site, it would be premature to suggest it as the location of ancient Nagar.

[383] ARET 1 45 §34″.

[384] MEE 2 41:obv.ix:15.

[385] Ḫarran, Ḫazuwan, Ḫalsum, Šanapsugum, Irritum, Dulu, Adarkizu; only the general location of Adarkizu cannot be figured out.

[386] Gelb 1957: 142-43; Gelb 1961: 35; *RGTC* 1:82. Pettinato, who transliterated *Kà-kà-ba-an*ki (in MEE 1 and 2), was the first to equate the city of the Ebla texts with its homonym in the Sargonic tablet from Tell Brak (MEE 2: p. 292).

[387] Gadd 1940: F.1153:11; Loretz 1969: pl. xxxv, no. 69; for the toponymic and geographical aspects of the tablet, see also Kessler 1984 and Charpin 1987b: 131–32.

inside the Ḫabūr Triangle,[388] so that Kakkabān, too, can with confidence be attributed to the same area. Moreover, there is a single Eblean reference to *ma-da* *ᵓÀ-bí-um*ᵏⁱ in the context of northwest Mesopotamian sites.[389] It may be identified with the locality and mountain called *A-ba-a* which the Old Babylonian Yale Itinerary mentions as a point of reference on the road from the headwaters of the Ḫabūr to Ḫarran and whose name, as suggested by Hallo, survives as Ṭiwāl el-ᶜAbā, the name of a ridge of hills between the Ḫabūr and the Balīḫ.[390] The area north and east of Ṭiwāl el-ᶜAbā abounds in wells and springs and is studded with large, strongly fortified mounds which flourished in the Early Dynastic and Sargonic ages.[391] One may suspect that some rarely mentioned cities, apparently outside the zone of Eblean supremacy, may have belonged to that area.[392]

The relations between Ebla and Nagar were close and friendly. We know the names of two kings of Nagar (Bakmiš and Maran). Numerous messengers (ḫ ú b) of Nagar came to Ebla; high-ranking Ebleans—an elder as a representative of Ibbi-Zikir,[393] Ibbi-Zikir himself,[394] and even the queen of Ebla[395]—traveled to Nagar. We hear of eleven caravans (k a s k a l) of (or to) the king of Nagar.[396] Standard gifts of clothing and silver were sent to Nagar, but we do not know what Ebla received instead. But we do have information on what looks like a large-scale joint operation by both kingdoms concerning, not unexpectedly, wool. As stated in passing above (n. 315), one hundred female and seventy male workers from Nagar, paid three shekels of silver apiece, were enrolled in three Eblean labor teams. It follows from the mention of a gift to the god Ada

[388] *Viz*., Nagar near the southern corner of the Triangle; Urkiš at Tell Muzān southeast of ᶜAmūdah; Lilabšinum east of Tell Barri (by no means at Tell Brak, as thought by Kessler); Šeḫna at Tell Leilān (also known as Šubat-Enlil); Ḫidar in the area of Tell Leilān (cf. ARMT 26/1 142:7 and A.988:13, quoted in ARMT 26/1 142); Tadum (Mariote Taᵓadum, Taᵓidum, Late Bronze Taᵓidi), in my opinion, at Tell Farfara, halfway between Tell Leilan and Tell Barri.

[389] ARET 1 3 §39″. For *ma-da* as 'land' cf. n. 182 above.

[390] Hallo 1964: 64 line 30: a stop *lìb-bi* KUR *A-sa-am ù A-ba-a* 'between the mountain(s?) of Asam and Abâ'; see Hallo 1964: 75–76 on the identity of Mount Asam with Mariote KUR *Ḫa-sa-am* and Neo-Assyrian ᵏᵘʳ*Ḫa-sa-mu* and ᵘʳᵘ*Ḫa-sa-me* east of Ḫarran. It should be added that *A-ba-a* recurs at Mari as KURⁱ *Ḫa-bi-im* (ARM 18 143:2′) and *Ḫa-ab-ba*ᵏⁱ (ARM 1 70:12′) and in Old Assyrian tablets as *Ḫa-ba-im* (*Inscriptions Cunéiformes du Kultépé* 1 189:19′; *Cuneiform Texts from Cappadocian Tablets* 5 48c:4).

[391] Van Liere and Lauffray 1955: 139–40 and map. Of these mounds, only Tell Ḫueyra has been excavated (by A. Moortgat and W. Orthman).

[392] Old Assyrian and Mariote data locate in that area the city of Mardaman, mentioned in Sargonic royal inscriptions and in later epic tales about Sargon and Naram-Sin. Strangely enough, *mar-da-ma-núm* appears at Ebla not as a toponym but as the designation of some kind of commodity, perhaps an article of clothing. The term is cited by Cagni 1984: 187 and n. 90 on the basis of unpublished texts of which he does not quote the inventory numbers. It is likely that the name of the merchandise, as often, derived from the city name.

[393] TM.75.G.554, quoted in MEE 1 222.

[394] TM.75.G.43, quoted in MEE 1 132 (issue of beer for the journey of Ibbi-Zikir to Mari and Nagar); ARET 7 122 (purchase of sixteen pieces of linen for the journey of Ibbi-Zikir to Nagar).

[395] TM.75.G.1633, quoted in MEE 1 1071 (date formula DIŠ m u d u - d u *ma-lik-tum Na-gàr*ᵏⁱ 'the year when the queen went to Nagar').

[396] ARET 1 45 §31″.

"from the king and Irᵓaq-Damu" in the same tablet[397] that this took place under the last Eblean king of the archives period. Now the text ARET 8 533, from the end of the same reign, records in §§62–63 a series of batches of collected wool, measured in $n a_4$[398] and systematically designated as either siki *Na-gàr*ᵏⁱ 'wool of Nagar', or siki si-lù-ur_4 'wool (delivered to) the si-lu-ur_4',[399] probably the wool collector, who received the freshly shorn wool from labor teams called *ìr-a-núm*.[400] Evidently teams from Nagar worked along with Eblean teams at the labor-intensive seasonal shearing campaign and received for their city a share of the produced wool.

As for Nagar's neighbor, Kakkabān, two of its six occurrences in Ebla texts record one and the same transaction—the purchase of 127 clothes for Kakkabān by the Eblean ur_4, Enᵓa-Damu;[401] a third one (all that remains of the tablet) says "Kakkabān: (account of) Zekam: total: two tablets, two years, two hundred [. . .]."[402] This implies regular trade connections between Ebla and Kakkabān. Both Enᵓa-Damu and Zekam are frequently mentioned in Eblean administrative texts, sometimes as recipients of travel allowances. It is significant that Zekam, although he was employed by the administration (sa-za_xᵏⁱ) of Ebla, is five times designated a man of Kakmium.[403]

The important royal city of Kakmium lay in all likelihood on the route leading to Nagar. Its importance for Ebla can be gauged from the fact that it is second only to Mari—and not by much—in the number of mentions in the texts. Names of persons from Kakmium are much fewer in number (about one hundred) than those of Mariotes but they far exceed the numbers of people from other sixteen cities around Ebla as compiled by Archi.[404] Of course the Kakmium of the Ebla texts is only a namesake of the Ur III Kakmi, Old Babylonian Kakmu(m) in the

[397] ARET 1 44 §19.

[398] See n. 366 above.

[399] The term is also found, in connection with wool, in ARET 4 11 and 25. The word contains the element ur_4 which designates an office (see n. 316 above). The passage ARET 4 25 §26, in which a quantity of wool has been purchased for (šè) a si-lu-ur_4, indicates that it did not designate a quality of wool. The word should not be italicized (as in ARET 4 and Archi 1988c), as though it were a Semitic word, for it appears in the Sumerian column of VE 1120, unfortunately without its Eblaic correspondence (it is followed by VE 1121, si-ur_4 = *me-a-gu-um*, which does not help). Sollberger, in ARET 8, transliterated it si-udu-ur_4. I shall not discuss here the possible meaning of si.

[400] On these detachments and their role in shearing sheep see Archi 1988c, in particular p. 133 with an excerpt from TM.75.G.10052, in which siki *Na-gàr*ᵏⁱ (here measured in "KIN"-units) is listed together with the wool gathered by labor teams (here é-$duru_5$).

[401] ARET 7 13 §11. The same deal has been inserted in an inventory of 4,007 pieces of clothing, ARET 1 28, from the time of Ibrium. Read there, §3, beginning: 1 *mi-at* 27 túg-⌜túg⌝/ *En-ᵓà-Da-mu*/ níg-sa_{10} *$iš_{11}$* ⟨*-ki*⟩ *Ga-ga-ba-*⌜an⌝ᵏⁱ.

[402] ARET 3 162.

[403] ARET 3 800:i; ARET 4 1 72; ARET 4 21 §§1, 20; ARET 8 521 §32. Cf. ARET 1 15 §35: *Du-bí* lú *Zé-kam*$_4$ sa-za_xᵏⁱ.

[404] Archi 1984b; these are, besides Kakmium: Abarsal (Abarsil), Absu (*et var.*), Adabig(u), Adu, Ama and Amat, Arḫatu, Dudulu (Tuttul), Dulu, Dub (Ṭub), Ḫarran, Ḫazuwan, Imar (Emar), Irritum, Gargamiš, Nagar, and Ursaᵓum (those of Ebal and Manuwat have not been collected). On the names of Mariotes see Archi 1985e.

Transtigris.[405] It was definitely a client kingdom of Ebla: it is very often listed among the more prominent cities of this rank, it paid tribute (m u - t ù) along with them,[406] it delivered the ceremonial, so-called oil-tribute (ì - g i š s a g) for the then crown prince Išʾar-Damu,[407] it sent some gifts "in the day of oil-offering in the temple of the god Kura,"[408] and it combined with the client kingdom of Dulu in producing the insignificant but symbolic gift of two pieces of apparel for the "pronouncement of oath."[409] Kakmium's partnership with Dulu (a city very certainly located in northwestern Mesopotamia, probably near the sources of the Balīḫ)[410] may suggest that it was one of the big Early Bronze mounds east of the Balīḫ, on the road to the headwaters of the Ḫabūr.[411] Just as Manuwat and Ebal owed their commercial prominence to their locations on the Euphrates trade artery,[412] so Kakmium's importance was due to its role of a transit point and intermediary on the principal east–west route.

This is all that is known of Ebla's connections beyond the sphere of its supremacy. It does not mean that some mysterious factors prevented Ebla from having relations with areas to its west (Mediterranean coast), north (Anatolia), and south (southern Syria and Palestine). Indeed, the Egyptian stone vases found in fragments in the ruins of palace G[413] must have come from the south, but by what route and through how many hands remains unknown. Despite claims to the contrary, Ugarit is not mentioned either in the great List of Geographical

[405] After some hesitation, Archi 1985c: 220 recognized that the Eblean Kakmium was distinct from the Transtigridian and tentatively placed the former near the area of the Ḫabūr. Sollberger, ARET 8: p. 46, said that the two sites had nothing in common but the name. Cf. n. 47 above. I have counted thirty-five cases (including Ebla itself) of complete or close homonymy between places in the Ebla Empire and those in the Transtigris.

[406] MEE 2 5:obv.i:1–4 = ARET 1 31 §1.

[407] MEE 2 1:rev.iii:1–7.

[408] ARET 3 800:i; one of the four men who delivered the gifts was Zekam who, as seen just above, also served Ebla.

[409] MEE 2 20:obv.vii:6–11 = ARET 1 14 §20: 2 m í - t u g *Kak-mi-um*^{ki} *wa Du-lu*^{ki} u d - d u$_{11}$- g a n a m - t a r / k u$_{5}$. For the reading and meaning of the last word cf. Astour 1988b: 149 and n. 77.

[410] *Du-lu*^{ki} should not be read *Gub-lu*^{ki} and identified with Gubla (Byblos), as only Pettinato and his students persist in asserting. The reason is not that DU was not read *gub* at the time of the Ebla archives, but the uncontroversial fact that Dulu is systematically listed in the context of Ḫarran, Irritum, and their constant companion Šunapsugum, also with Carchemish, Raʾaq, and Emar on the Euphrates, with Kakmium and Nagar—nothing reminiscent of Phoenicia. An Eblean conjuration of serpents (text *g* of the é n - é - n u - r u collection published by Pettinato 1979d: 344–45) begins with é n - é - n u - r u k i é n - é - n u - r u ^{d}*Ba-li-ḫa-a* 'conjuration by the Earth, conjuration by the Divine Balīḫ' and is concerned with š u - r a m u š - m u š g á n a - k e š d a g á n a - k e š d a *Du-lu*^{ki} 'smiting the serpents in the fields of Dulu'. The conjuration may have been composed at Dulu (and cf. the payment of one piece of clothing to *Puzur*$_{4}$*-ra-Ma-lik Du-lu*^{ki} (for) ud-du$_{11}$-ga muš 'conjuration of serpents'), and the invocation of the divinized river Balīḫ may point to Dulu's location near it, which would perfectly agree with what is otherwise known about the general location of Dulu. See already Astour 1988b: 145 n. 46.

[411] Cf. n. 391 above.

[412] Cf. p. 57 above.

[413] Described and studied by Scandone Matthiae 1979, 1981, and 1988.

Names (of southern Mesopotamian provenance)[414] or in three administrative tablets of Ebla.[415] In the northern direction, no point north of the Taurus or west of the Amanus is attested in Ebla texts. A city *Ga*-NI-*šu*^{ki} is listed as one of "seventeen 'countries' in the hand of the king of Ebla";[416] Pettinato identified it with the well-known Kaniš (Kültepe) and stated: "The presence of the city of Kaniš in central Turkey gives an idea of the true political expansion of Ebla,"[417] and even stronger: "In the north, the geographical boundaries enclose almost all of modern Turkey: we remind that Kaniš was subject to Ebla."[418] Pettinato's disciple Davidović tried to strengthen his Anatolian attribution of *Ga*-NI-*šu*^{ki} by finding more Anatolian, or supposedly Anatolian, places in the list of the "seventeen 'countries,'" and at the same time to make his extreme assertion more acceptable by reducing these places to Ebla's "commercial colonies."[419] Neither approach works, the former because of its geographical inconsistence,[420] the

[414] First published by Pettinato 1978, then as MEE 3 56, parallel with copies of the same work found at Abū Ṣalābīḫ and of earlier dates than the Ebla copy. It has been proven that the list is of southern Mesopotamian composition and comprises only Mesopotamian and Transtigridian place names; see Steinkeller 1986: 31–40; a complete comparative edition of the list has been prepared by Douglas Frayne but has not yet appeared as of this writing. No. 5 of the list is *U*$_9$*-ga-ra-at*^{ki} (the corresponding entry is destroyed in the Abū Ṣalābīḫ copies). It was believed to stand for Ugarit, but a mention of a single Syrian city in the list would not agree with its geographical framework. Steinkeller 1986: 37 equated it with *Wa-ga-la-at*^{ki} in the Transtigris.

[415] ARET 3 939:obv.iii: *Ù-gú-ra-tum*^{ki}; ARET 8 524 §7: *Ù-gú-ra-tum* (without ki, but the context is the same as in the previously cited text); ARET 7 71 §3: *Ù-gú-ra-at*^{ki}. Archi 1987h: 186 thought it possible that this place, unlike that of the List of Geographical Names, could be identical with Ugarit. But it appears in the context of direct possessions of Ebla; in the last quoted passage its administrator is none other than Ibrium. Even its etymology is different. *Ugarit* is formed with the Akkadian loanword *ugāru* 'field' (cf. the Ugaritic dyad of minor gods, *Gpn w Ugr* 'vine and field'); *Ugurāt*(*um*), on the other hand, should be understood as /uqqurātum/, epenthetic form of Old Assyrian *waqqurtum/uqqurtum* 'dear one [fem.]'; cf. Eblean PN *Ù-gú-ra* and, for linguistic affinities between Eblaic and Old Assyrian, Parpola 1988.

[416] TM.75.G.2136, published by Pettinato 1978: 51–52. *Ga*-NI-*šu*^{ki} is no. 12 of the list; no. 13 is destroyed; nos. 1 and 3 "are not read correctly by Pettinato," according to Archi 1981a: 1 n. 2, but the correct readings are not cited.

[417] Pettinato 1979a: 111.

[418] Pettinato 1979a: 206; the entire section is repeated in Pettinato 1986: 215–16. Few scholars outside Pettinato's immediate circle agree with his sweeping generalization; see, e.g., Diakonoff 1985: 320 on Kaniš.

[419] Davidović 1989: 10–12 and 23 nn. 67–70.

[420] In addition to *Ga*-NI-*šu* = Kaniš, Davidović equated *Ḫu-bù-ša-an*^{ki} with Ḫubišna, *Du-nu*^{ki} with Tuna (both in southern Cappadocia of Hittite and Classical times), *Al-šúm*^{ki} with Alši (actually east of Diyarbakir and north of the upper Tigris), *Za-bur-rúm*^{ki} and *Zi-rí-ba*^{ki} with Zaburu and Ziriba of Hittite texts (which is true, except that both of these towns belonged to the Hittite appanage kingdom of Carchemish and were thus located in historical Syria and not in Anatolia), *Lu*$_5$*-a-tum*^{ki} with Luḫitim or Eluḫat (actual location between Urfa and Mardin, thus in historical upper Mesopotamia), *Gi-za-nu*^{ki} with modern Tell Hizan, fifteen km southeast of Harran (which is phonetically unacceptable), *Du-wu-um*^{ki} (misprinted *Du-wu-mu*) vaguely in "the south-east region located east of the upper course of the river Euphrates." Now five towns of the list—*Lu*$_5$*-a-tum*^{ki}, *Zi-rí-ba*^{ki}, *Ḫu-bù-ša-an*^{ki}, *Ti-na-ma-zu*^{ki}, and *Gi-za-nu*^{ki}—are listed in TM.75.G.1975 (published by Archi 1981a: 1–3) as belonging to one and the same district, that of Luʾatum. Can one imagine

latter because the phrase *in* šu, or *in* 2 šu, 'in the hand(s)' means 'possession, full property, jurisdiction', which is inapplicable to commercial establishments in foreign countries.[421] In point of fact, the crucial *Ga*-NI-*šu*ki recurs in a Hittite text—not as Kaniš in Cappadocia but as uru*Ka-an-ni-še* in the far northwest of Syria.[422] In the southern direction, one must agree—though for a different reason—with Archi's conclusion that the geographical horizon of the Ebla texts reached no further than the area of Ḥomṣ.[423] Pettinato's alleged discoveries of several Phoenician and biblical Palestinian cities as parts of his Eblean super-empire[424] need no refutation: it suffices to read the texts in which they appear.[425]

What caused this strange ignorance of regions adjacent to Ebla on the north, west, and south? Diakonoff surmised that "apparently, the road to the sea toward Ugarit was barred by some other important city-state—perhaps Ḫalab, or maybe Armanum, mentioned by Naram-Suen of Akkad along with Ebla."[426] A glance at the map shows that Ḫalab (Aleppo) is not situated between Ebla and Ugarit; besides, the entire Quweiq Valley directly belonged to the Kingdom of Ebla proper. Moreover, as evidenced by a considerable number of Eblean place-names which recur in the outer districts acquired by the Kingdom of Ugarit in the fourteenth century,[427] the territory of Ebla abutted on the territory of Ugarit on the latter's east (the Bargylus Range) and north (the area of Basiṭ and Baer).[428] Archi, on his part, made a suggestion why there may have been no "intense relations with places further to the South: we must keep in mind that, even at present . . . almost 150 km of desert in a straight line stretch between Homs and the oasis of Damascus."[429] This is true, but the desert stretch in question never stopped the connections between the north and the south of Syria: the ancient arterial road turned southwestward from Ḥomṣ and proceeded via Qidši (Kadesh-on-the-Orontes) and the Biqāᶜ Valley to Galilee and the coast of Palestine.

The explanation may be simpler. The archives of Ebla were found not in one but in six separate places in royal palace G.[430] Moreover, three well-preserved

---

a district of which one town is located in Cappadocia and another in the central part of northern Mesopotamia? My view of the location of the district of Luᵓatum in general and of several of its towns in particular has been given in Astour 1988b: 142–43 and n. 29.

[421] Pettinato's and Davidović's views of Ebla's role in Anatolia look like a revival of the old theory, of which Julius Lewy was the last and staunchiest defender, that Cappadocia was an "Assyria on the Halys" and formed, with the "Assyria on the Tigris," the "Old Assyrian Empire," on which cf. Garelli 1963: 25–27.

[422] See on it (and on *Al-šúm*ki) Astour 1988b: 153; read there *Ga*-NI-*šu*ki instead of *Gá*-NI-*šu*ki.

[423] Archi 1984b: 229; Archi 1985c: 221; cf. Astour 1988b: 145 and n. 41.

[424] Pettinato 1979a: 206, expanded in his 1983 article and 1986: 244–58.

[425] A characteristic of Pettinato's way of reaching his conclusions is given in the review of his 1986 book by Heimpel 1989.

[426] Diakonoff 1985: 330.

[427] As explained in Astour 1981a: 20–21 and Astour 1981b.

[428] Astour 1988b: 144–45. A full list of Eblean-Ugaritic toponymic correspondences may be presented at another opportunity.

[429] Archi 1980b: 3.

[430] Archi 1986b.

tablets, typologically different from the other archival texts, were discovered in the southern part of the palace in 1982 and may have belonged to the archive of a separate sector of the administration.[431] The bulk of the earlier uncovered archives is heavily slanted toward the eastern possessions of Ebla and their neighboring states. Records on deals with other regions may have been stored in some as-yet-unexcavated part of the palace or in another administrative building on the Acropolis. They may or may not be recovered in the future. There are also other major gaps in our knowledge of Ebla's foreign trade. We ignore the provenance of gold, silver, tin, and copper which show up so prominently in the texts. Perhaps the relevant records were kept in the é-am, but it is interesting to note that the same absence of information exists in the chronologically close Sargonic commercial texts, though they were written by the merchants themselves rather than by royal recorders.[432] Cuneiform texts, from the Sargonic period on, testify to the timber wealth of northern Syria, sometimes referring specifically to Ebla, and this has been confirmed by TM.82.G.266 (an annual balance of the property owned, or administered, by Ibbi-Zikir), which includes the item "1700 minas of silver, price [níg-sa_{10}] of boxwood [^{giš}taškarin] (and) cypress [^{giš}ir-nun] (of) Ibbi-Zikir."[433] This is a very large monetary amount, but does it represent the market value of the timber or its actual sale, and if the latter, to whom? Other Ebla texts published so far record few and small sales of wood.[434] In brief, the material at our disposal is limited, but it is all we have.[435] In presenting, on these pages, a sketch of Ebla's foreign trade, I followed the example of W. F. Leemans, who wrote his classical work on Old Babylonian foreign trade strictly on the basis of inscriptional evidence.[436]

TO BE CONTINUED

431 Matthiae 1983: 548–49, assisted by information from Archi. Short quotations from all three tablets were given in Archi 1988a: 209, and of one of them in Archi 1987f: 121–22.

432 "There seems to be no records of bulk purchases of copper or silver, but only records of transactions and stocks at hand, sometimes very large and often in the hands of private people"; Foster 1977: 37.

433 Quoted in Archi 1988a: 209. For the latter tree, cf. VE 470: giš-nun-ir = *i-dum*, and the explanation of the latter word as Akkadian *imdu/endu* by Fronzaroli 1988: 10; according to *AHw* 211, *s.v. emdu(m)*, *endu* II, it is an evergreen cypress.

434 It should be noted that on the receiving end of timber trade, in Sargonic southern Mesopotamia, "while shipments of wood do occur in the records, these are in small quantities and seem to be private enterprise on a modest scale"; Foster 1977: 37.

435 Most articles on Ebla's foreign trade miss the mark. Pettinato 1979c presented, instead of documentation on international commerce, some lengthy records which belong to the categories of noncommercial distributions listed on pp. 57–58 above. Pinnock 1985 is a cautious but general discussion with few specifics, unlike her 1988 article which deals with lapis-lazuli trade. Van Lerberghe 1988 suggests some possible, but inscriptionally unconfirmed, sources of Ebla's tin. Klengel 1988 deals with the economic potential of Syria at large and with its international road connections as revealed mainly by later sources, rather than with the actual written material from Ebla itself.

436 Leemans 1960.

Bibliography

Abu al-Soof, Behnam

1966 "Short Sounding at Tell Qalinj Agha (Erbil)." *Sumer* 22:77–82, pls. i–vi.

1969 "Excavations at Tell Qalinj Agha (Erbil), Summer, 1968: Interim Report." *Sumer* 25:3–42, pls. viii–xx.

Abu al-Soof, Behnam, and Shah es-Siwwani

1967 "More Soundings at Tell Qalinj Agha (Erbil)." *Sumer* 23:69–75, pls. i–v.

Algaze, Guillermo

1986 "Habuba on the Tigris: Archaic Nineveh Reconsidered." *JNES* 45:125–37.

1989a "Tigris-Euphrates Reconnaissance Project, 1988." *Mār Šipri* 2/1:1, 3, 7–8.

1989b "A New Frontier: First Results of the Tigris-Euphrates Archaeological Reconnaissance Project, 1988." *JNES* 48:241–81.

Arcari, Elena

1988 "The Administrative Organization of the City of Ebla." Pp. 125–29 in *Wirtschaft und Gesellschaft von Ebla: Akten der Internationalen Tagung, Heidelberg 4.–7. November 1986.* Edited by Harold Hauptmann and Hartmut Waetzoldt. Heidelberg.

Archi, Alfonso

1979a "An Administrative Practice and the 'Sabbatical Year' at Ebla." *SEb* 1/5–6:91–95, 2 pls.

1979b "Diffusione del culto di dNI-*da-kul*." *SEb* 1/7–8:105–18, 2 pls.

1980a "Materiale epigrafico ittita da Tell Fray." *Studi Miceni ed Egeo-Anatolici* 22:31–32, pls. i–ii.

1980b "Notes on Eblaite Geography." *SEb* 2/1:1–16, 4 pls.

1981a "Notes on Eblaite Geography II." *SEb* 4:1–17, 7 pls.

1981b "Kiš nei testi di Ebla." *SEb* 4:77–87.

1981c "I rapporti tra Ebla e Mari." *SEb* 4:129–66, 13 pls.

1982 "About the Organization of the Eblaite State." *SEb* 5:201–20.

1984a "A Recent Book on Ebla." *SEb* 7:23–43.

1984b "The Personal names in the Individual Cities." Pp. 225–51 in *Studies on the Language of Ebla.* Edited by Pelio Fronzaroli. Quaderni di Semitistica 13. Florence.

1984c "Allevamento e distribuzione del bestiame ad Ebla." *Seb* 7:45–81, 10 pls.

1985a "Le synchronisme entre les rois de Mari et les rois d'Ebla au IIIe millénaire." *MARI* 4:47–51.

1985b "Les rapports politiques et économiques entre Ebla et Mari." *MARI* 4:63–83.

1985c "L'organizzazione politica della Siria nell'età di Ebla." ARET 1: 219–25.

1985d "Mardu in the Ebla Texts." *Or* 54:7–13.

1985e "Les noms de personnes mariotes à Ebla (IIIème millénaire)." *MARI* 4:53–58.

1986a "Die ersten zehn Könige von Ebla." *ZA* 76:213–17, 1 pl.

1986b "The Archives of Ebla." Pp. 72–86 in *Cuneiform Archives and Libraries: Papers read at the 30e Rencontre Assyriologique Internationale, Leiden, 4–8 July 1983.* Edited by Klaas R. Veenhof. Istanbul/Leiden.

1987a "Ebla and Eblaite." *Eblaitica* 1:7–17.

1987b "Reflections on the System of Weights from Ebla." *Eblaitica* 1:47–89.

1987c "The 'Sign-List' from Ebla." *Eblaitica* 1:91–113.

1987d "Les titres de en et lugal à Ebla et des cadeaux pour le roi de Kish." *MARI* 5:37–52.

1987e "More on Ebla and Kish." *Eblaitica* 1:125–40.

1987f "Gifts for a Princess." *Eblaitica* 1:115–24.

1987g "gín DILMUN 'sicle pesé, standard.'" *RA* 81:186–87.

1987h "Ugarit dans les textes d'Ebla?" *RA* 81:185–86.

1988a "Studies in Eblaite Prosopography." Pp. 205–85 (§§1–14), 1 pl., in *Eblaite Personal Names and Semitic Name-Giving: Papers of a Symposium held in Rome, July 15–17, 1985.* Edited by Alfonso Archi. Archivi Reali di Ebla—Studi 1. Rome.

1988b "Ḫarran in the III Millennium B.C." *UF* 20:1–8.

1988c "Zur Organisation der Arbeit in Ebla." Pp. 131–38 in *Wirtschaft und Gesellschaft von Ebla: Akten der Internationalen Tagung, Heidelberg 4.–7. November 1986*. Edited by Harold Hauptmann and Hartmut Waetzoldt. Heidelberg.

ARES 1 Archivi Reali di Ebla—Studi 1: *Eblaite Personal Names and Semitic Name-Giving: Papers of a Symposium Held in Rome, July 15–17, 1985*. Edited by Alfonso Archi. Rome 1988.

Arnaud, Daniel

1986 *Emar VI: Textes sumériens et accadiens*. 3 vols. Recherches au pays d'Aštata. Paris.

1987 "La Syrie du Moyen-Euphrate sous le protectorat hittite: contrats de droit privé." *Aula Orientalia* 2:211–41.

Astour, Michael C.

1968 "Mesopotamian and Transtigridian Place Names in the Medinet Habu Lists of Ramses III." *JAOS* 88:733–52.

1971 "Tell Mardīḫ and Ebla." *UF* 3:9–19.

1972 "New Works on Ancient Syria and the Sea Peoples: Review Article." *JAOS* 92:447-59.

1977a "Continuité et changement dans la toponymie de la Syrie du Nord." Pp. 117–41 (with map) in *La toponymie antique: Actes du Colloque de Strasbourg, 12–14 juin 1975*. Leiden.

1977b "Tunip-Hamath and Its Region: A Contribution to the Historical Geography of Central Syria." *Or* 46:51–64.

1978 "The Rabbeans: A Tribal Society on the Euphrates from Yaḫdun-Lim to Julius Caesar." *Syro-Mesopotamian Studies* 2/1:1–12.

1981a "Ugarit and the Great Powers." Pp. 3–29 (map) in *Ugarit in Retrospect: Fifty Years of Ugarit and Ugaritic*. Edited by Gordon D. Young. Winona Lake, IN.

1981b "Les frontières et les districts du royaume d'Ugarit (Éléments de topographie historique régionale." *UF* 13:1–12.

1987 "Semites and Hurrians in Northern Transtigris." Pp. 3–68 in *Studies in the Civilization and Culture of Nuzi and the Hurrians*, vol. 2. Edited by D. I. Owen and M. A. Morrison. Winona Lake, IN.

1988a "Toponymy of Ebla and Ethnohistory of Northern Syria: A Preliminary Survey." *JAOS* 108:545–55.

1988b "The Geographical and Political Structure of the Ebla Empire." Pp. 139–58 in *Wirtschaft und Gesellschaft von Ebla: Akten der Internationalen Tagung, Heidelberg 4.–7. November 1986*. Edited by Harold Hauptmann and Hartmut Waetzoldt. Heidelberg.

1989 *Hittite History and Absolute Chronology of the Bronze Age*. Studies in Mediterranean Archaeology, Pocket-book 73. Partille, Sweden.

Balty, Jean C.

1972 "Le problème de Niya." Pp. 53–63 in *Colloque Apamée de Syrie: Bilan des recherches archéologiques 1969–1970*. Brussels.

1981 *Guide d'Apamée*. Photographs by Jean C. Balty Wilfried van Rengen. Brussels.

Bauer, Josef

1969 "Zum Totenkult im altsumerischen Lagasch." Pp. 107–14 in *XVII. Deutscher Orientalistentag vom 21. bis 27. Juli 1968 in Würzburg*. Zeitschrift der Deutschen Morgenländischen Gesellschaft Supplement 1. Wiesbaden.

Behm-Blancke, Manfred R.

1988 "Periphere Ninive-5-Keramik am Oberen Euphrat." *MDOG* 120:159–72.

Bell, Gertrude Lowthian

1910 "The East Bank of the Euphrates from Tell Ahmar to Hit." *Geographical Journal* 36:513–37, map.

1911 *Amurath to Amurath*. 2d ed. London.

Biga, Maria Giovanna

1988 "Studies in Eblaite Prosopography." Pp. 285–87, 291–306 (§§15, 17–19) in *Eblaite Personal Names and Semitic Name-Giving: Papers of a Symposium Held in Rome, July 15–17, 1985*. Edited by Alfonso Archi. Archivi Reali di Ebla—Studi 1. Rome.

Biga, Maria Giovanna, and Francesco Pomponio

1987 "Iš˒ar-Damu, roi d'Ebla." *NABU* 1987/106.

Biggs, Robert D.

1982 "The Ebla Tablets: A 1981 Perspective." *Bulletin: The Society for Mesopotamian Studies* (Toronto) 2:9–24.

Boese, Johannes

1982 "Zur absoluten Chronologie der Akkad-Zeit." *Wiener Zeitschrift für die Kunde des Morgenlandes* 74:33–55.

Bordreuil, Pierre, and Dennis Pardee

1982 "Le rituel funéraire ougaritique RS.34.126." *Syria* 59:121–28.

Bottéro, Jean

1965 "Syria during the Third Dynasty of Ur" (§4 of G. Posener, J. Bottéro, and Kathleen M. Kenyon, "Syria and Palestine, c. 2160–1780"). *CAH*² fasc. 29:30–37 = *CAH*³, 1/2 (1971): 559–66.

Boulanger, Robert

1966 *The Middle East: Lebanon–Syria–Jordan–Iraq–Iran*. Hachette World Guides. Translated by J. S. Hardmann. Paris.

Bounni, Adnan

1979 "Campaign and Exhibition from the Euphrates in Syria." *AASOR* 44:1–7.

Bounni, Adnan, and Paolo Matthiae

1980 "Tell Fray, ville frontière entre Hittites et Assyriens au XIIIᵉ siècle av. J.-C." *Archaeologia* 140 (1980): 30–39.

Braidwood, Robert J., and Linda S. Braidwood

1960 *Excavations in the Plain of Antioch*, 1: *The Earlier Assemblages, Phases A–J*. Oriental Institute Publications 61. Chicago.

Buccellati, Giorgio

1966 *The Amorites of the Ur III Period*. Naples.

1983 *Terqa: An Introduction to the Site*. Preprint on the Occasion of the Symposium of Der ez-Zor, October 1983.

Burney, Charles

1980 "Aspects of the Excavations in the Altinova, Elaziğ." *Anatolian Studies* 30:157–67.

Cagni, Luigi

1984 "Il lessico dei testi amministrativi e dei testi bilingui di Ebla." Pp. 371–91 in *Il Bilinguismo a Ebla: Atti del Convegno Internazionale (Napoli, 19–22 aprile 1982)*. Edited by Luigi Cagni. Naples.

Charpin, Dominique

1987a "Tablettes présargoniques de Mari." *MARI* 5:65–127.

1987b "Šubat-Enlil et le pays d'Apum." *MARI* 5:129–40.

Chesney, Francis Rawdon

1850 *The Expedition for the Survey of the Rivers Euphrates and Tigris, Carried on the Order of the British Government, in the years 1835, 1836, and 1837*. London (vols. 1, 2, and a vol. of maps all that was published).

Civil, Miguel

1967 "Šū-Sîn's Historical Inscriptions: Collection B." *JCS* 21:24–38.

1983 "The sign LAK 384." *Or* 52:233–34.

1984 "Bilingualism in Logographically Written Languages: Sumerian in Ebla." Pp. 75–97 in *Il Bilinguismo a Ebla: Atti del Convegno Internazionale (Napoli, 19–22 aprile 1982)*. Edited by Luigi Cagni. Naples.

1987 "The Early History of HAR-ra: The Ebla Link." Pp. 131–58 in *Ebla 1975–1985: Dieci Anni di Studi Linguistici e Filologici; Atti del Convegno Internazionale (Napoli, 9–11 ottobre 1985).* Edited by Luigi Cagni. Naples.

Courtois, Jacques-Claude

1973 "Prospection archéologique dans la moyenne vallée de l'Oronte (El Ghab et Er Roudj—Syrie du nord-ouest)." *Syria* 50:54–99, pls. i–ii.

Davidović, Vesna

1988 "Guruš in the Administrative Texts from Ebla." Pp. 199–204 in *Wirtschaft und Gesellschaft von Ebla: Akten der Internationalen Tagung, Heidelberg 4.–7. November 1986.* Edited by Harold Hauptmann and Hartmut Waetzoldt. Heidelberg.

1989 "Trade Routes between Northern Syria and Central Anatolia in the Middle of the III Millennium B.C." *Acta Sumerologica (Japan)* 11:1–26.

De Graeve, Marie-Christine

1981 *The Ships of the Ancient Near East (c. 2000–500 B.C.).* Orientalia Lovaniensia Analecta 7. Louvain.

Demiel, Anton

1920 "Die Listen über den Ahnenkult aus der Zeit Lugalandas und Urukaginas." *Or* [old series] 2:32–51.

Dhorme, Édouard

1949 *Les religions de Babylonie et d'Assyrie.* Pp. 1–330 of *Mana: Les anciennes religions orientales* 1/2. Paris.

Diakonoff, Igor M.

1959 *Obščestvennyj i gosudarstvennyj stroj drevnego Dvureč'ja: Šumer* [Society and state in ancient Mesopotamia: Sumer]. Moscow.

1985 "Značenije Èbly dlja istorii i jazykoznanija" [The importance of Ebla for history and linguistics]. Pp. 318–49 in *Drevnjaja Èbla (Raskopki v Sirii)* [Ancient Ebla (Excavations in Syria)]. Edited by P. Matthiae and I. M. Diakonoff. Moscow. English translation in *Eblaitica* 2:3–29.

Dornemann, Rudolph H.

1985 "Salvage Excavations at Tell Hadidi in the Euphrates River Valley." *BA* 48:49–59.

Dossin, Georges

1939 "Benjaminites dans les textes de Mari." Pp. 981–96 in *Mélanges syriens offerts à M. René Dussaud.* Paris.

van Driel, G.

1980 "The Uruk Settlement on Jebel Aruda: A Preliminary Report." Pp. 75–93 in *Le Moyen Euphrate: Zone de contact et d'échange; Actes du Colloque de Strasbourg, 10–12 mars 1977.* Leiden.

1983 "Seal and Sealings from Jebel Aruda 1974–1978." *Akkadica* 33:34–62.

van Driel, G., and C. van Driel-Murray

1979 "Jebel Aruda 1977–1978." *Akkadica* 12:2–28, 3 pls.

1983 "Jebel Aruda, the 1982 Season of Excavation, Interim report." *Akkadica* 33:1–26, 1 plan.

Durand, Jean-Marie

1987 "Villes fantômes de Syrie et autres lieux." *MARI* 5:199–234.

Edzard, Dietz Otto

1957 *Die "zweite Zwischenzeit" Babyloniens.* Wiesbaden.

1981a "Der Text TM.75.G.1444 aus Ebla." *SEb* 4:35–60.

1981b "Neue Erwägungen zum Brief des Enna-Dagan von Mari." *SEb* 4:89–97.

1988 "Semitische und nichtsemitische Personennamen in Texten aus Ebla." Pp. 25–44 in *Eblaite Personal Names and Semitic Name-Giving: Papers of a Symposium Held in Rome, July 15–17, 1985.* Edited by Alfonso Archi. Archivi Reali di Ebla—Studi 1. Rome.

Fales, Frederick Mario
1973 *Censimenti e catasti di epoca neo-assira.* Rome.
1988 "Formationa with *m*-Prefix in the Bilingual Vocabularies." Pp. 205–9 in *Wirtschaft und Gesellschaft von Ebla: Akten der Internationalen Tagung, Heidelberg 4.–7. November 1986.* Edited by Harold Hauptmann and Hartmut Waetzoldt. Heidelberg.

Fielden, K.
1981 "A Late Uruk Pottery Group from Tell Brak." *Iraq* 43:157–66.

Finet, André
1957 "Les médecins au royaume de Mari." *Annuaire de l'Institut de Philologie et d'Histoire Orientales et Slaves 1*14 (1954–1957): 123–44, pls. i–iv.
1975 "Les temples sumériens de Tell Kannâs." *Syria* 52:157–74.
1978 Note on the exhibition of the excavations at Habuba Kabira, Berlin. *Akkadica* 10: 24–27.
1979 "Bilan provisoire des fouilles belges du Tell Kannâs." *AASOR* 44:79–95.

Finkelstein, Jacob Joel
1962 "Mesopotamia." *JNES* 21:73–92.
1966 "The Genealogy of the Hammurapi Dynasty." *JCS* 20:95–118.

Foster, Benjamin R.
1977 "Commercial Activity in Sargonic Mesopotamia." Pp. 31–43 in *Trade in the Ancient Near East: Papers Presented to the XXIII Rencontre Assyriologique Internationale, University of Birmingham, 5–9 July, 1976.* Edited by J. D. Hawkins (= *Iraq* 39 [1977]). London.

Frankfort, Henri
1951 *The Birth of Civilization in the Near East.* London. [Cited according to paperback edition, Garden City, NY, no date.]

Fronzaroli, Pelio
1977 "West Semitic Toponymy in Northern Syria in the Third Millennium B.C." *Journal of Semitic Studies* 2:145–66.
1979 "Un atto reale di donazione dagli archivi di Ebla (TM.75.G.1766)." *SEb* 1/1:1–16, 2 pls.
1980 "Un verdetto reale dagli Archivi di Ebla (TM.75.G.1452)." *SEb* 3/3–4:33–52, 2 pls.
1981 "La conguinzione eblaita *ap.*" *SEb* 4:167–76.
1982 "Per una valutazione della morfologia eblaita." *SEb* 5:93–120.
1984a "The Eblaic Lexicon: Problems and Appraisals." Pp. 117–57 in *Studies on the Language of Ebla.* Edited by Pelio Fronzaroli. Quaderni di Semitistica 13. Florence.
1984b "Materiali per il lessico eblaita, 1." *Seb* 7:145–90.
1984c "Disposizioni reali per Tiṭaw-Liᵓm (TM.75.2396, TM.75.G.1986+)." *SEb* 7:1–22.
1988 "Il culto dei re defunti in *ARET* 3.178." Pp. 1–33 in *Miscellanea Eblaitica* 1. Quaderni di Semitistica 15. Florence.
1989 "A proposito del culto dei re defunti a Ebla." *NABU* 1989/2.

Fugmann, E.
1958 *L'architecture des périodes pré-hellenistiques (Hama: Fouilles et Recherches 1931–1938, II 1).* Copenhagen.

Gadd, Cyril J.
1940 "Tablets from Chagar Bazar and Tall Brak." *Iraq* 7:22–61, pls. i–v.

Garelli, Paul
1963 *Les Assyriens en Cappadoce.* Paris.

Gaz.Syr. *Gazetteer No. 104: Syria: Official Standard Names, Approved by the U.S. Board on Geographic Names.* 2d ed. Department of Interior. Washington, DC. 1983.

Gelb, Ignace J.
1954 "Two Assyrian King Lists." *JNES* 13:209–30.
1957 *Glossary of Old Akkadian.* Materials for the Assyrian Dictionary 3. Chicago.
1961 "The Early History of the West Semitic Peoples." *JCS* 15:27–47.

1962 "Ethnic Reconstruction and Onomastic Evidence." *Names* 10:45–52.

1972 "From Freedom to Slavery." Pp. 81–92 in *Gesellschaftsklassen im Alten Zweistromland und in den angrenzenden Gebieten: XVIII. Rencontre assyriologique internationale, München, 29. Juni bis. 3. Juli 1970.* Edited by D. O. Edzard. Munich.

1973 "Prisoners of War in Early Mesopotamia." *JNES* 32:70–98.

1977 "Thoughts about Ibla: A Preliminary Evaluation, March 1977." *Syro-Mesopotamian Studies* 1/1:3–30.

1980 *Computer-aided Analysis of Amorite.* With the assistance of Joyce Bartels, Stuart-Morgan Vance, and Robert M. Whiting. Assyriological Studies 31. Chicago.

1981 "Ebla and the Kish Civilization." Pp. 9–73 in *La Lingua di Ebla: Atti del Convegno Internazionale (Napoli, 21–23 aprile 1980).* Edited by Luigi Cagni. Naples.

1986 "Ebla and Lagash: Environmental Contrast." Pp. 157–67 in *The Origins of Cities in Dry-Farming Syria and Mesopotamia in the Third Millennium* B.C. Edited by Harvey Weiss. Guilford, CT.

1987 "The Language of Ebla in the Light of the Sources from Ebla, Mari, and Babylonia." Pp. 49–74 in *Ebla 1975–1985: Dieci Anni di Studi Linguistici e Filologici; Atti del Convegno Internazionale (Napoli, 9–11 ottobre 1985).* Edited by Luigi Cagni. Naples.

Geller, Markham J.

1987 "The Lugal of Mari at Ebla and the Sumerian King List." *Eblaitica* 1:141–45.

Goetze, Albrecht

1953 "Four Ur Dynasty Tablets Mentioning Foreigners." *JCS* 7:103–9.

1959 "Amurrite Names in Ur III and Early Isin Texts." *Journal of Semitic Studies* 4: 193 203.

Gordon, Cyrus H.

1987 "Introduction." *Eblaitica* 1:1–5.

Grayson, Albert Kirk

1975 *Assyrian and Babylonian Chronicles.* Texts from Cuneiform Sources 5. Locust Valley, NY.

Grégoire, Jean-Pierre, and Johannes Renger

1988 "Die Interdependenz der wirtschaftlichen und gesellschaftlich-politischen Struktur von Ebla: Erwägungen zum System der Oikos-Wirtschaft in Ebla." Pp. 211–24 in *Wirtschaft und Gesellschaft von Ebla: Akten der Internationalen Tagung, Heidelberg 4.–7. November 1986.* Edited by Harold Hauptmann and Hartmut Waetzoldt. Heidelberg.

Hallo, William W.

1964 "The Road to Emar." *JCS* 18:57–88.

1971 *Mesopotamia and the Asiatic Near East.* Pp. 1–183 in William W. Hallo and William Kelly Simpson, *The Ancient Near East: A History.* New York.

Hawkins, John David

1980 "The 'Autobiography of Ariyahina's Son': An Edition of the Hieroglyphic Luwian Stelae *Tell Ahmar* 1 and *Aleppo* 2." *Anatolian Studies* 30:139–56.

Hecker, Karl

1981 "Eigennamen und die Sprache von Ebla." Pp. 165–75 in *La Lingua di Ebla: Atti del Convegno Internazionale (Napoli, 21–23 aprile 1980).* Edited by Luigi Cagni. Naples.

Heimpel, Wolfgang

1989 Review of *Ebla: Nuovi orizzonti della storia*, by G. Pettinato. *JAOS* 109:120–23.

Hinz, Walter

1971 "Persia *c.* 2400–1800 B.C." *CAH*[3] 1/2:644–80.

Hirsch, Hans

1963 "Die Inschriften der Könige von Agade." *AfO* 20:1–82.

Hitti, Philip K.

1968 *History of the Arabs from the Earliest Times to the Present.* 9th ed. New York.

Holland, T. A.

1976 "Preliminary Report on Excavations at Tell es-Sweyhat, Syria, 1973–4." *Levant* 8:36–70, pls. iv–viii.

1977 "Preliminary Report on Excavations at Tell es-Sweyhat, Syria 1975." *Levant* 9:36–65, pls. viii–x.

Honigmann, Ernst

1923 *Historische Topographie von Nordsyrien im Altertum.* Leipzig. [Reprinted from *Zeitschrift des Deutschen Palästina-Vereins* 46 (1923) 149–93, 47 (1924) 1–64.]

1935 *Die Ostgrenze des byzantinischen Reiches.* Vol. 3 of A. A. Vasiliev, *Byzance et les Arabes.* Brussels.

Hood, Sinclair

1951 "Excavations at Tabara el Akrad, 1948–49." *Anatolian Studies* 1:113–47.

van Huÿssteen, Pieter J. J.

1984 " 'EN-ZI' or 'RU_{12}-ṢÍ': A Short Note on Variant Readings of Certain Ebla Personal Names." *SEb* 7:227–30.

Isserlin, B. S. J.

1956 "Place Names Provinces in the Semitic Speaking Ancient Near East." *Proceedings of the Leeds Philosophical Society* (Literary and Historical Section) 8:83–110.

Jacobsen, Thorkild

1939 *The Sumerian King List.* Assyriological Studies 11. Chicago.

1970 *Toward the Image of Tammuz and Other Essays on Mesopotamian History and Culture.* Harvard Semitic Studies 21. Cambridge, MA.

Kessler, Karlheinz

1984 "Nilabšinu und der altorientalische Name des Tell Brak." *Studi Micenei ed Egeo-Anatolici* 24:21–31.

Kienast, Burkhart

1980 "Der Feldzugsbericht des Ennadagan in literarischhistorisher Sicht." *OA* 19:247–61.

1984 "Zum Feldzugsbericht des Ennadagān." *OA* 23:19–32.

Kitchen, Kenneth A.

1977 "The King List of Ugarit." *UF* 9:131–42.

Klengel, Horst

1988 "Ebla im Fernhandel des 3. Jahrtausends." Pp. 245–51 in *Wirtschaft und Gesellschaft von Ebla: Akten der Internationalen Tagung, Heidelberg 4.–7. November 1986.* Edited by Harold Hauptmann and Hartmut Waetzoldt. Heidelberg.

Kohlmeyer, Kay

1984 "Euphrat-Survey: Der mit Mitteln der Gerda Henkel Stiftung durchgeführte archäologische Geländebegehung im syrischen Euphrattal." *MDOG* 116:95–118.

1986 "Euphrat-Survey 1984. Zweiter Vorbericht über die . . . archäologische Geländebegehung im syrischen Euphrattal." *MDOG* 118:51–65.

Kraus, Fritz R.

1965 "Könige, die in Zelten wohnen: Betrachtungen über den Kern der assyrischen Königslisten." *Mededelingen der Koninklijke Nederlandse Akademie van Wettenschappen, Aft. Letterkunde*, Nieuwe Reeks 28/2:123–40, 1 chart.

1972 *Altbabylonische Briefe in Umschrift und Übersetzung*, 5: *Briefe aus dem Istanbuler Museum.* Leiden.

Krebernik, Manfred

1982/83 "Zu Syllabar und Orthographie der lexikalischen Texte aus Ebla." I: *ZA* 72:178–236; II: *ZA* 73:1–47.

1988a "Prefixed Verbal Forms in Personal Names from Ebla." Pp. 45–69 in *Eblaite Personal Names and Semitic Name-Giving: Papers of a Symposium Held in Rome, July 15–17, 1985.* Edited by Alfonso Archi. Archivi Reali di Ebla—Studi 1. Rome.

1988b *Die Personenamen der Ebla-Texte: Ein Zwischenbilanz.* Berliner Beiträge zum Vorderen Orient 7. Berlin.

Krecher, Joachim

1984 "The Preposition /min(u)/ 'from' and Ì.TI 'he was (present).'" Pp. 71–83 in *Studies on the Language of Ebla.* Edited by Pelio Fronzaroli. Quaderni di Semitistica 13. Florence.

1988 "Observations on the Ebla Toponyms." Pp. 173–90 in *Eblaite Personal Names and Semitic Name-Giving: Papers of a Symposium Held in Rome, July 15–17, 1985.* Edited by Alfonso Archi. Archivi Reali di Ebla—Studi 1. Rome.

Kupper, Jean-Robert

1957 *Les nomades en Mésopotamie au temps des rois de Mari.* Bibl. de la Fac. de Philos. et Lettres de l'Univ. de Liège 142. Paris.

Lambert, Maurice

1970 "Les inscriptions des temples d'Ishtarat et de Ninni-zaza." *RA* 64:168–71.

Lambert, Wilfred George

1985 "The Pantheon of Mari." *MARI* 4:525–39.

Lambert-Karlovsky, Carl C.

1978 "The Proto-Elamites on the Iranian Plateau." *Antiquity* 52:114–20.

Leemans, Wilhelmus François

1960 *Foreign Trade in the Old Babylonian Period as Revealed by Texts from Southern Mesopotamia.* Studia et documenta ad iura Orientis antiqui pertinentia 6. Leiden.

van Lerberghe, Karel

1988 "Copper and Bronze in Ebla and in Mesopotamia." Pp. 253–55 in *Wirtschaft und Gesellschaft von Ebla: Akten der Internationalen Tagung, Heidelberg 4.–7. November 1986.* Edited by Harold Hauptmann and Hartmut Waetzoldt. Heidelberg.

Lewy, Julius

1951 "Tabor, Tibar, Atabyros." *Hebrew Union College Annual* 23 (1951–52): 357–86.

Lieberman, Stephen J.

1969 "An Ur III Text from Drēhem Recording 'Booty from the Land of Mardu.'" *JCS* 22:53–62.

van Liere, W. J.

1963 "Capitals and Citadels of Bronze-Iron Age Syria in Their Relationship to Land and Water." *Annales Archéologiques de Syrie* 13:107–22, map, 4 pls.

van Liere, W. J., and J. Lauffray

1955 "Nouvelle prospection archéologique dans la Haute Jezireh syrienne: Compte-rendu provisoire." *Annales Archéologiques de Syrie* 4–5 (1954–55): 120–48, 4 pls., map.

Lloyd, Seton

1938 "Some Ancient Sites in the Sinjar District." *Iraq* 5:123–42.

van Loon, Maurits L.

1967 *The Tabqa Reservoir Survey 1964.* Direction Générale des Antiquités, Musée National. Damascus.

Loretz, Oswald

1969 *Texte aus Chagar Bazar und Tell Brak,* vol. 1. Alter Orient und Altes Testament 3/1. Kevelaer and Neukirchen-Vluyn.

de Maigret, Alessandro

1978 "Fluttuazioni territoriali e caratteristiche tipologiche degli insediamenti nella regione di Matah (Siria): Nota preliminare." *Atti del I° convegno italiano sul Vicino Oriente Antico.* Orientis Antiqui Collectio 13. Rome.

1981 "Il fattore idrologico nell'economia di Ebla." *OA* 20:1–36.

1984 "La paleoecologia di Ebla alla luce dei testi amministrativi." Pp. 329–35 in *Il Bilinguismo a Ebla: Atti del Convegno Internazionale (Napoli, 19–22 aprile 1982).* Edited by Luigi Cagni. Naples.

Mallowan, M. E. L.

1947 "Excavations at Brak and Chagar Bazar." *Iraq* 9:1–259, pls. i–lxxxvi.

1970 "The Development of Cities from al-ᶜUbaid to the End of Uruk 5." *CAH*³ 1/1:327–462.

Margueron, Jean
1982 "Mari: originalité ou dépendance?" *SEb* 5:121–44.

Matthiae, Paolo
1980 "Ittiti ed Assiri a Tell Fray: Lo scavo di una città medio-siriana sull'Eufrate." *Studi Miceni ed Egeo-Anatolici* 22:35–51, pls. i–x.
1981 *Ebla: An Empire Rediscovered.* Translated by Christopher Holme. Garden City, NY.
1983 "Fouilles de Tell Mardikh-Ébla en 1982: nouvelles recherches sur l'architecture palatine d'Ébla." *Compte Rendu Académie des Inscriptions et Belles-Lettres* 1983: 530–54.
1987 "Les dernières découvertes d'Ébla en 1983–1986." *Compte Rendu Académie des Inscriptions et Belles-Lettres* 1987: 135–61.

Mayer, Walter
1986 "Die Tontafelfunde von Tall Munbāqa 1984." *MDOG* 118:126–31.

Mellink, Machteld J.
1985 "Archaeology in Anatolia." *American Journal of Archaeology* 89:547–67, pls. 61–66.
1988 "Archaeology in Anatolia." *American Journal of Archaeology* 92:101–31.
1989 "Archaeology in Anatolia." *American Journal of Archaeology* 93:105–33.

Meskéné-Emar
À l'Occasion d'une Exposition: Meskéné-Emar: Dix ans de travaux, 1972–1982. Textes réunis par Dominique Beyer. Mission archéologique de Meskéné-Emar. Paris 1982.

Michalowski, Piotr
1988 "Thoughts about Ibrium." Pp. 267–77 in *Wirtschaft und Gesellschaft von Ebla: Akten der Internationalen Tagung, Heidelberg 4.–7. November 1986.* Edited by Harold Hauptmann and Hartmut Waetzoldt. Heidelberg.

Milano, Lucio
1987a "OAkk. BAN-*ḫa-tum = tirḫatum* 'bridal price.'" *Or* 56:85–86.
1987b "Barley for Rations and Barley for Sowing (*ARET* II 51 and Related Matters)." *Acta Sumerologica (Japan)* 9:177–201.
1987c "Food Rations at Ebla: A Preliminary Account of the Ration Lists Coming from the Ebla Palace Archive L.2712." *MARI* 5:519–50.
1988 "Studies in Eblaite Prosopography." Pp. 288–90 (§16) in *Eblaite Personal Names and Semitic Name-Giving: Papers of a Symposium Held in Rome, July 15–17, 1985.* Edited by Alfonso Archi. Archivi Reali di Ebla—Studi 1. Rome.

Monchambert, Jean-Yves
1984 "Prospection archéologique sur l'emplacement du futur lac du Moyen Khabour." *Akkadica* 39:1–7.

Moortgat, Anton
1960 *Tell Chuēra in Nordost-Syrien. Vorläufiger Bericht über die zweite Grabungskampagne 1959.* Wiesbaden.
1962 *Tell Chuēra in Nordost-Syrien. Vorläufiger Bericht über die dritte Grabungskampagne 1960.* Cologne and Opladen.

Müller, Hans-Peter
1988 "Zur Bildung der Verbalwurzeln im Eblaitischen." Pp. 279–82 in *Wirtschaft und Gesellschaft von Ebla: Akten der Internationalen Tagung, Heidelberg 4.–7. November 1986.* Edited by Harold Hauptmann and Hartmut Waetzoldt. Heidelberg.

Müller, W. Max
1906 *Egyptological Researches: Results of a Journey in 1904*, vol. 1. Washington, DC.

Musil, Alois
1927 *The Middle Euphrates: A Topographical Itinerary.* New York.
1928 *The Manners and Customs of the Rwala Bedouins.* New York.

Nikolskij, M. V.
1908 *Dokumenty xozjajstvennoj otčetnosti drevenejšej èpoxi Xaldei iz sobranija N. P. Lixačeva*, vol. 1 [Documents of economic accounting from the most ancient epoch of Chaldea in the collection of N. P. Lixačev]. St. Petersburg.

1915 *Dokumenty xozjajstvennoj otčetnosti drevnej Xaldei iz sobranija N. P. Lixačeva*, vol. 2 [Documents of economic accounting from ancient Chaldea in the collection of N. P. Lixačev]. Moscow.

Nougayrol, Jean

1968 "Textes suméro-accadiens des archives et bibliothèques privées d'Ugarit." Pp. 1–446 in *Ugaritica* 5. Paris.

Oates, David

1977 "Excavations at Tel Brak, 1976." *Iraq* 39:233–44.

1982 "Excavations at Tell Brak, 1978–81." *Iraq* 44:187–204, pls. vii–xv.

1983 "Tell Brak: The Most Recent Discoveries." *Annales Archéologiques de Syrie* 33/1:83–92.

1985 "Excavations at Tell Brak, 1983–84." *Iraq* 47:159–73.

Owen, David I., and R. Veenker

1987 "MeGum, the First Ur III Ensi of Ebla." Pp. 263–91 (pls. i–ii) in *Ebla 1975–1985: Dieci Anni di Studi Linguistici e Filologici; Atti del Convegno Internazionale (Napoli, 9–11 ottobre 1985)*. Edited by Luigi Cagni. Naples.

Palmieri, Alba

1981 "Excavations at Arslantepe, Malatya." *Anatolian Studies* 31:101–19, pls. xiii–xvi.

Pardee, Dennis

1988 *Les textes paramythologiques de la XXIVe campagne*. Ras Shamara-Ougarit 4. Paris.

Parpola, Simo

1988 "Proto-Assyrian." Pp. 293–98 in *Wirtschaft und Gesellschaft von Ebla: Akten der Internationalen Tagung, Heidelberg 4.–7. November 1986*. Edited by Harold Hauptmann and Hartmut Waetzoldt. Heidelberg.

Parrot, André

1953 "Les fouilles de Mari: Huitième campagne (automne 1952)." *Syria* 30:196–221, pls. xxi–xxvi.

1967 *Les temples d'Ishtarat et de Ninni-Zaza*, with G. Dossin and L. Laroche. Mission archéologique de Mari 3. Paris.

1974 *Mari, la capitale fabuleuse*. Paris.

Parrot, Andre, and Jean Nougayrol

1948 "Un document de fondation hurrite." *RA* 42:1–20.

Pettinato, Giovanni

1975 "Testi cuneiformi del 3. millennio in paleo-cananeo rinvenuti nella campagna 1974 à Tell Mardikh = Ebla." *Or* 44:361–74.

1977a "Relations entre les royaumes d'Ebla et de Mari au troisième millénaire, d'après les Archives Royales de Tell Mardikh–Ebla." *Akkadica* 2:20–28.

1977b "Gli archivi reali di Tell Mardikh-Ebla." *Rivista Biblica Italiana* 25:225–43.

1977c "Il Calendario di Ebla al Tempo del Re Ibbi-Sipis sulla base di TM.75.g.427." *AfO* 25 (1974/1977): 1–36.

1978 "L'Atlante Geografico del Vicino Oriente Antico attestato ad Ebla e ad Abū Ṣalābīkh (I)." *Or* 47:50–73, pls. vii–xii.

1979a *Ebla: Un impero inciso nell'argilla*. Milan.

1979b "Culto ufficiale ad Ebla durante il regno di Ibbi-Sipiš." *OA* 18:83–215, pls. i–xii.

1979c "Il commercio internazionale di Ebla: economia statatale e privata." Pp. 171–233 in *State and Temple Economy in the Ancient Near East*, vol. 1. Edited by Edward Lipiński. Louvain.

1979d "Le collezioni é n - é - n u - r u di Ebla." *OA* 18:328–51, pls. xxxvi–xlii.

1980 "Bolletino militare della campagna di Ebla contra la città di Mari." *OA* 19:231–45, pls. xiv–xv.

1981 "Gasur nella documentazione epigrafica di Ebla." Pp. 297–304 in *Studies on the Civilization and Culture of Nuzi and the Hurrians: In Honor of Ernest R. Lacheman*. Edited by M. A. Morrison and D. I. Owen. Winona Lake, IN.

1983 "Le città fenicie e Byblos in particolare nella documentazione epigrafica di Ebla." Pp. 107–18 in *Atti del I Congresso Internazionale di Studi Fenici e Punici*, vol. 1. Rome.

1986 *Ebla: nuovi orizzonti di storia.* Milan.

1987 "Dieci anni di studi epigrafici su Ebla." Pp. 1–35 in *Ebla 1975–1985: Dieci Anni di Studi Linguistici e Filologici; Atti del Convegno Internazionale (Napoli, 9–11 ottobre 1985).* Edited by Luigi Cagni. Naples.

1988 "Nascita, matrimonio, malattia e morte ad Ebla." Pp. 299–316 in *Wirtschaft und Gesellschaft von Ebla: Akten der Internationalen Tagung, Heidelberg 4.–7. November 1986.* Edited by Harold Hauptmann and Hartmut Waetzoldt. Heidelberg.

Pettinato, Giovanni, and Paolo Matthiae

1976 "Aspetti amministrativi e topografici di Ebla nel III millennio Av. Cr." *Rivista degli Studi Orientali* 50:1–30.

Pfälzner, Peter

1988 "Tell Bdēri 1985: Bericht über die erste Kampagne." With Cornelia Becker, Heike Dohmann, and Sabina Kulemann. *Damaszener Mitteilungen* 3:223–386, pls. 49–60.

Pinnock, Frances

1985 "About the Trade of Early Syrian Ebla." *MARI* 4:85–92.

1988 "Observations on the Trade of Lapis Lazuli in the III[d] Millennium B.C." Pp. 107–11 in *Wirtschaft und Gesellschaft von Ebla: Akten der Internationalen Tagung, Heidelberg 4.–7. November 1986.* Edited by Harold Hauptmann and Hartmut Waetzoldt. Heidelberg.

Pomponio, Francesco

1980 "AO 7754 ed il sistema ponderale di Ebla." *OA* 19:171–86.

1987 "La datazione interna dei testi economico-amministrativi di Ebla." Pp. 249–62 in *Ebla 1975–1985: Dieci Anni di Studi Linguistici e Filologici; Atti del Convegno Internazionale (Napoli, 9–11 ottobre 1985).* Edited by Luigi Cagni. Naples.

1988 "Gli ugula nell'amministrazione di Ebla." Pp. 317–23 in *Wirtschaft und Gesellschaft von Ebla: Akten der Internationalen Tagung, Heidelberg 4.–7. November 1986.* Edited by Harold Hauptmann and Hartmut Waetzoldt. Heidelberg.

Porada, Edith

1965 "The Relative Chronology of Mesopotamia, Part I." Pp. 133–200 in *Chronologies in Old World Archaeology.* Edited by Robert W. Ehrich. Chicago.

Reiner, Erica

1956 " 'Lipšur' Litanies." *JNES* 15:129–49.

Roux, Georges

1980 *Ancient Iraq.* 2d ed. Harmondsworth.

Rowton, Michael B.

1952 "The Date of the Hittite Capture of Babylon." *BASOR* 126:20–24.

Saporetti, Claudio

1981 "Una considerazione sul testo N. 6527 del catalogo di Ebla." Pp. 287–89 in *La Lingua di Ebla: Atti del Convegno Internazionale (Napoli, 21–23 aprile 1980).* Edited by Luigi Cagni. Naples.

Sauren, Herbert

1966 *Topographie der Provinz Umma nach den Urkunden der Zeit der III. Dynastie von Ur*, 1: *Kanäle und Bewasserungsanlesen.* Dissertation Heidelberg.

Scandone Matthiae, Gabriella

1979 "Vasi iscritti di Chefren e Pepi I nel Palazzo Reale G di Ebla." *SEb* 1/3–4:33–43, 3 pls.

1981 "I vasi egiziani di pietra dal Palazzo Reale G." *SEb* 4:99–127.

1988 "Les relations entre Ébla et l'Egypte au III[éme] et au IIème millénaire avant J.-C." Pp. 67–73 (pls. xi–xv) in *Wirtschaft und Gesellschaft von Ebla: Akten der Internationalen Tagung, Heidelberg 4.–7. November 1986.* Edited by Harold Hauptmann and Hartmut Waetzoldt. Heidelberg.

Schneider, Nikolaus

1930 *Das Drehem- und Djoḫaarchiv*, 6: *Die Geschäftsurkunden aus Drehem und Djoḫa in den Staatlichen Museen (VAT) zu Berlin*. Reprinted from *Orientalia* 47–49 (1930). Rome.

1931 *Die Drehem- und Djoḫa-Urkunden der Strassburger Universitäts- und Landesbibliothek in Autographie und mit systematischen Wörterverzeichnissen*. Analecta Orientalia 1. Rome.

Sigrist, R. Marcel

1982 "Miscellanea." *JCS* 34:242–52.

Simons, Joseph

1937 *Handbook for the Study of Egyptian Topographical Lists Relating to Western Asia*. Leiden.

von Soden, Wolfram

1981 "Das Nordsemitische in Babylonien und in Syrien." Pp. 355–61 in *La Lingua di Ebla: Atti del Convegno Internazionale (Napoli, 21–23 aprile 1980)*. Edited by Luigi Cagni. Naples.

1987 "*Itab/pal* und *Damu*: Götter in den Kulten und in den theophoren Namen nach den Ebla-Texten." Pp. 75–90 in *Ebla 1975–1985: Dieci Anni di Studi Linguistici e Filologici; Atti del Convegno Internazionale (Napoli, 9–11 ottobre 1985)*. Edited by Luigi Cagni. Naples.

1988 "Ebla, die früheste Schriftkultur Syriens." Pp. 325–32 in *Wirtschaft und Gesellschaft von Ebla: Akten der Internationalen Tagung, Heidelberg 4.–7. November 1986*. Edited by Harold Hauptmann and Hartmut Waetzoldt. Heidelberg.

Sollberger, Edmond

1965 "Three Ur-Dynasty Documents." *JCS* 19:26–30.

1980 "The So-Called Treaty between Ebla and 'Ashur.'" *SEb* 3/9–10:129–55.

Sollberger, Edmond, and Jean-Robert Kupper

1971 *Inscriptions royales sumériennes et akkadiennes*. Littératures Anciennes du Proche-Orient, 3. Paris.

Speiser, Ephraim A.

1941 *Introduction to Hurrian*. AASOR 20 (1940–41). New Haven.

Steiner, Gerd

1986 "Der Grenzevertrag zwischen Lagaš und Umma." *Acta Sumerologica (Japan)* 6: 219–300.

Steinkeller, Piotr

1984 "Old Akkadian Miscellanea." *RA* 78:83–88.

1986 "Seal of Išma-Lim, son of the Governor of Matar." *Vicino Oriente* 6:27–40.

1987 "Battering Rams and Siege Engins at Ebla." *NABU* 1987/27.

Strommenger, Eva

1960 "Das Menschenbild in der altmesopotamischen Rundplastik von Mesilim bis Hammurapi." *Baghdader Mitteilungen* 1:1–103, charts 1–19, maps 1–2.

1979 "Ausgrabungen der Deutschen Orient-Gesellschaft in Ḥabuba Kabira." *AASOR* 44: 63–78.

1980 *Habuba Kabira: Eine Stadt vor 5,000 Jahren*. Mainz.

Stucky, Rolf A.

1973 "Ausgrabungen auf Tell el Hajj 1971 und 1972." *Antike Kunst* 16:83–86, pl. 15.

Tefnin, Roland

1978 "L'or et le sel: Note sur l'ecologie d'une région de l'ancienne Syrie." *Annales Archéologiques de Syrie* 27–28 (1977–78): 198–206.

1980 "Deux campagnes de fouilles au Tell Abou Danné, 1975–1976." Pp. 179–99 in *Le Moyen Euphrate: Zone de contact et d'échange; Actes du Colloque de Strasbourg, 10–12 mars 1977*. Leiden.

Thureau-Dangin, François
1907 *Die sumerischen und akkadischen Königsinschriften.* Vorderasiatische Bibliothek 1/1. Leipzig.
Veenhof, Klaas R.
1972 *Aspects of Old Assyrian Trade and its Terminology.* Leiden.
Voûte, Pauline H. E.
1972 "Chronique des fouilles et prospections en Syrie de 1965 à 1970." *Anatolica* 4 (1971–72): 83–133, map.
Waetzoldt, Hartmut
1984 " 'Diplomaten', Boten, Kaufleute und Verwandtes in Ebla." Pp. 405–37 in *Il Bilinguismo a Ebla: Atti del Convegno Internazionale (Napoli, 19–22 aprile 1982).* Edited by Luigi Cagni. Naples.
1987 "Frauen (dam) in Ebla." Pp. 364–77 in *Ebla 1975–1985: Dieci Anni di Studi Linguistici e Filologici; Atti del Convegno Internazionale (Napoli, 9–11 ottobre 1985).* Edited by Luigi Cagni. Naples.
Wäfler, Markus
1980 "Der Becher MBQ 23/35–62 (= 71 MBQ 59)." *MDOG* 112:9–11.
Watson, Patty Jo
1965 "The Chronology of North Syria and North Mesopotamia from 10,000 B.C. to 2,000 B.C." Pp. 61–100 in *Chronologies in Old World Archaeology.* Edited by Robert W. Ehrich. Chicago.
Weidner, Ernest F.
1936 "Aus den Tagen eines assyrischen Schattenkönigs." *AfO* 10 (1935–36): 1–48.
1959 *Die Inschriften Tukulti-Ninurtas I. und seiner Nachfolger*, with Heinrich Otten. AfO Beiheft 12. Graz.
Weiss, Harvey
1983 "Excavations at Tell Leilan and the Origins of North Mesopotamian Cities in the Third Millennium B.C." *Paléorient* 9/2:39–52.
Weiss, Harvey, and T. Cuyler Young Jr.
1975 "The Merchants of Susa: Godin V and Plateau-Lowland Relations in the Late Fourth Millennium B.C." *Iran* 13:2–17, pls. i–v.
Wirth, Eugen
1971 *Syrien: Eine geographische Landeskunde.* Wissenschaftliche Länderkunden 4/5. Darmstadt.
Wiseman, Donald John
1953 "Texts and Fragments." *JCS* 7:108–9.
1956 *Chronicles of the Chaldaean Kings (626–556) in the British Museum.* London.
Woolley, Leonard
1952 *Carchemish: Report on the Excavations at Djerabis on Behalf of the British Museum*, 3: *The Excavations in the Inner Town*, by Sir Leonard Woolley; and *The Hittite Inscriptions*, by R. D. Barnett. London.
1953 *A Forgotten Kingdom: Being a Record of the Results Obtained from the Excavation of Two Mounds, Atchana and Al Mina, in the Turkish Hatay.* Harmondsworth/Baltimore.
Zaccagnini, Carlo
1984 "The Terminology of Weight Measures for Wool at Ebla." Pp. 189–204 in *Studies on the Language of Ebla.* Edited by Pelio Fronzaroli. Quaderni di Semitistica 13. Florence.

Ebla and the Amorites

GIORGIO BUCCELLATI

The Terms of the Problem

The Ebla *querelle*, if one may so term the sharply divergent opinions which have come to be voiced about the nature of the language and culture of third-millennium Ebla, is happily on the wane. Happily, because little scholarly benefit came from it; and on the wane, because the difficult task of philological documentation is absorbing the better part of the effort being currently expended in this area. While it is not my intent to review here any of the aspects of this affair, I will refer to it at certain junctures, from the following perspective: the internal dynamics of the *querelle* as a form of scholarly discourse has, in my view, led to a certain crystallization of substantive and methodological presuppositions, which have been at times accepted too soon and too uncritically. The resulting scholarly perception has to be taken into consideration as a sort of mindset which conditions the direction taken by the research, through the assumptions it posits (often tacitly) upstream of any interpretation. In other words, while the *querelle* may well have subsided, the factors which led to its coming into being are still operative and should be addressed on their scholarly merits.

Two important objective factors[1] are (1) the very early date of Ebla archives (Pre-Sargonic or early Sargonic) and (2) the fact that their findspot is found so far to the west of any other third-millennium cuneiform corpus. An important concomitant factor should also be stressed, namely (3) the material consistency and homogeneity of the archives. Such homogeneity heightens, on the one hand, the significance of its early date: this is not a scattered group of texts, without a clear

Author's note: The text of this article follows that of a paper delivered at the Center for Ebla Research at New York University, at the invitation of Prof. Cyrus H. Gordon on February 25, 1990. I retain the discursive nature of the presentation, and adduce only a minimum of documentary and bibliographical references; a fuller presentation of my argument and of the relevant data will be undertaken as a part of my research on Khana mentioned below, n. 6. I am grateful to Prof. Gordon and to Prof. Baruch Levine for their hospitality in New York, and to Prof. Gordon in particular for his further hospitality on the pages of his series *Eblaitica*.

[1] I will not take up here the issue of the connections that have been suggested between the Ebla texts and the Bible. For some considerations which have a bearing on the argumentation given below and which pertain to the patriarchal tradition see Buccellati 1990a.

archeological context, but rather one of the largest and best preserved cuneiform archives ever, excavated within a well-stratified and culturally impressive setting. Thus it is that in Ebla we have, as the fountainhead of Semitic documentary evidence, a fully developed scribal practice—or, to put it differently, what we find *at* the beginning is by no means *the* beginning, but rather a full-blown and sophisticated tradition. The homogeneity of the archives also heightens, on the other hand, the significance of their western provenience: the lopsided position of Ebla *vis-à-vis* the rest of the Mesopotamian epigraphic evidence looms even larger when one considers that the great Sumerian centers of the south, far as they are geographically from Ebla, are also just about as distant from it in terms of the wealth and cohesiveness of their epigraphic yield. In other words, there is no epigraphic continuum, in either the constitution of the archives or the geographical distribution of the finds, between the south and Ebla—Mari itself being in effect isolated, and with an even greater distance intervening between Mari and Ebla than between Mari and the southern centers.

To recapitulate, the Ebla archives are a typological unicum whose very uniqueness lends an almost dramatic dimension to their equally impressive early date and their very isolated geographical position. Interestingly, these factors were as operative before the discovery of the archives in downplaying the significance of Ebla as they were going to be afterward in raising scholarly and public temperatures to a feverish level. For it should not be forgotten that archeological Ebla, as a rich urban culture, had been "discovered" considerably before the archives were—and yet scholarly attention could hardly be said to have focused sharply on its extremely important architecture and statuary until the tablets came along. "What good could possibly come from a third-millennium place in western Syria?" seems to have been the underlying, unspoken consensus. Now, if there was any justification to such an attitude it was the lack of a documentary continuum between Ebla and the Mesopotamian south: under such conditions it did strain the imagination to assume an Ebla where we know Ebla to be today. Of course, such a continuum is in effect, except for Mari,[2] still lacking today.

One important exception that one would have expected before the epigraphic discoveries at Ebla pertained to linguistic categories. Amorite, generally regarded as a West Semitic dialect, was found in the latter part of the third millennium in the southern cities—and yet, being a *West* Semitic dialect, would naturally be expected to originate in the western regions, that is, precisely in that part of Syria where Ebla was. Such was the logical expectation expressed,

[2] More third-millennium epigraphic data from Mari have been found in the meantime. Also, a whole new epigraphic region seems to be opening up in the Khabur plains with the recent discoveries of new third-millennium tablets at Tell Brak and Tell Mozan: these finds, too, will cause a new appreciation of important third-millennium sites long since known archeologically, like Tell Brak itself and Tell Chuera.

for instance, in the first preliminary report of the excavations (ten years before the discovery of the texts), where it was hypothesized that the ethnic affiliation of the inhabitants of Ebla may have been Amorite.[3] In point of fact, the Mesopotamian evidence alone seemed even then to contradict this assumption, and it was on that basis that at about the same time I expressed my doubts about considering as Amorite the language of the western cities, including Ebla.[4] Yet, a general perceptual atlas of the third millennium would clearly have retained the notion of Amorite as the overall language of the west and would have split Syro-Mesopotamia in two halves, more or less along the lines of modern boundaries, calling the western half, with Ebla as one of its centers, Amorite, and the eastern half Akkadian. It was therefore surprising, from such a perspective, when it soon became apparent that the divergent picture I had in mind in 1967 was in fact correct, since hardly any evidence of Amorite presence was found at Ebla—be it in the form of individuals qualified as MAR.TU, or in the form of onomastic items.[5]

It is in the light of such considerations that the terms of the problem addressed in the title of this article acquire their significance: Why is it that the earliest known strand of western Semitic (Amorite) left no trace in the first major archives excavated in the west? It is just this issue that I intend to take up here, with a view toward clarifying both terms of the problem, that is, Ebla *and* the Amorites. One important result will be a new understanding of the early history of Semitic languages in general. I now take up these three points in sequence, beginning with a revised reconstruction of the history of the Amorites,[6] showing then how this affects our interpretation of the history of Ebla, and bringing out in the end the pertinent conclusions for Semitic linguistics.

[3] Liverani 1965: 122–23: "La popolazione doveva essere, a nostro avviso, amorrea: Amorrei i sedentari agricoltori asserragliati entro le mura, Amorrei i pastori nomadi che premevano fuori di esse."

[4] This was my conclusion published shortly after the initial publication of the first preliminary report, Buccellati 1966, where I wrote (p. 247) that "this reconstruction [i.e., an Amorite linguistic affiliation for Ebla], which undoubtedly deserves serious consideration, seems on this point to be at variance with the Mesopotamian evidence . . . , especially with the fact that in the Sumerian texts the Amorites are never connected with Western cities in contrast to the other people of the West who usually are."

[5] For a good review of the evidence see Archi 1985.

[6] I give here a concise summary of a long-term research that I have been carrying out on the kingdom of Khana, as a follow-up of my earlier interest in the Amorites (Buccellati 1966 and 1967) and in conjunction with my archeological work at Terqa. In this study I utilize not only the archeological and linguistic, but also the geographical evidence, in an attempt to understand the latter in terms of the perceptual categories of the ancients. A number of articles have appeared or are in press for my Khana series (1988, 1990a, 1990b, 1990c, 1990d, and forthcoming). I plan to eventually integrate these articles into a full-length monograph, where I will also take up the issues discussed in this article, and provide a complete documentation, including detailed photographic illustrations of the pertinent geographical phenomena. For now, one will find in the articles cited above the preliminary documentation on which the conclusions summarized here are based.

A Revised History of the Amorites

Perhaps because the cuneiform documentation of Mari, as well as Terqa, is so squarely within the limits of the Mesopotamian scribal tradition, we tend to view the region of which these two cities were successively the capitals as practically identical in their geopolitical and sociopolitical structure with the rest of Mesopotamia. In fact, however, there are strong differences which lend to the Middle Euphrates and Lower Khabur region a very unique geomorphological physiognomy. What will be relevant in the present context are some observations on the way in which the peculiar character of the territory affected the sociopolitical structure of the people living within it, and in particular the interaction between the urban and the rural populations.

While both regions (i.e., the Mesopotamian south on the one hand and the Middle Euphrates/Lower Khabur on the other) are "arid" in that they lie below the 250 mm isohyet, there is a subtle but fundamental difference in the relief, which causes a sharp differentiation between the two zones. The south is entirely alluvial, that is, it is entirely irrigable, while the Middle Euphrates and Lower Khabur basin is irrigable only along a very narrow strip, called in Arabic the *zôr*, and in Akkadian the *aḫ Purattim*.[7] No amount of hydrological work could have raised the river water above the escarpment which, with varying degrees of steepness, bound the valley trough on either side. It is interesting to remark in this connection that the location of Mari corresponds to the southern end of this trough: just below Mari, at a point neatly in line with the modern border between Syria and Iraq, the trough becomes so constricted as to provide practically no land base at all for any real agriculture. Thus Mari, instead of being central, is located at the effective southern border of the agricultural strip and at the mouth of the few canals which were possible in the valley trough. (Similarly, in this respect, Terqa was located near the mouth of the Khabur, and Tuttul/Tell Bia^c near the mouth of the Balikh.)

Another difference in the relief, minor as it may seem at first in terms of absolute elevation, sets the Khabur plains apart from the Lower Khabur basin. The minor ranges of the Jebel Abd el-Aziz and the Jebel Sinjar constitute in fact a powerful environmental boundary, in that they correspond to the 250 mm isohyet, and thus they mark the southern border of the dry-farming area. It is perceptually very impressive for someone traveling from the alluvial strip of the *zôr* to the rolling plains of the northern Khabur plains to see wheat grow on *rolling* plains, that is, uphill from any water body; it just seems miraculous!

An important implication of this environmental situation pertains to our understanding of animal husbandry. The close interaction between farming and animal husbandry is rooted in the different but related utilization of the same environment. In the Middle Euphrates/Lower Khabur basin the narrowness of the agricultural strip placed severe limits on the development of both economic

[7] As I have suggested in Buccellati 1990b.

activities and led to the exploitation of the immense "backyard," as it were, of the valley floor: the steppe.

I interpret the evidence of the Mari texts as showing a special phenomenon of land reclamation, whereby the peasants of the *aḫ Purattim* were induced, by the very narrowness of the irrigated area available and the consequent rapid saturation of the agrarian rural landscape, to discover the potential of the steppe by tapping its water table through the systematic development of a network of wells. This allowed them to utilize fully the abundant ground cover of the steppe for their herds—a phenomenon which corresponds in terms of cultural history to the development of irrigation in the river basins. Just as irrigation led to the development of a rural class which remained through time under the direct control of the urban elite, so the development of the wells led to the establishment of a rural class which came to be more and more autonomous of urban controls, since city-based administration and military power never effectively extended (or even tried to extend) to the steppe. Instead of "sedentarization of the nomads" we should speak, I believe, of "nomadization of the peasants."[8]

In their early stages, possibly down to the Ur III period (the end of the third millennium), these peasant-herders or agro-pastoralists remained essentially agrarian in character, that is, based in the *aḫ Purattim*, and used the steppe only as an extension of their narrow farming strip (the *aḫ Purattim*), so that as a result the state never found it necessary to establish firm controls on this pasture land so ephemeral in use. The Mari texts still represent this by showing how all confrontations of the state with the peasant-herders or agro-pastoralists took place in the agrarian *aḫ Purattim* and never in the pastoral steppe. And yet, given the abundant possibility of long-term survival in the steppe, these agro-pastoralists developed into a formidably autonomous rural class, such as neither the irrigated south nor the rainfed north and northwest had ever known. In other words, their effective potential of turning into full "pastoralists" gave them a degree of political power which resulted eventually in the establishment of the so-called Amorite dynasties.

The term MAR.TU or *Amurru* 'Amorites' refers, in the view just outlined, to this rural class of nomadizing peasant-herders, a class that is developing an

[8] In some respects, this perspective builds on the extensive research undertaken by Rowton (I will quote here only one of the more recent among his many articles on the subject, Rowton 1978), which emphasizes the closeness between settled and nomadic elements of the population, and which has been further developed by others. See for instance how the problem is phrased by Liverani 1970: 10–11: the difference between nomads and settled populations is not so much ethnic or linguistic, as rather one between lifeways of different groups of the same populations; what linguistic differences there may be, will derive more from the difference in lifestyle rather than in origin. On the other hand, the nomads are still viewed precisely as such, i.e., as nomads whose sedentarization is not so much a migratory as a social phenomenon (Liverani 1970: 11). My interpretation adds an even narrower dimension to the nature of the interaction between herding and farming (which are viewed as concomitant functions carried out by the same group of people rather than as specialized professions carried out by two distinct groups) and to an understanding of the origin of (organized) nomadism as a relatively late phenomenon. The difference in interpretation is more clearly in evidence in a more-recent statement by Liverani 1988: 299.

ethnic identity as a result of the particular circumstances which define the strength and limits of the group solidarity felt by its members. The sociopolitical, or "tribal," groups that emerge in the process (such as Khaneans or Suteans) are smaller than the broader group subsumed under the terms for Amorites. The latter, then, remains a term that describes the lifestyle of these individuals as much as it refers to their broad ethnic identity.[9] Why is it, then, that by the Old Babylonian period it becomes an archaic term, when the class of people to which it refers is more in evidence than ever? In my opinion, it was replaced by two terms, which are normally understood as tribal names: *banū Yamina* and *banū Samʾal*. These convey, I submit, the same semantic range that the term *Amurru* had in earlier times, except that they split it in two: the "sons of the right river bank" and the "sons of the left river bank" correspond to what in Arabic is known today as the *shamia* and the *jezira*, respectively, that is, the steppe to the south and west of the Euphrates in its middle course, and the steppe to the north and east, contained by a "meso-potamian (i.e., inter-riverine) island" (which is the literal meaning of *jezira*) between the Euphrates and the Tigris.[10] These two worlds, quite similar in many respects but still perceived today as quite different, and separated by what in ancient times would have been a formidable gap, the Euphrates, are the proper habitat of these incipient nomads: the more the steppe, or "steppes," become their proper environment, the more closely identified they become with it. Thus the "sons of the steppe lying off the left or right river bank" are terminologically (as well as, in my understanding, genetically) very closely related to the "sons of the irrigation district" (*mārū ugārim*), as Old Babylonian Akkadian says of the settled farmers.

If one plots on a map (fig. 1) not only the 250 mm isohyet, but also the line between arid/irrigable plain and arid/nonirrigable plateau (the steppe), one will notice an interesting distributional pattern in the relationship between major urban centers and the size of their rural hinterland. The region controlled by Mari and then Terqa is proportionately much larger than that controlled by other single urban centers with political autonomy. Alternatively, one may say that the density of urban political centers (i.e., of cities which served as capitals of independent kingdoms) is much higher in either the irrigated alluvium to the south or the dry-farming plains to the north, whereas the entire region in between has effectively only *one* political center, Mari first and then Terqa.

The kingdom of Khana appears then to be coterminous with a whole and very distinctive geopolitical region, one which is characterized on the one hand by a special relationship to water resources and land exploitation, and on the other hand by a distributional pattern of urban centers which differs from the rest of the Syro-

[9] This is somewhat similar to a specific connotation that the term *ʿArab* has today, where in the language of settled (Arab) people it refers to the nomadic (Arab) people, i.e., to the Bedouin.

[10] My (preliminary) arguments for this hypothesis are to be found in Buccellati 1990b. Note how, in this perspective, the renderings *banū*, *mārū*, or, for that matter, the shortened *marmū* for *mārū Yamina* are all equivalent and therefore perfectly interchangeable.

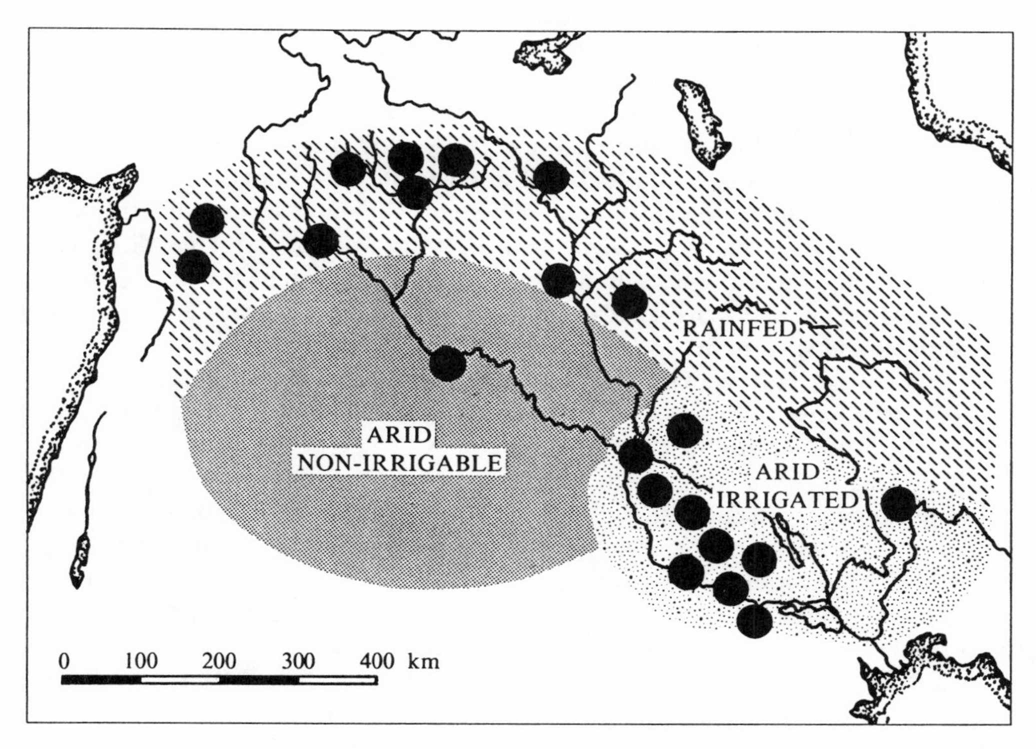

FIGURE 1. *Schematic Climatological Map of Syro-Mesopotamia (black dots are major urban centers).*

Mesopotamian world. Significantly, this geopolitical region is almost entirely included within the modern political boundaries of the Syrian Arab Republic.

At first, the vastness of the territory may appear to be illusory, precisely on account of the limited presence of urban centers within its boundaries. But, we should not think of the steppe either as an empty quarter or as a territory belonging to nomadic tribes rather than to the kingdom based in the *aḫ Purattim*. While incapable of sustaining urban life as such, the steppe was an integral resource of the kingdom and one that made it possible for it to develop an economic base otherwise unmatched by the farming resources of the *aḫ Purattim*. From the Mari texts we know that Khana territorial control over the steppe (in Mari's times at least) extended all the way to the west, since Mari was directly in contact with Qatna over matters pertaining to herds and their grazing rights. Neither Tadmor/Palmyra nor any other oasis had achieved anything even remotely approaching an urban status in the second millennium: the steppe was effectively a vast rangeland, exploited by peasant-herders more or less dependent on the central state power in the *aḫ Purattim*. In this respect, Mari and Terqa seem to have controlled the entire environmental niche represented by the steppe, and to have aptly subsumed it under the geopolitical term Khana.

Rather than viewing Mari as an outpost, however important, of Mesopotamian civilization, and Terqa as the minor provincial center of a petty local kingdom, we may, in the light of the foregoing discussion, obtain a better perception of the uniqueness of the region of Khana and its kingdom. Distinctive for the geographical zone it occupies and with which it is almost entirely coterminous; distinctive for the mode of adaptation to the environmental situation, from which possibly pastoral nomadism began to evolve from an early agro-pastoralist stage; distinctive for the peculiar pattern of interaction between urban and rural populations—the region and kingdom of Khana stands as a major autonomous component within the geopolitical and sociopolitical makeup of the ancient Near East.

Thus, rather than viewing the Amorites as nomads or seminomads who are threatening Khana from the outside, we should understand them as the unique outgrowth, from within, of the rural class of Khana. The Ur III texts from the south give us a glimpse into the formative period of this process, when the Amorites appear both as scattered individual immigrants settled in the Sumerian cities and as a threatening military force at the kingdom's northern boundary.[11] The early second-millennium texts from Mari, on the other hand, as well as the contemporary onomastics from all of Syro-Mesopotamia, open a larger window onto the climactic stages of this process: the rural classes of the *aḫ Purattim* have achieved a sociopolitical autonomy of their own, in fact they have established an ethnic and tribal identity which they carry much beyond the boundaries of their initial habitat and in numbers much greater than in the late third millennium at the time of the kingdom of Ur III.

Significance for the History of Ebla

Considering the difference in date between the period of Ebla (mid-third millennium) and the events described above (end of the third and early part of the second millennium), what is the import of the argumentation adduced above with regard to our assessment of the history and language of Ebla? The answer has both historical and linguistic dimensions.

At first, one may be tempted to answer the question about the lack of an Amorite presence at Ebla in chronological terms: the Amorites are not mentioned because *there were no Amorites* at the time of the archives. But we know better. On the one hand, Amorites are mentioned in the south as far back as the Fara period and a few, at least, do appear in the Ebla archives as well. On the other hand, there is an important reference from the south that refers back to about 2200 B.C., the year-name of Šar-kali-šarri which records a victory achieved by that king "over the Amorites in the mountain of *Ba-sa-ar*."[12] What is particularly

[11] That the Ur III MAR.TU are few is not an accident in the recovery of the evidence, since the individuals of Amorite origin are still qualified as such, precisely through the use the apposition MAR.TU appended after their name. Such a qualification is no longer used in the later periods because the sheer number of Amorite individuals robs the qualification of its original distinctiveness.

[12] For the references see Buccellati 1966: 236, 327.

remarkable about this event is that the conflict took place *in* the hilly region known today as Jebel Bishri,[13] at some distance from the *aḫ Purattim* which is, one should remember, the only place where conflicts between the Mari government and its own rural class (the so-called "nomads") were to take place in later periods. In other words, in the time of the Mari archives direct royal control (including military deployment) did not extend much further than the first line of wells about twenty to thirty km on either side of the valley trough.[14] However, some four hundred years earlier a king from the south claims to have gone some one hundred km into the steppe, where no Mari king ever took his troops. Whether this was because of the superior tactical and strategic capability of the Akkadian king *vis-à-vis* the Mari kings, or (more likely) because of the as yet lesser degree of strength and cohesiveness achieved by the agro-pastoralist of the *aḫ Purattim*, who simply withdrew to their inland wells in front of their attacker, who in turn successfully pursued them there—the net result is that we have here a strong indication of the sense of identity which the Amorites projected even then, enough to be registered in the southern perception as something worthy of designating a year-name.

If the Amorites have such a standing some two centuries after the period of the Ebla archives, and since they are after all mentioned, however scantily, in the same archives, the question of their relative absence at Ebla cannot be explained on the basis of their simply not having as yet come into existence. So the problem reproposes itself—with a likely solution emerging from the historical reconstruction I have proposed above for the origin and nature of the Amorites. To pursue this solution I wish to contrast different patterns of interaction between the urban centers and their rural hinterland in early Syro-Mesopotamia, which are strongly conditioned by the different environmental conditions described above, and which are represented schematically in figure 2.

In pattern A, documented in the arid and irrigated southern regions of Syro-Mesopotamia, the territories occupied by the urban and rural populations are practically coterminous: this means that urban, and therefore state, controls extend to every aspect of rural life, so that there is no possibility left for the rural classes to develop any meaningful distinctiveness, economic, political or otherwise. An argument *ex silentio* is that we hardly ever hear in texts from the south about any type of political initiative on the part of the local rural classes, nor do we have ethnic terms that seem applicable to them. More positively, we

[13] The Jebel Bishri is not a mountain in the sense of either absolute elevation or difficulty of access—as the Taurus is to the north. It is a relatively low and mildly sloped range, dotted with wells and lined with wadis. It does, however, like the Jebel Hamrin on the Tigris, impress somebody coming from the alluvial south as the first major rise to incise the skyline even on the distant horizon.

[14] This buffer zone along the river banks was called in Mari *baṣʾatum* in the singular and *baṣaʾātum* in the plural; see Buccellati 1990b: 95. It is conceivable that the defensive line established by the kings of the Ur III kingdom against the Amorites, called *Murīq-Tidnim*, was in effect a similar buffer zone of wells and defensive stations, cutting transversely across the Euphrates basin rather than alongside it, like the *baṣaʾātum* in Mari.

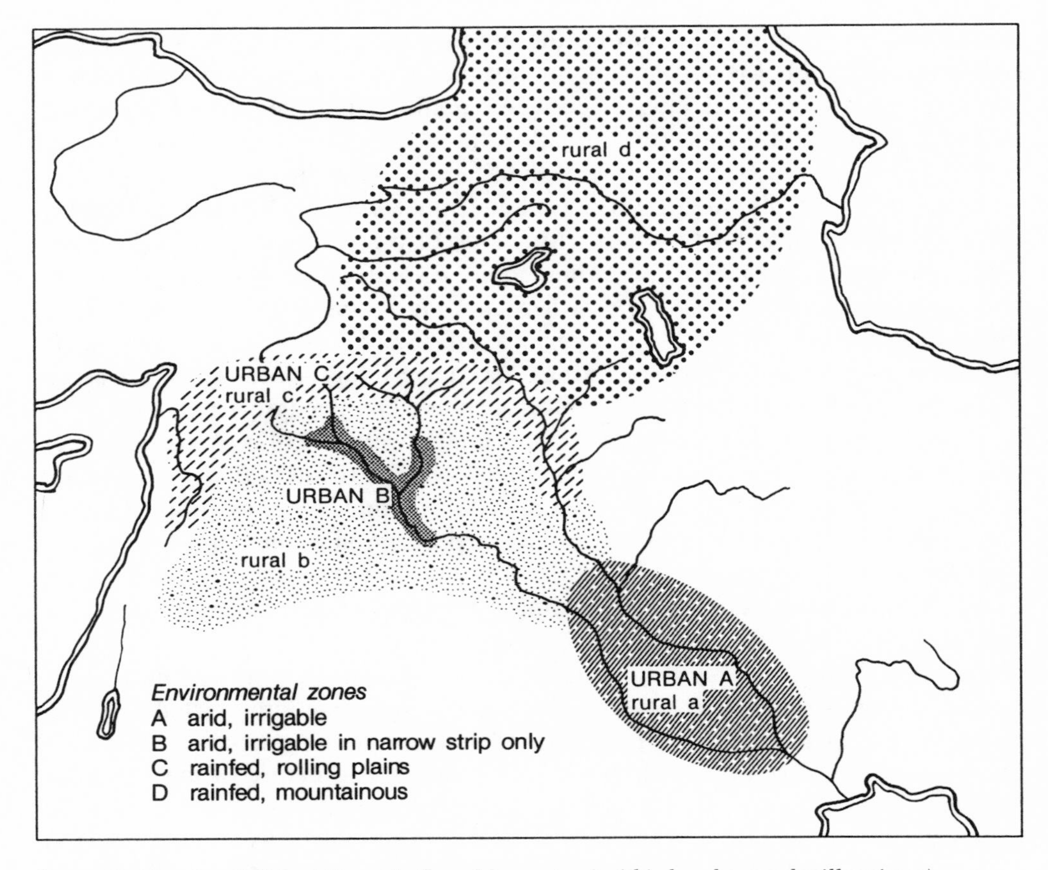

FIGURE 2. *Rural and Urban Zones in Syro-Mesopotamia (third and second millenniums).*

know that the state exercised a very close control not only on agriculture but also on herding.

Pattern B is found in the arid and minimally irrigable area of the Middle Euphrates and the steppe: this situation defines Khana in a uniquely distinctive way, since it does not apply to any other region. Here I view the rural population as appropriating the steppe resources for its herding needs. Technically, this appropriation results in an expansion of territorial control on the part of the state: since the rural population is subject to state control, the territory it exploits is in turn of direct pertinence to the state. There is however one major difference *vis-à-vis* other situations: the rangeland in the steppe is so vast and its human occupation so fluid that actual military and administrative presence on the part of the state is practically ruled out. What is more, it appears to be unnecessary as well—at least as long as the herdsmen responsible for its exploitation are firmly rooted among the rural classes at home in the alluvial strip, the *aḫ Purattim*. This means in fact that their presence in the steppe is by definition ephemeral, and that they remain, in principle, under the direct and immediate control of the state on all occasions when they return to the *aḫ Purattim*. The change intervenes when they realize that they in fact are not in any immediate and direct *need* to return to the *aḫ Purattim*, if they choose otherwise: partly, the resources of the steppe may be exploited longer than on a seasonal basis, partly their contacts with the states on the other side of the steppe gives them autonomous contacts with foreign, independent states—such as no other rural population can enjoy. This process, which I consider to be one of partial and selective nomadization, may well be the locus where pastoral nomadism on a systematic scale had its origin,[15] but it provides in any case an insight into a wholly unique dimension that characterizes the region of Khana. The urban-rural pattern of interaction was so completely different from that of the other regions that its rural class left an indelible mark in the historical development of the Near East, in marked contrast with the rural classes of the southern alluvium or the northern rainfed plains. This entire region was firmly under the control of Mari (and of Terqa after the destruction of Mari) in the early second millennium. In the third millennium the situation was probably analogous, as may be assumed from the extraordinary significance of Mari in the texts of the royal archives of Ebla: Emar (by the big bend of the Euphrates) and Tuttul (at the mouth of the Balikh) may have controlled a portion of the steppe, but at most as far as the ranges of Palmyra and the Jebel Bishri, below which the control of Mari presumably extended already as far as the Orontes basin—making Mari a kingdom directly bordering Ebla.

Pattern C is found in the area of rainfed, undulating plains and low hills from the Orontes basin to the Khabur plains, bounded by the Jebel Ansariya and the Taurus. It is the least well known at present, and is proposed here somewhat hypothetically (with the expectation that the study of the texts of Ebla might provide substantive clarification, corroborated hopefully by any new texts which might come from the numerous and major excavations currently taking place in the Khabur plains).[16] I assume on the one hand a large rural population under the direct and close control of the state, somewhat as in zone A. But I am also assuming that this rural population had close links with the mountain-based, nonurban population of the Taurus, perhaps all the way up to the Caucasus (shown as zone D in fig. 2). They served as the suppliers of metals, stones, and timber to the great urban centers of the south—Ebla and the cities in the Khabur plains serving as the gateway for the rest of the ancient Near East. While Ebla and the cities in the Khabur plains belong to the same zone, it is interesting to note what seems to be a real lack of references in Ebla to the great urban centers of the upper Khabur (such as Chuera, Mozan, Leilan and possibly even Brak).[17]

[15] On this see Buccellati 1990b: 98–102.

[16] Besides Tell Brak, Tell Mozan has also begun to yield third-millennium tablets: they have been published in Milano 1991.

[17] This is hypothesized on the basis of the geographical horizon which can be reconstructed for geographical names mentioned in Ebla. Brak has a special position, being the southernmost of the great third-millennium cities in the Khabur plains, controlling the road that leads to the Sinjar

The northern cities were, to judge from the archeological evidence, on the same level of sophistication and urban development as Ebla, but were not, it seems, part of the commercial network utilized by Ebla. It is possible that both Ebla and the Khabur cities had independent access to the raw materials in the Anatolian plateau, and that they were, in this respect, competitors for the same supply centers in the north and the same markets to the south.

In the light of the above remarks about the different patterns of rural/urban interaction we may now better understand the relative absence of the Amorites at Ebla. If the Amorites were the rural class of the *aḫ Purattim* that were in the process of reclaiming the steppe on a systematic basis, the kingdom administration of Ebla would have had no reason to deal with them directly, since its Mari contacts were maintained through diplomatic channels directly with the urban center of the *aḫ Purattim* kingdom. There is no more reason for the Amorites to be prominently mentioned in the Ebla archives than there would be for a mention of Terqa—which we know existed at that time as an urban center of a certain size and with massive defensive walls, but which was undoubtedly no more than an important provincial city under the political control of the capital, Mari. The contacts between Ebla and Mari would presumably have been carried out along the Ephrates route, that is, the route which was secure because under the direct military, logistic, and administrative control of Mari, possibly already all the way from the mouth of Balikh to the mouth of the Khabur and further south. The situation might be similar to that of the king of Qatna who, in the Old Babylonian period, writes to the king of Mari about matters pertaining to Mari herdsmen interacting, all the way across the vast expanse of the steppe, with Qatna herdsmen.[18] As the crow flies, Qatna and Mari are somewhat closer than Ebla and Mari, but in terms of a direct and secure road along the Euphrates, Ebla is in fact much closer.

In line with the reconstruction proposed above, we may say that Ebla had a direct control over both agriculture *and* herding[19] in its territory, and left no room for the development of autonomous tendencies in its rural population. To the extent that the Amorites are a rural population with an independent base for economic growth and a concomitantly growing sense of socioethnic independence, there are no Amorites in Ebla. The Amorites in the steppe are just beyond the boundaries of Ebla's territory,[20] and thus much closer to Ebla, in terms of

passes. If Archi's assumption (1984: 233, 240) is right, that Kakmium, east of the Tigris, was important as a station "along the commercial road which led to the Iranian plateau," then it is possible that such a road would have gone north of Mari along the Khabur, and then across the lower limit of the northern plains, presumably controlled by Brak. Whether or not this portion of the route remained within the territory controlled by Mari, and thus skirted Brak and its territory, we do not know, but the first alternative seems more likely, since the Ebla horizon as we know it at present does not seem to include cities in the Khabur plains in general.

[18] See Buccellati 1990a: 240–41.

[19] See Archi 1980 and Milano 1984.

[20] The Mari hinterland reaches all the way to a point where the steppe meets the dry-farming region controlled by Ebla, somewhere between the Palmyrenean ranges and the river basins.

physical proximity, than their urban counterparts in Mari. But these same Amorites were actually very distant from Ebla in terms of diplomatic contacts, which were carried out at the level of palace-to-palace interaction. The Amorites were physically around the corner, but perceptually it was as if they did not exist, except for the few occasions when some chiefs of the incipient tribal groups (qualified as "kings" in the Ebla texts) appeared on a stray visit in the capital. It was, we may presume, in the interest of the Ebla kings to keep the independent herdsmen of the steppe away from their own rural classes, lest these too should develop an unwelcome sense of independence from the central Ebla government. It was just as much in the interest of the Mari kings to keep their subjects away for as long as they could from any foreign capital, lest they should add a dimension of political prestige to their already growing socioeconomic independence.

Significance for Semitic Linguistics

I have summarized the overall thrust of my theory in a series of schematic charts and maps (figs. 3–6). These should be taken as no more than a graphic index to the argumentation, without any claim at precision in the quantification of the details: within the purview of the present study I have not yet undertaken a full tabulation of the data, which requires a considerable amount of research because of uncertainties in the analysis of third-millennium data and because of the bulk of the evidence in the case of the second-millennium data. Such tabulations will derive from further studies which my students and myself are currently devoting to the topic.[21] For the time being, these maps will serve a dual purpose. On the one hand they will help visualize a certain range of perceptions with regard to the data, with a degree of quantification which should for now simply be taken to reflect the order of magnitude that is applicable. The second purpose is to emphasize the direction which, I submit, study of the data should take: rather than assuming a dichotomy between east and west in the early period, we should envisage a greater Syro-Mesopotamian unity with finer internal differentations.

One way to emphasize this point is by considering the following unconventional hypothesis. If exactly the same texts as those found in the royal archives of Ebla had been excavated in the Zab rather than the Orontes basin, less would have been made of the West Semitic, let alone biblical, connections. In other words, the geographical and archeological circumstances of the finds have, in my view, weighed more heavily on a linguistic interpretation of the data than the more

[21] The following doctoral dissertations are underway at UCLA: James H. Platt on Ebla graphemics (his work deals extensively with onomastics, particularly with regard to variant spellings of the same name); Joseph M. Pagan on Ebla Semitic onomastics; Mark A. Arrington on name-giving (Ebla, Old Akkadian, and Amorite); and Terrence Szink on Ebla non-onomastic Semitic. On these studies see my article "The Ebla Electronic Corpus: Onomastic Analysis" (below). I plan a fresh study on Amorite onomastics within the purview of my research on Khana, which will include an analysis of the new data not only from the third millennium (Ebla to Ur III), but also from Mari, Šubat-Enlil, and Terqa.

properly linguistic reality reflected in the texts. In order to better understand the point I am trying to make it will be useful to visualize what I consider to be a diffused scholarly perception of the Semitic linguistic areas in the third millennium.

A modern perceptual map of such Semitic areas in the third millennium (fig. 3) would assume a basic twofold division between east and west. In this perspective, the boundary runs somewhere along the modern boundary between Syria and Iraq. The western area includes the steppe and/or the desert (generally, the difference between the two is not clearly articulated, particularly not in terms of ancient perceptions and modes of land utilization), and in some less-defined way the urban areas in the rainfed or irrigated zones. Mari is the major ancient point of reference on this great divide between east and west: it is considered an outpost of Mesopotamian civilization on the one hand, and on the other a major window onto the West Semitic west. When the texts of Ebla were first discovered it seemed natural that one should seek to fit them into this picture. They were found in the west (geographical considerations), and they represented a cultural unicum in terms of their archival setting (archeological considerations). Hence, two tenacious—and pugnacious—scholarly perceptions. First, Eblaite was immediately viewed as a separate language (it was found far in the west and it was embodied in an incredibly rich epigraphic documentation). Second, and consequent to the first point, the identification of its linguistic relationship to other languages became a major research priority—with an initial irresistible tendency to emphasize the links with (later) West Semitic languages, much at the expense of the (more readily apparent) links with Akkadian. The general scholarly perception as I represent it in figure 3 is heavily influenced by an undue projection into the past of two situations obtaining at a later point in time.[22]

The first of these later situations is the genuine linguistic distinction between East and West Semitic that obtained in the late second and then in the first millennium.[23] There is then a clear distinction between Standard and Neo-Babylonian or Neo-Assyrian attested primarily in the east (though the imperial expansion exports these dialects to the west), on the one hand, and on the other Hebrew, Phoenician, and Aramaic, attested primarily in the west (though Aramaic spreads throughout the east and becomes the lingua franca throughout the Near East). This distinction, which is both linguistic and geographical (West Semitic spoken primarily in the west and East Semitic spoken primarily in the

[22] For a similar caution against projecting back in time the later distinction between Aramaic and Canaanite (both of which derived in fact from Amorite), see Liverani 1970: 19; and 1973: 107–8.

[23] In point of fact, the difference between East and West Semitic even in the later periods must also be viewed in a more-nuanced way than is usually the case. Akkadian in the first millennium was progressively becoming a cultural relic from the live linguistic organism that it had once been (something which, of course, has nothing to do with the size of the scribal documentation, that in fact increased during that period of time). In this respect, rather than speaking of East and West Semitic, we should speak of surviving third/second-millennium Semitic and new first-millennium Semitic. But such a topic is clearly beyond the scope of the present inquiry.

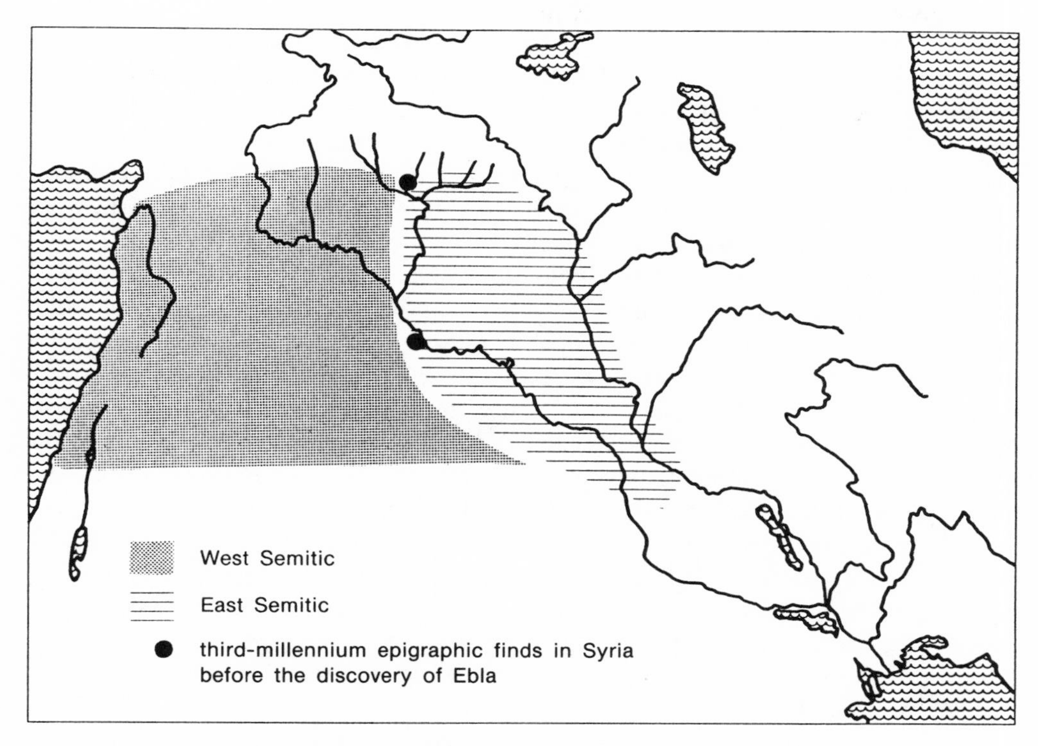

FIGURE 3. *Perceptual Map of East and West Semitic.*

east) is telescoped back to the third and early second millennium: Amorite is West Semitic spoken in the west and Akkadian is East Semitic spoken in the east.

The second situation telescoped back in time is the ethnolinguistic distinctiveness of sizable human groups living in the steppe and then in the desert from the late second millennium on. Appropriately, in this respect, the first kingdom which develops *in* the steppe proper was called *Amurru*. I have tried to show elsewhere how this kingdom developed not from an earlier political presence in the steppe, but rather as a complete political innovation resulting from the deurbanization of the Middle Euphrates and Lower Khabur in the second half of the second millennium.[24] And so, while the kingdom of Amurru of the Amarna age does in no way provide evidence for the existence of an earlier Amorite entity in the west, it has come instead to be perceived in just such a light: the faint remnant of an assumed strong, earlier West Semitic presence situated in the west. This perception was putatively confirmed by the continued presence in later periods of human groups in the steppe (and desert), from the Akhlamu and Arameans all the way down to the early Arabs.

What is the alternative that I wish to propose for the map we have been discussing? There are three basic elements to my answer. (1) We should not be unduly conditioned by the geographical or archeological setting of the corpus in

[24] Buccellati 1990a: 240–46.

assessing its linguistic affiliation: just because it is in the west, and separated by a considerable documentary gap from the south, the language of Ebla need not be automatically considered west Semitic. (2) The strong links with Akkadian ought to be assessed on the basis of a structural comparison, rather than in an ad hoc fashion.[25] (3) The acknowledged links with later West Semitic should be understood within the framework of the historical links with the Amorites, as brought out in the reconstruction presented here.

Amorite, being tied linguistically to the nomadizing rural classes of the *aḫ Purattim* and the steppe, was more conservative than its urban counterparts, and thus remained more archaic in its typological features. Of these urban counterparts, the earliest is Eblaite. Being the earliest in time, it is also more closely related to the typologically archaic Amorite—not because they are West Semitic, but because they are both archaic. The geographical dimension is pertinent in the following measure: at home in the rural enclaves of the *aḫ Purattim* but especially in the steppe, Amorite had its own distinctive area where it was presumably shielded from its urban counterparts. Yet Amorite-speaking individuals were perfectly at home in the settled urban and farming areas, where their language was perceived, presumably, more as a kindred socio-lect than as a foreign dialect. Both Amorite and its urban counterparts belong, in this sense, to a broader linguistic unity, which I wish to call here, for ease of reference, early North Semitic.[26] Its development through five successive stages is represented schematically in figure 4.

(1) The earliest stage can only be reconstructed on the basis of comparative criteria between Amorite and its urban counterparts. Amorite being the more archaic of the two, it would have retained closer links with "proto–North Semitic."[27] (2) At the beginning of our documentation, about the mid-third millennium, early North Semitic is especially attested in its urban embodiment—Eblaite and Pre-Sargonic Akkadian;[28] urban Semitic in this second stage

[25] As is more and more the case, following especially the seminal studies of Gelb 1980 and 1981. A particularly significant contribution is Pennacchietti 1981.

[26] It could also be called early Syro-Mesopotamian Semitic, taking Syro-Mesopotamia in the precise sense which I have defined in Buccellati 1990a: 229–31. Either term may appear to contradict the caveats I have discussed earlier about a geographical conditioning in our perception of linguistic reality. But this is not so. I have argued against an uncritical equation between the geographical provenience of the documentation with the geographical area where a language is spoken. In fact, as I will argue below, Amorite was *not* initially spoken at all in the West (i.e., the Syro-Palestinian west), and thus it is precisely on geographical grounds that it should not be called a western language.

[27] This point, which needs more research, is in contrast, for instance, with the position of Garbini 1981: 77, who considers Eblaite as the oldest Semitic language (or Semitic *tout court*) and Amorite as the innovative language.

[28] The difference between Pre-Sargonic and Sargonic Akkadian on the one hand, and the closer kinship between Pre-Sargonic Akkadian and Eblaite on the other, has been forcefully and convincingly argued by Gelb 1981; see also Westenholz 1988. For the archaic nature of Eblaite see also, e.g., Conti 1984 and Fronzaroli 1984. An intriguing, if highly tentative, hypothesis may be ventured as a footnote to Westenholz's comments on the religious conception evidenced, in his view by Pre-Sargonic onomastics. If the Pre-Sargonic pantheon was structurally restricted in scope and gave maximum prominence to a double (masculine/feminine) hypostasis of the divine,

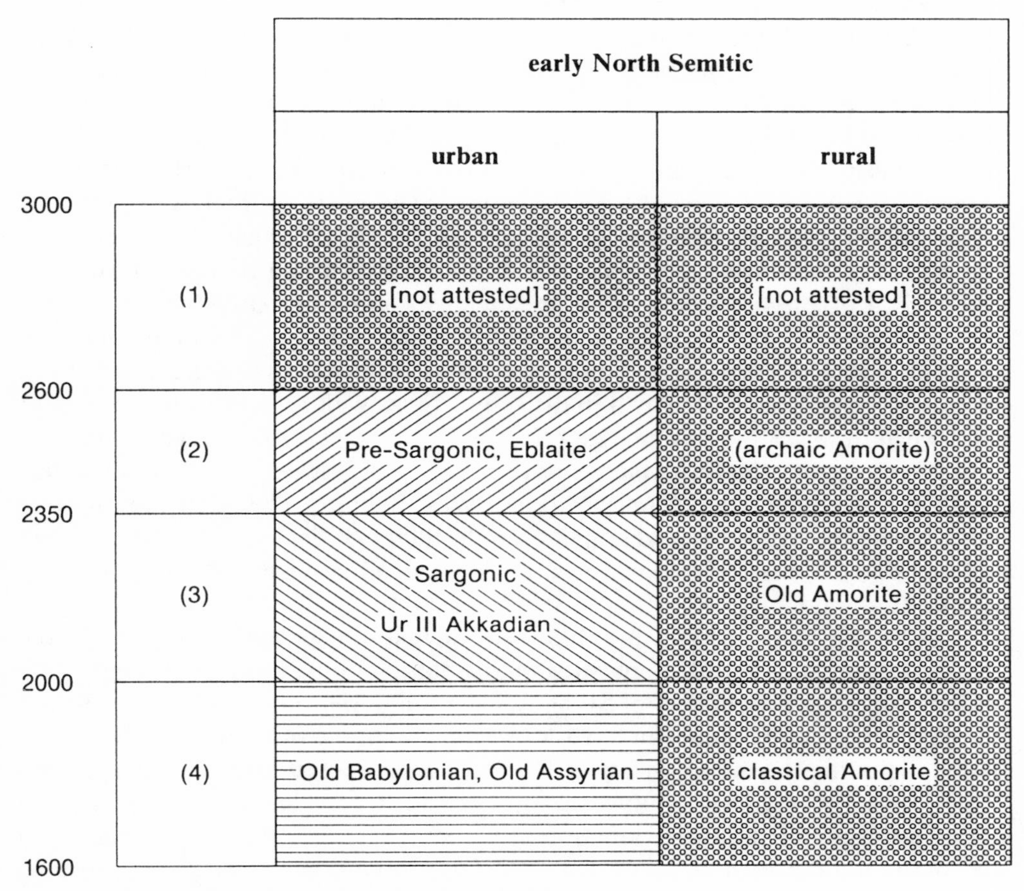

FIGURE 4. *Developmental Stages of Early North Semitic.*

corresponds to what Gelb has so eloquently described as the language of the Kish civilization.[29] We know from a few references that Amorite existed, and we can assume that its structure was close to what we know about it from later evidence, or if anything only more archaic. (3) During the Sargonic period, urban

a hypostasis later abandoned as being too lofty and distant from the needs of the people; if Amorite society was more conservative in its religious tradition as it was in its language, and thus more apt to retain early beliefs which it originally shared with its counterpart urban society; and if the patriarchal tradition of the Bible reflects certain survivals of early Amorite traditions—could there be some degree of continuity from the earliest (Pre-Sargonic) to the later Semitic conception of the divine? Aware as I am of the speculative and fragile nature of these wide-ranging connections, and aware as I am in particular of current views about a late date for both the patriarchal tradition and the development of Israelite monotheism, I still do not consider this hypothesis as totally fanciful, and for all the expressed caveats I do not advance it lightly. But any possible merit of such a line of reasoning can only be gauged from a much-fuller and more-nuanced argumentation than would ever be possible here.

[29] See especially Gelb 1981.

North Semitic undergoes a major development, largely affected, no doubt, by the expansionist policy of the kings of Akkad, which rested on strongly centralized administrative policies. (4) Somewhere between the collapse of the Akkadian "empire," the Guti invasion, the temporary pan-Mesopotamian resurgence of the Ur III dynasty, and the political climax of the Amorites in the early part of the second millennium, profound transformations take place in the development of urban Semitic, which emerges essentially as Old Babylonian.[30] Evidence for Amorite is at its fullest for this same period: unlike its urban counterpart, this rural survival of early North Semitic presumably had hardly any stimulus toward change, and thus had retained a strongly archaic and conservative linguistic structure. (5) The even-greater transformations of the second millennium bring about a more-profound upheaval in the linguistic as well as sociopolitical map of southwestern Asia[31]—and marks effectively the end of the development of North Semitic. For the first time we have a true split between East Semitic (Middle Babylonian and Middle Assyrian) and West Semitic. The latter is in part an heir to Amorite, whose speakers had brought their political weight to bear more and more on the western regions, as a result of the effective deurbanization of the Middle Euphrates.

By way of conclusion, I provide two schematic maps which summarize the data pertaining to Semitic onomastic documentation in the third and early second millennium. The first map (fig. 5) shows the relative proportion of Amorite vs. non-Amorite Semitic names in Syro-Mesopotamia in the third millennium, down to and including the third dynasty of Ur (the reader is again reminded that the pie charts are only intended to give an approximation of relative proportions, and not an accurate quantitative valuation of percentages). For the documentation in the south only those names are given that either are qualified as MAR.TU or can be analyzed linguistically as Amorite. Also shown are the major findspots of epigraphic finds in the north during the same period. The only sizable Amorite presence is found in the Sumerian texts of the Ur III dynasty, particularly those from Puzriš-Dagan. The most-noticeable gap in the documentation pertains to Mari, from where we have relatively few texts, and of a type which is not as apt to yield onomastic information as the letters and administrative texts of the Old Babylonian period. Since the Ur III texts suggest a provenience for the Amorites from precisely the region of Mari, and since the situation found in the Old Babylonian period does not seem to presuppose a major break in historical development, it seems logical to presuppose that third-millennium Mari may have already exhibited a situation similar to that of the early second millennium—to presuppose, in other words, the presence of a local rural population with an Amorite linguistic affiliation. Be that as it may, we have otherwise positive evidence for the fact that Amorite is barely to be found elsewhere, and clearly not

[30] The typological links between Eblaite and Old Assyrian, for which see especially Parpola 1988, fit nicely into this picture, in the measure in which peripheral areas (in this case the Orontes and the Zab basins) tend to remain linked typologically (in their retention of archaic traits) in spite of their geographical distance.

[31] I have dealt with these and the following issues in Buccellati 1990a.

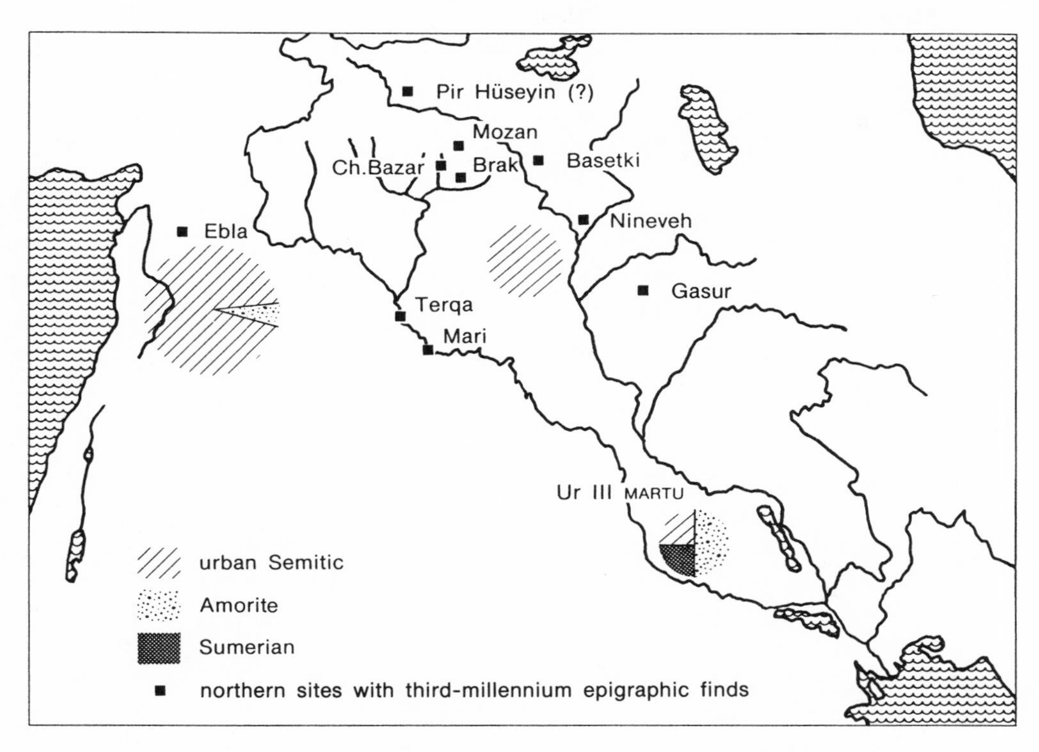

FIGURE 5. *Distribution of Semitic PNs in the Third Millennium (plus Sumerian names for individuals qualified as* MAR.TU*).*
Note: Graphic rendering of relative proportions is only indicative of order of magnitude and does not reflect actual percentages.

in the western region of Ebla. Also pertinent in this respect is the well-known fact that western toponomastics, indicative of the earliest linguistic presence in the area, is not Semitic.[32]

The situation in the Old Babylonian period (fig. 6) is so completely altered that this is often referred to as the *Amorite* period. There is a clear prevalence of Amorite names in Mari, the Khabur, and the west, and a strong presence, if not a majority, in the south. There are also indications that Amorite influence wanes, in onomastics, during the course of the Old Babylonian period. The important point is that an overlay of the maps shows a situation of change: the Amorite presence in the west was not there in the mid-third millennium, and came into being only between the end of the third and the beginning of the second millennium. This ties in well with the notion proposed above about a spread of the agro-pastoralists of the *aḫ Purattim* from the Middle Euphrates to the neighboring regions, as a result of the process of nomadization and crystallization of ethnic consciousness.

[32] See especially Gelb 1961 and Archi 1984: 228.

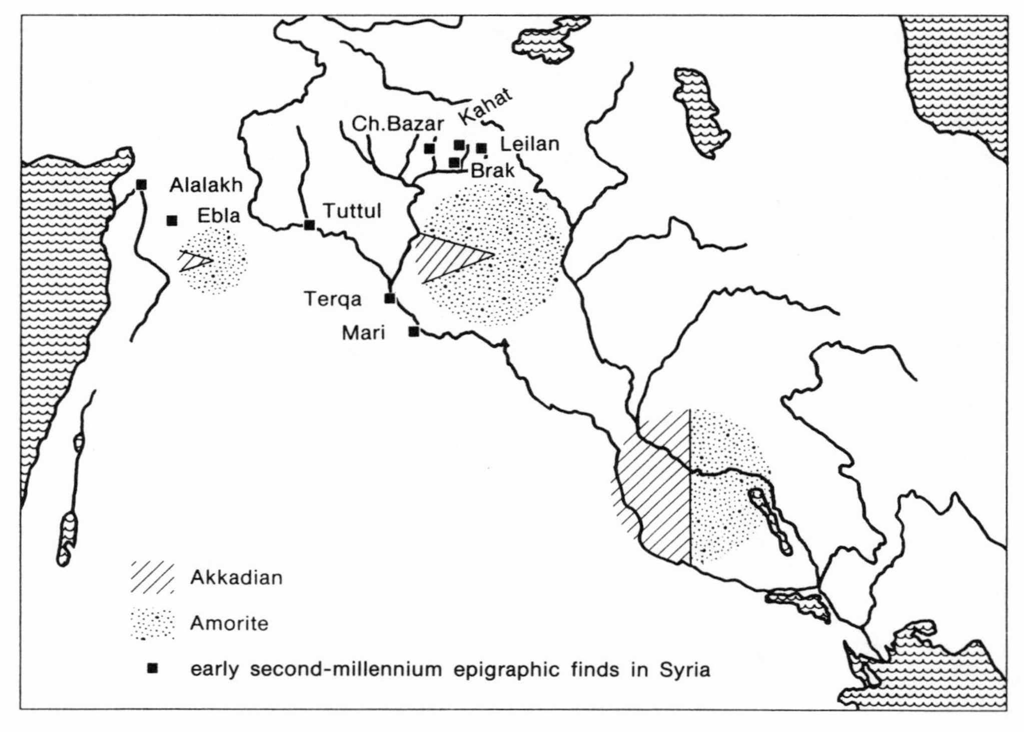

FIGURE 6. *Distribution of Semitic PNs in the Early Second Millennium.*
Note: Graphic rendering of relative proportions is only indicative of order of magnitude and does not reflect actual percentages.

While predictably controversial in its central thrust, in need of further elaboration on several points of detail, and clearly open to revisions with regard to the nature of the argumentation and the specifics of the documentation—the broad reconstruction I have proposed here will hopefully serve as a catalyst in promoting a fresh perspective on the historical and linguistic setting of both Ebla and the Amorites, and thereby of ancient Syro-Mesopotamia as a whole. Venturing as scholars in the wondrous maze of the Ebla archives, we may sympathize with those first few Amorites who were physically venturing in the maze of this sophisticated ancient city. We come from beyond the borders not only of space and time, but also of established mindsets and perceptual world views. I hope that we may be as successful in bringing to bear our scholarly analysis on the Ebla evidence as the ancient Amorites were in eventually clamping their indelible sociopolitical imprint on it!

References

Archi, A.

1980 "Allevamento e distribuzione del bestiame ad Ebla." *Annali di Ebla* 1:1–33. Reprinted in *SEb* 7 (1984) 45–81.

1984 "The Personal Names in the Individual Cities." Pp. 225–51 in *SLE.*

1985 "Mardu in the Ebla Texts." *Or* 54:7–13.

Buccellati, G.

1966 *The Amorites of the Ur III Period.* Ricerche 1. Naples.

1967 "Archaeological Survey of the Palmyrene and the Jebel Bishri." *Archaeology* 20:305–6 (with Marilyn Kelly-Buccellati).

1988 "The Kingdom and Period of Khana." *BASOR* 270:43–61.

1990a "From Khana to Laqē: The End of Syro-Mesopotamia." Pp. 229–53 in *De la Babylonie à la Syrie, en passant par Mari* (J. R. Kupper Festschrift). Edited by Ö Tunca. Leiden.

1990b "'River Bank,' 'High Country' and 'Pasture Land': The Growth of Nomadism on the Middle Euphrates and the Khabur." Pp. 87–117 in *Tell al-Hamidiyah 2.* Edited by S. Eichler, M. Wäfler, and D. Warburton. Göttingen.

1990c "The Rural Landscape of the Ancient Zôr: The Terqa Evidence." In *Les techniques et les pratiques hydro-agricoles traditionelles en domaine irrigué.* Bibliothèque Archéologique et Historique. Edited by B. Geyer. Damascus.

1990d "Salt at the Dawn of History: The Case of the Bevelled Rim Bowls." In *Resurrecting the Past: A Joint Tribute to Adnan Bounni.* Edited by M. Van Loon et al. Leiden.

forthcoming "A Note on the *Muškēnum* as a Homesteader." In *MAARAV* 7–8 (Stanley Gevirtz Festschrift). Edited by B. Zuckerman et al.

Conti, Giovanni

1984 "Archaismi in eblaita." Pp. 159–72 in *SLE.*

Fronzaroli, P.

1984 "The Eblaic Lexicon: Problems and Appraisal." Pp. 117–57 in *SLE.*

Garbini, G.

1981 "Considerations on the Language of Ebla." Pp. 75–82 in *Lingua.*

Gelb, Ignace J.

1961 "The Early History of the West Semitic Peoples." *JCS* 15:27–47.

1980 *Thoughts about Ibla: A Preliminary Evaluation, March 1977.* Syro-Mesopotamian Studies 1/1. Malibu.

1981 "Ebla and the Kish Civilization." Pp. 9–73 in *Lingua.*

Liverani, M.

1965 "I tell pre-classici." Pp. 107–33 in *Missione archeologica italiana in Siria: Rapporto preliminare della campagna 1964.* Edited by P. Matthiae et al. Rome.

1970 "Per una considerazione storica del problema amorreo." *OA* 9:5–27.

1973 "The Amorites." Pp. 100–133 in *Peoples of Old Testament Times.* Edited by D. J. Wiseman. Oxford.

1988 *Antico Oriente: Storia, società, economia.* Bari.

Milano, L.

1984 "Distribuzione di bestiame minuto ad Ebla: criteri contabili e implicazioni economiche." Pp. 205–24 in *SLE.*

1991 *Mozan 2. The Epigraphic Finds of the Sixth Season.* Syro-Mesopotamian Studies 5/1. With contributions by G. Buccellati, M. Kelly-Buccellati, M. Liverani, Malibu.

Parpola, Simo

1988 "Proto-Assyrian." Pp. 293–98 in *WGE.*

Pennacchietti, Fabrizio A.
1981 "Indicazioni preliminari sul sistema preposizionale dell'eblaita." Pp. 291–319 in *Lingua.*

Rowton, M. B.
1978 "Pastoralism and the Periphery in Evolutionary Perspective." Pp. 291–301 in *L'Archéologie de l'Iraq.* Colloques Internationales du C.N.R.S. 580. Paris.

Westenholz, A.
1988 "Personal Names from Ebla and in Pre-Sargonic Babylonia." ARES 1:99–117.

The Ebla Electronic Corpus: Onomastic Analysis

GIORGIO BUCCELLATI

1. The Ebla Electronic Corpus

This article is in the nature of an interim report on a project of onomastic analysis of the Ebla personal names, which is in turn part of a larger project called *Cybernetica Mesopotamica*.[1] The purpose of this paper is to outline the conceptual and technical aspects of the onomastic data base;[2] while a fuller assessment of the system will be possible only upon its publication in a complete version, this interim report will focus on the methodological presuppositions. This seems warranted by the fact that a considerable number of names has already been analyzed[3] and that the linguistic coding of the same has been thoroughly tested. It is especially the linguistic and data-processing aspects of the project that I intend to illustrate in this article, using by way of reference some of the preliminary results derived from our analysis of the data elaborated so far.[4]

Author's note: This paper is the second in a series of "Studies in Ebla Onomastics," of which the first (the text of a paper presented in Rome in May 1980) is due to appear in *Studi Eblaiti*. The present text is a revised version of the paper presented at the Center for Ebla Research at New York in February 1990. I am grateful to Prof. Cyrus H. Gordon for his kindness in inviting me to participate in the series of lectures sponsored by his center, and for his interest in seeing this article through to publication.

[1] For the most-recent presentation of the project *Cybernetica Mesopotamica* as a whole see Buccellati 1990a.

[2] For a parallel presentation of the graphemic aspects of the *Ebla Electronic Corpus* project, see Buccellati 1990b.

[3] The analysis and data entry of the Ebla texts and names has been undertaken by my students J. H. Platt, J. M. Pagan, and, in part, M. A. Arrington, who are currently completing their dissertations on Ebla graphemics, onomastics, and name-giving, respectively, and who have been preparing the electronic publication of the data base with the assistance of Alfonso Archi and Lucio Milano. See for now Platt 1988; Platt and Pagan 1990.

[4] I wish to stress that my personal contribution has been in the articulation of the overall system design for both *Cybernetica Mesopotamica* as a whole and the *Ebla Electronic Corpus* in particular; in the definition of the linguistic codes illustrated here, with regard to both their internal coherence as a unified linguistic system and their suitability for electronic data processing; and in the writing of the programs which allow the preliminary manipulation and publication

I will first address some preliminary issues which pertain to general concepts of data processing of cuneiform texts, as I have been applying them within the framework of *Cybernetica Mesopotamica.* The most-apparent dimension of the project is the publication of data in machine-readable format. Simply put, this means that data are distributed on disk,[5] practically at no cost and with all the attendant advantages made possible through the kind of electronic processing that can be applied to them. But three concomitant factors are, in my view, of even greater significance for such an endeavor to be truly successful. The first is the care taken in designing the format the data should take; the second, the substantive shape of the data themselves; and the third, the identification of channels for proper data utilization.

As for the first point, the coding of the data is much more complex than a simple matching of computer characters with diacritical marks or the introduction of ad hoc codes to express grammatical parsing. To achieve a more-effective manipulation of the data, it is important that the coding be construed as a regular grammar, aiming for both substantive comprehensiveness and structural coherence. It is also important that such coding be as transparent as possible and clearly documented, so that users may handle it to their best advantage and so that updates may easily integrate not only new data but also new codes as part of a coherent and well-designed system. This concern for structural coherence is particularly important if one wishes for the electronic analysis of the data to be far-reaching and fully effective.

---

of the data. The substantive research on the data themselves, with all the attendant philological questions that this entails, is, on the other hand, the primary work of Platt, Pagan, and, to a lesser extent, Arrington; my former student J. H. Hayes was also involved in a very active role during the formative stages of the project. Thus the data which are used as exemplification in this article derive from their own work—which hopefully will be ready for publication in the not-too-distant future. It should also be stressed that these data, still preliminary in their present form, ought to be viewed in any case only as a help in illustrating the methods and techniques which are properly the focus of my paper, and not for their substantive import. In point of fact, the system as I have designed it is applicable to all cuneiform corpora and was initially applied to Old Babylonian data. I wish to thank here my four UCLA collaborators for their sustained commitment to the project, for their philological contributions, and for their suggestions in matters of linguistic analysis and interpretation, and to thank Platt in particular for his stewardship in coordinating the logistic aspects and his acumen in identifying all the proper intellectual priorities. Finally, I wish to remember with strong feelings of gratitude and sorrow for his untimely passing, the profound impact that I. J. Gelb had on the initial stages of the project. Both the conceptual design of the research and the articulation of our basic presuppositions owe much to his influence, which sadly could not be continued in time to affect our current operational stage.

[5] The first two groups of texts which have been published in this format are Buccellati, Podany, and Roualt 1987 and Saporetti, Platt, and Pagan 1987. Since our work began at an early date, before the advent of personal computers, some of the early corpora were made available to colleagues on an ad hoc basis either on tape for use on mainframe computers or in the forms of custom prepared printouts. The major corpora which were so prepared were the Old Babylonian letters and the Western Akkadian texts. These data have now been transferred to a format suitable for use with personal computers, and are currently being updated for eventual distribution in a format compatible to the one here described for the *Ebla Electronic Corpus.*

As for the second point, the data that we present in disk format are veritable text editions, with a strong emphasis on the philological dimension. This is apparent in a number of ways. The production of detailed word and sign indexes highlights inconsistencies of transliteration which are either harmonized or corrected, as the case may be; a large number of collations were initiated as part of this process of text editing, and while this has required much time and coordination of efforts with Archi and Milano, it has resulted in a vastly improved documentary base. It also appeared desirable to include in the electronic transliteration system a higher degree of precision in rendering graphic details, whether or not they are of immediate graphemic import—for instance in rendering cuneiform digital notation. While these details render the electronic transliteration more complex than its standard printed counterpart, they may be filtered out at will depending on the degree of precision one wishes in analyzing the data.

As for the third point, the issue is: what kind of utilization can best be made of data published in the electronic medium? Even a minimum of computer literacy indicates that one can easily perform such tasks as word searches, not otherwise possible when data are available only in standard printed format. More complex tasks, on the other hand, require both a certain expertise in data processing and a considerable time expenditure in "massaging" the data, as the lingo puts it, that is, in adapting the continuous text string to the requirements of any given program. It is just such preliminary "massaging" that I intend to perform for the user's benefit. My goal, then, is to accompany the data with a minimum of attendant programs, which will assist users in preparing the data for utilization with other programs of their choice; beyond that, my programs also allow a "turn-key" type of utilization, that is, one that can be implemented without programming expertise by following step-by-step instructions. The first type of program does such manipulation as filtering codes and characters, or formatting the data for utilization with standard word processors and data-base management systems. The second type of program provides indexes, concordances, and simple computations of the type illustrated in part in the printouts given in the tables below. These outputs are fairly rigid in scope, in that parameters are fixed and allow relatively few choices; but they meet the basic needs for which the data base has been designed in the first place, and well demonstrate the real quantum leap that is possible in data analysis through electronic data processing.

One further aspect that distinguishes the *Ebla Electronic Corpus* is that our project is being developed in close concert with the team from the University of Rome that is responsible for the primary publication of the data, and is thus in effect an official publication of the Ebla expedition itself. This guarantees a unique degree of control on the documentary accuracy of the data; it also means that we are able to include names from texts currently being prepared for publication as well as from texts already published. An important consequence of this coordination with the Rome team is that the flow of primary data is on a par with the publication of the texts in the series *Archivi Reali di Ebla: Testi*, making our data base uniquely comprehensive and up-to-date.

Finally, the point should be made that, while the emphasis of the project is on the publication of computer disks, there will also be accompanying volumes (to appear in the series *Cybernetica Mesopotamica: Manuals*) which will serve especially in the initial stages to present in traditional style the data provided on disk and the results which can be derived from the application of the relevant programs. As both aspects (data structure and program application) become more familiar to scholars, one will be able to dispense more and more with the printed version and to rely almost exclusively on disks.

The correlation of the various goals indicated above has entailed a certain delay in the progress of our work. The first objective of the *Ebla Electronic Corpus* is the primary publication of the data. The disks with the electronic version of ARET 1–4 have been ready for a while, except for a number of collations that need to be added. We also need to complete an accompanying volume which will explain in detail the nature of the data on the disks.[6] The volume, ARET 9 (Milano 1990), is accompanied by a disk edition which is distributed simultaneously with the printed volume.

The second objective of the *Ebla Electronic Corpus* is the application of special types of analysis to the data. The two major types underway at present are graphemic and onomastic analysis. It is on the latter aspect that the rest of this article will concentrate.

Work on the *Ebla Electronic Corpus* has been carried out so far with the financial assistance of the Packard Humanities Institute, the Academic Senate of the University of California, Los Angeles, and the Ambassador International Cultural Foundation. Funding is, however, limited, and this has slowed the progress of our project. Fortunately we can count on the very active collaboration not only of graduate students who are working on their dissertations (Platt, Pagan, and Arrington), but also of our colleagues in Rome, Archi and Milano. Pelio Fronzaroli has also indicated his willingness to assist us, as the project advances, in the area of linguistic analysis of the onomastic data. To all these institutions and individuals I wish to express my heartfelt personal gratitude.

2. *Onomastic Analysis of Ebla Personal Names: Linguistic Considerations*

An in-depth analysis of the personal names from Ebla will provide the single most important resource for a fuller understanding of the linguistic reality at Ebla, since the onomastic data are the major source of information in that respect. While indexes of names are published with every new text edition,

[6] Platt, Pagan, and Arrington forthcoming. An ancillary publication which is almost completely ready for publication is Platt forthcoming; it contains an exhaustive bibliographical listing of more than one thousand titles of all publication of primary data on Ebla, and all pertinent secondary literature. Those interested in further information on these publications and wishing to be placed on a mailing list for future announcements should write to J. H. Platt, Assistant Editor, Cybernetica Mesopotamica, IIMAS, POB 787, Malibu, CA 90265.

the linguistic interpretation that accompanies them is generally selective. And while important and comprehensive studies on Ebla onomastics have appeared, they either stress the interpretive and linguistic aspects more than the documentary aspect (such as the many important studies of Gelb and Fronzaroli) or they provide a preliminary overview rather than a systematic handling of the data (such as Krebernik 1988). Our project aims at filling this gap by establishing an all-inclusive repertory of text occurrences and of linguistic interpretations for the Ebla corpus as a whole. *Onomastic Repertory of Ebla* is based on a systematic culling of the data from the text editions and of the interpretations from the available secondary literature, with a special effort at integrating the underlying graphemic and prosopographic dimensions.

The *Repertory* is conceived as the publication of a system of interrelated data bases. While publication as such will only be possible at some later date, the criteria which define its format are already well established since they have been designed as a function of data entry, and *vice versa*. In point of fact, the published *Repertory* and the computer data bases are mirror images of each other, or different embodiments of the same conceptual design. In the presentation that follows I will describe this conceptual design by referring to both the *Repertory* as a static published volume and to the data bases as dynamic electronic files.

2.1. Primary Data Used

The *Repertory* will include all personal names contained in specified segments of the inventory of the Ebla texts, and it will provide a systematic linguistic analysis for all such names in the measure in which they are understood. While our main interest, and the largest body of evidence in the corpus, pertains to Semitic personal names, we will include in the documentary section all proper names, that is, divine names, geographical names, and month names, as well as personal names. The textual segments, or sub-corpora, chosen for analysis will be closely correlated to the program of publication of definitive text editions, both in printed form as ARET and in electronic format as *Cybernetica Mesopotamica: Texts* (*CMT*).

Specifically, the *Repertory* will cull all the names contained in ARET 1–4 and 7–10. We will also excerpt names from other publications of texts, as well as from articles which make available primary editions of specific texts (especially from the journal *Studi Eblaiti*). Some of the ARET volumes in course of publication will be available to the project in manuscript or proof form, in particular volumes 9–10. In every case, we will rely heavily on collations from the original, so as to insure an even philological quality to our collection of names.

The total number of name occurrences which have already been entered in the documentary data file by Platt and Pagan is about twenty thousand items.[7]

[7] The section from the documentary data base given as table 1 includes 15,039 names, but this particular listing was produced in 1988.

An approximate estimate of the number of names as distinct linguistic items is about five thousand. It is difficult to gauge the eventual total with any degree of precision before the research is actually completed, because the concept of "element," as explained below, includes components of personal names which will be isolated from the names following our research; also, part of the data on which the project will draw is still in course of publication.

The pertinent secondary literature will also be studied systematically, and all acceptable interpretations included and acknowledged. References to such interpretations will be given in the final version of the *Repertory* (they are not included in the samples given below) and will be part of a special section of the data base, so that not only the primary data (i.e., the names themselves) but also the interpretive references will be available on magnetic media for easy updating. Where multiple interpretations are possible, they will all be included side by side, using our judgment as to which ones are most plausible.

2.2. *Methods of Analysis*

The following major levels of analysis are being applied systematically to the writing and the language of the names: graphemics, paleography, phonology, morphology, syntax or name formation, and semantics. We include prosopographic information to the extent described below. We only occasionally address questions of semiotics (name-giving)[8] and the like.

Prosopography will play a significant role insofar as it will assist in identifying different text occurrences of a name as belonging to the same name-bearer, thus requiring that they be considered as linguistic variants of the same name (except in cases of nicknames, double names, or the like). For instance, when the same individual is called *Iš-da-ma-*^{d}KU.RA, *Uš-du-*^{d}KU.RA, and *Uš-dum-*^{d}KU.RA in three different texts,[9] one must find an onomastic solution for the divergence of forms attributed (prosopographically) to the same name-bearer.

Graphemic control is of paramount importance for a correct evaluation of the onomastic evidence, as the evidence just adduced from prosopography makes amply evident. Besides correlation of variant writings for names attributed to the same individual, the more general concern must be to establish patterns of distributional correlations among signs. The fully computerized data base of Ebla texts already at our disposal and on which Platt is currently working provides the best tool for such an assessment of distributional possibilities.

Paleographical and *philological* questions that arise from an in-depth onomastic analysis are given particular attention, and in this respect the collaboration of Archi and Milano is especially invaluable. Both through their direct

[8] My student Mark Arrington is working on a doctoral dissertation dealing with name-giving as found in the third-millennium Semitic milieu.

[9] ARET 9:37, 38, and 40, respectively. The names belong to a list of DAMS of Irkab-Damu, and they occur each time in the same relative position in the list. I owe this example to the courtesy of Platt and Pagan, who have established a long list of such correlations.

oversight of the expedition archives (photographs and files), and through Archi's work at the museums in Aleppo and Idlib where the original tablets are stored, collations are an integral part of the way in which our data base is established.

The *grammatical* analysis is based on a coding system which identifies each significant element on the phonological, morphological, syntactic (i.e., pertaining to name composition), and lexical level. The encoding manual, the use of which is exemplified in the brief samples given below, already has been tested over a relatively long period of time, and should serve well for speedy and effective data entry. In practice, the manual translates (with modifications suited to accommodate Eblaite and Amorite peculiarities) into a coherent system the overall structural understanding of Akkadian which I have developed in my forthcoming *Structural Grammar of Babylonian*. I will not illustrate here the nature and structure of this coding system, because to do so would require an amount of detail clearly beyond the scope of the present article, but full details will eventually accompany the publication of the onomastic data base. The various interpretations found in the literature are being translated into this system, in order to provide comprehensive access to the current scholarly understanding of Ebla onomastics. Beyond that, our own analysis is given wherever possible. The published data base will include both the body of scholarly interpretations and our own, according to selective criteria which will be decided upon as the work progresses. The process of data entry is being carried out by Pagan.

The data are filed in three major, interrelated data bases—one dealing with documentary and prosopographic evidence, the second with whole names as linguistic items, and the third with individual elements as linguistic components of the names. More details on the contents of these data bases and on their interconnections will be given presently. At this point, it may be well to address the issue of the depth and scope of the analysis planned for the names. In general, the approach we propose to follow is situated half-way between that represented by extensive name indexes (such as the Mari *Répertoires*) on the one hand and fully analytical studies on the other (such as my own *Amorites of the Ur III Period*, H. Huffmon's *Amorite Personal Names*, or similar studies on onomastics). It will thus be similar to that followed by Gelb in his *Computer-Aided Analysis of Amorite*, except that it will be more extensive in its linguistic categorization and fully documented for its interpretive choices in terms of comparative materials. In any case, the final result will be much more than a glossary, because it will include a full grammatical categorization, with corresponding sorts by pertinent categories.

2.3. *The Documentary Data Base (Table 1)*

The structure of the individual data bases and the nature of their interrelationship may be discerned by viewing the tables included with this article. These sample printouts present the data as they will eventually appear in the printed *Repertory*, and are a distillate of the most-important categories contained in the data bases. While they do not exhaust by any means the potentiality of the

TABLE 1. *Documentary Data Base: Text Occurrences and Prosopography*

				Text				Name-bearer[f]		
Template[a]	Sq#[b]	Reference	Transliteration	Pub[c]	Txt[d]	Prv[e]	Date	Sex[g]	■a Age[h] ■k Kin ■o Occup[i] ■p Prov[j]	Notes[k]
ʾa$_3$-da-hu	15	3.800.r.3,6′	ʾa$_3$-da-hu	T	txtls	E			■p du-ub	
*4	16	3.2.r.3,7′	ʾa$_3$-da-hu	T	txtls	E			■p du-ub	
	17	3.63.r.3,6	ʾa$_3$-d[a-hu]	T	txtls	E			■p du-ub	
	18	4.19.r.1,5	ʾa$_3$-da-hu	T	txtls	E			■p du-ub	
ʾa$_3$-da-LUM	19	8.540.v.17,8	ʾa$_3$-da-*LUM	T	txtls	E				
ʾa$_3$-da-mi-gu	20	1.8.v.7,20	ʾa$_3$-da-mi-gu	T	txtls	E	ITI ZA-*LUL		■k ib-dur-da-gan DUMU-NITA ʾa$_3$ ■o NAR	
	21	7.81.r.1,3	ʾa$_3$-da-mi-gu	T	metals	E			■o NAR	
ʾa$_3$-da-mi-gu$_2$	22	3.498.v.2,2′	ʾa$_3$-da-mi-gu$_2$	T	txtls	E			■o NAR	
ʾa$_3$-da-ri$_2$-ba	23	1.15.r.8,3	ʾa$_3$-da-ri$_2$-ba	T	txtls	E	ITI ig-za		■p ar-ha-du	
ʾa$_3$-da-rum$_2$	24	4.11.r.2,13	ʾa$_3$-da-rum$_2$	T	txtls	E			■o LU$_2$ iš-ra-il	
ʾa$_3$-da-ša	25	1.4.v.6,6	ʾa$_3$-da-ša	T	txtls	E			■k ŠEŠ-2-IB	
*72	26	1.4.v.7,5	ʾa$_3$-da-ša	T	txtls	E			■k LU$_2$ ib-gi	
ʾa$_3$-da-še$_3$	98	1.2.r.5,6	ʾa$_3$-da-še$_3$	T	txtls	E	ITI MAXGANA$_2$-GUDU$_4$			
*17	99	1.6.v.5,9	ʾa$_3$-da-še$_3$	T	txtls	E	ITI za-*LUL		■k ŠEŠ-2-IB	
ʾa$_3$-daš	120	9.66:v.5,15	ʾa$_3$-daš	T	rations	E				
*30	121	9.68:v.8,5	ʾa$_3$-daš	T	rations	E	ITI-^{d}*AMA-ra			
ʾa$_3$-daš-še$_3$	151	3.458.r.4,10	ʾa$_3$-daš-še$_3$	T	txtls	E			■k ŠEŠ-2-IB	
a-a-lu	536	3.644.r.2,5	a-a-lu	T	txtls	E		m	■k A-MU in-gar$_3$ ■o LU$_2$-KAR ■p kak-mi-um	
a-bu$_3$-uš-gu$_2$	786	1.4.v.9,12	a-bu$_3$-uš-gu$_2$	T	txtls	E			■p zu-gu$_2$-lu	
a-mur-da-mu	1264	8.521.r.7,6	a-mur-da-mu	T	txtls	E			■o LU$_2$ KAS$_4$-KAS$_4$ ■p ma-ri$_2$	
ar-si-a-hu	1915	8.523.r.7,3	ar-si-a-hu	T	txtls	E			■o MAŠKIM ■p gar$_3$-ga-mi-is	
*14	1919	76.G.2143.r.1,4	ar-si-a-hu	T	agr	E	ITI za-*LUL		■p ib-la	
ba-du-lum	2030	2.23.r.2,4	ba-du-lum	T	anim	E	ITI I$_3$-NUN	m	■o UGULA ENGAR	
bu-$_3$-da-*NI	2553	3.460.r.3,4	bu$_3$-da-*NI	T	list	E	ITI za-ʾa$_3$-tum		■o UGULA ŠE ʾa$_3$-mi-zu	
bu$_3$-da-na-im		1.8.v.13,22	bu$_3$-da-na-im	T	txtls	E			■p *HUB$_2$.*KI u$_3$-ti-gu$_2$	
da-hir$_2$-li-im	2828	75G.1452.r.4,2	da-hir$_2$-li-im	T	legal	E		f	■k DUMU-MI$_2$ i-ri$_2$-ik-da-mu ■p ib-la	
du-bi$_2$-zi-kir	3518	3.59.r.6,4′	du-bi$_2$-zi-kir	T	txtls	E	1 MU TIL ma-ri$_2$		■o UGULA KA$_2$ kak-mi-um	
du-bu$_3$-i-sar	3802	1.17.r.9,9	du-bu$_3$-i-sar	T	txtls	E			■k DUMU-NITA il$_2$-zi ■o LU$_2$ du-nu	
*2	3803	3.59.r.7,3′	du-bu$_3$-i-sar	T	txtls	E	ITIgi-*NI		■k DUMU-NITA *NE-zi ■o LU$_2$ du-nu	
du-si-gu$_2$	3896	3.660.r.2,1′	du-si-gu$_2$	T	txtls+	E		f	■k AMA-GAL EN ■p ib-la	
en-na-BE	4210	3.585.r.2,5	en-na-BE	T	metals	E	ITI i-si	m	■o UGULA SIMUG	

TABLE 1. (*cont'd.*)

Template[a]	Sq#[b]	Reference	Transliteration	Text: Pub[c]	Text: Txt[d]	Text: Prv[e]	Text: Date	Name-bearer[f]: Sex[g]	Name-bearer[f]: ■a Age[h] ■k Kin ■o Occup[i] ■p Prov[j]	Notes[k]
*84	4265	75G.1353.v.1,7	en-na-BE	T	metals	E		m	■k ŠEŠ ri$_2$-ma ■o ha-su-wa-an	
en-na-da-gan	4311	75.G.2367.r.1,2	en-na-da-gan	T	letter	M		m	■o EN ma-ri$_2$ ■p ma-ri$_2$	
en-na-*NI	4642	1.1.v.9,5	en-na-*NI	T	txtls	E			■o DI-KU$_5$	
*6	4643	1.1.v.9,9	en-na-*NI	T	txtls	E	ITI za-*LUL		■p ma-za-lum du-lu	
	4676	2.6.r.4,4	en-na-*NI	T	metals	E	ITI za-*LUL		■o MAŠKIM SAGI	
	4816	4.15.r.10,10	en-na-*NI	T	txtls	E			■o da-nu	
gal-iš-hi	5647	75.G.1233.r.7,2	gal-iš-hi	T	metals	E			■p MA$_2$-HU mu-nu-ti-um	
i-da-ki-mu	6792	75.G.521.v.6,2	i-da-ki-mu	T	rations	E			■p ib-la	
i-de$_3$-ni-ki-mu	6866	1.8.v.8,6	i-de$_3$-ni-ki-mu	T	txtls	E	ITI ŠE-GUR$_{10}$		■a *NE.*DI TUR	
i-sa-ni-ki-mu	7319	1.17.r.9,14	i-sa-ni-ki-mu	T	txtls	E	ITI gi-*NI		■a LU$_2$ gu$_2$-*LUM ■o SA-ZA$_0$(LAK384)	
i-ti-^{d}eš$_4$-dar	7578	1.5.5.v.11,23	i-ti-^{d}eš$_4$-dar	T	txtls	E	ITI gi-*NI	m	■k DUMU-NITA wa-ra-an ■p bur-ma-an	
i-za-iš-lu	7976	2.44.v.3,2	i-za-iš-lu	C	metals	E	ITI za-*LUL			
ir$_3$-am$_6$-da-mu	9783	3.877.v.1,3′	ir$_3$-am$_6$-da-mu	T	txtls	E			■p LU$_2$-KAR a-la	
ir$_3$-am$_6$-gu$_2$-nu	9816	8.527.r.12,2	ir$_3$-am$_6$-gu$_2$-nu	T	txtls	E			■o MASKIM ki-ti-ir ■p a-du-bu$_3$	
ir$_3$-kab-da-mu	10109	75.G.2342.r.4,6	ir$_3$-kab-da-mu	T	letter	E		m	■o EN ib-la ■p ib-la	

a. The word *template* refers to the transliteration without breaks, emendations, punctuation marks, and the like. For names which share the same template, the template itself appears only in the first line, followed by the total number of text occurrences.

b. "Sq#" refers to the internal sequential number of name occurrences. At this point, the number is that of our preliminary list of 15,309 name occurrences. The selection of names given here was so chosen as to give an idea of the organization of the material.

c. "Pub" refers to the type of publication available for the text in question.

d. "Txt" refers to the type of text to which the text in question belongs. Categories given here are self-explanatory. It is expected that finer differentiations will be made in the final version of the *Repertory*.

e. "Prv" refers to the provenience of the text: in the present sample only E for Ebla and M for Mari are given. In the final version, finer differentiation will be made, as far as possible: for instance, a distinction will be made between the archival provenience within Ebla itself.

f. Prosopographic information is given here. Since one hardly ever finds information about each of the subcategories listed below, they are lumped together in sequential order, separated only by a distinctive graphic marker. The data base on disk has of course different field entries for each subcategory.

g. This is not the grammatical gender of the name, but the sex of the name-bearer when known.

h. Direct or indirect notes about age as apparent from the text.

i. The profession or occupation of the name-bearer as given in the text.

j. Provenience of the name-bearer as explicitly given in the text.

k. A further field of remarks will be added here in the final version of the *Repertory*. The actual remarks will be given in a separate text file to which an appropriate number will refer in this column.

electronic exploitation of such data bases, they serve to convey an image of their configuration.

The first major component contains the documentary data base. As seen in table 1, this data base provides an alphabetical list of all name occurrences, with textual and prosopographic information. Names are subsumed under individual graphemic "templates," that is, a standardized form of transliteration which omits information about textual details such as paleographical variations, breaks, or emendations. Where more than one text occurrence is found for a template, the total is given. It must be noted that such a template is not necessarily identical with the concept of a name as a linguistic item; rather, it must be understood as a graphemic concept, which subsumes textual, but not phonemic variants. Thus from the examples given in table 1, the graphemic templates *ʾa*$_3$*-da-ša,* *ʾa*$_3$*-da-še*$_3$*,* *ʾa*$_3$*-daš,* and *ʾa*$_3$*-daš-še*$_3$ may all correspond to an individual onomastic item, but they are graphemically distinct, and are so identified in the data base.

Text occurrences are sorted by publication reference within templates (some occasional discrepancies in the sample on table 1, e.g., the entry with sequential number 15, reflect the fact that the list used for the sample is taken from our actual working files, which have not yet been fully edited). An internal sequential number is assigned to each text occurrence, for ease of reference.

Details of textual information are listed in tabular form under the categories of publication type, text type, provenience of the text, and date of the text (a brief explanation of these categories is provided in the footnotes to table 1). The final edition will, of course, contain a full discussion of these categories, as well as a listing of the codes for each category. An interesting utilization of this kind of information for onomastic analysis is provided in table 7, which shows the distribution of names that occur exclusively or prevalently in the "small" archive at Ebla. (This table is an indication of the type of specialized elaboration that users will be able to perform on the data distributed as electronic files on disk.)

Prosopographic details are contained under the heading "Name-bearer" in table 1. In the interest of space economy, these data are not listed in tabular form, since it is seldom that information is actually found for each of the categories envisaged. The format of the final publication may change even further in this respect if it turns out that available information is so scarce that too much empty space would occur on each page. An alternative way of presenting this information might then be in the form of footnotes.

An important category omitted in the present layout of table 1 is a column referring to notes (see tables 2–3). These will be presented in discursive format at the bottom of each page and will either expand on coded information as tabulated in the charts, or contain information about categories which cannot be conveniently presented in tabular form.

2.4. The First Onomastic Data Base: Names (Table 2)

The second major component contains two interrelated data bases, which deal with onomastic analysis proper. The first onomastic data base includes the names as linguistic terms (an example of this format is found in table 2). The names are here listed by graphemic template, split into its component elements. Doublets, that is, multiple graphemic templates of what is assumed to be the same name, are so identified. Alternative linguistic interpretations are possible, on two levels, graphemic or phonemic. As an example of alternative graphemic interpretation one may quote *I-bi*$_2$*-Si-piš* and *I-bi*$_2$*-Zi-kir* (this example is used only for the sake of argument, since the former reading is no longer plausible). As an example of alternative phonemic interpretation one may quote *ˀamur-Damu* (with short *a*, for the imperative) and *ˀāmur-Damu* (with long *ā*, for the preterite). While our working data base contains all possible interpretations, the published version will be edited so as to avoid fanciful and improbable interpretations.

The name transcription encapsulates the linguistic interpretation of the name, which is given in more detail for each component in the element data base (see §2.5).

The next column identifies the structure of the name, by indicating the nature of the elements and their sequential order. The elements are identified as to the part of speech (verb, noun, etc.) with some additional information (e.g., the person for a finite form of the verb), depending on the frequency of each type.

Since hypocoristic afformatives are to be understood at the level of the name as a whole rather than as separate elements, they are identified in a separate column within this data base.

Interpretive references are added wherever pertinent. These references will also include sigla of individual contributors to the project when their interpretation is considered to be significantly personal.

One last column (which is missing in the sample given on table 1) will contain references to discursive notes on specific topics which cannot otherwise be given in tabular form. The notes will appear eventually at the bottom of the page.

2.5. *The Second Onomastic Data Base: Elements (Table 3)*

The second onomastic data base of the individual elements as linguistic components of the names is found in table 3. The elements are listed alphabetically according to their graphemic template. Where graphemic boundaries do not overlap with phonemic boundaries, a vertical bar | is used; for example, within the name *a-mu-rum*$_2$ we may isolate a hypocoristic ending *-um* which does not correspond to an autonomous grapheme; hence the template for the name will be rendered as *a-mu-r|um*$_2$.

Primacy is given to the graphemic template rather than to the transcription for two reasons. First, this maintains a clearer distinction between the interpretive and the documentary level. Second, it will be easier to relate each element to the documentary data base, where full information can be found for textual and prosopographic matters (to test for instance whether certain linguistic features occur only with certain types of name-bearers or certain types of texts).

TABLE 2. *Onomastic Data Base: Names*

<table>
<tr><th colspan="4">Template[a]</th><th></th><th></th><th></th><th></th><th></th><th></th></tr>
<tr><th>Elem. 1</th><th>Elem. 2</th><th>Elem. 3</th><th>Hypoch.</th><th>Db</th><th>Gr</th><th>Mr[b]</th><th>Transcription[c]</th><th>NmStr[d]</th><th>Notes[e]</th></tr>
<tr><td>a-ha</td><td>ka</td><td>il</td><td></td><td></td><td></td><td></td><td>aha-ka-il</td><td>n–pp–dn</td><td></td></tr>
<tr><td>a-mu-r|</td><td></td><td></td><td>|um$_2$</td><td>1</td><td></td><td>a</td><td>ʾāmur-um</td><td>v1–HY</td><td></td></tr>
<tr><td>a-mu-r|</td><td></td><td></td><td>|um$_2$</td><td>1</td><td></td><td>b</td><td>ʾamur-um</td><td>v2–HY</td><td></td></tr>
<tr><td>a-mu-r|</td><td></td><td></td><td>|u$_{12}$-um</td><td>2[f]</td><td></td><td>a</td><td>ʾāmur-um</td><td></td><td></td></tr>
<tr><td>a-mu-r|</td><td></td><td></td><td>|u$_{12}$-um</td><td>2</td><td></td><td>b</td><td>ʾ-amur-um</td><td></td><td></td></tr>
<tr><td>dar-kab</td><td>da-mu</td><td></td><td></td><td></td><td></td><td></td><td>tarkab-damu</td><td>v3–dn</td><td>Fronzaroli 1979: 275</td></tr>
<tr><td>i-bi$_2$</td><td>da-mu</td><td></td><td></td><td></td><td></td><td></td><td>ibbi-damu</td><td>v3–dn</td><td></td></tr>
<tr><td>i-bi$_2$</td><td>ku-ra</td><td></td><td></td><td></td><td></td><td></td><td>ibbi-kura</td><td>v3–dn</td><td></td></tr>
<tr><td>i-bi$_2$</td><td>*ZI-*KIR</td><td></td><td></td><td></td><td>A[g]</td><td></td><td>ibbi-sipiš</td><td>v3–dn</td><td>cf. Gelb 1981: 21–22</td></tr>
<tr><td>i-bi$_2$</td><td>*ZI-*KIR</td><td></td><td></td><td></td><td>B</td><td></td><td>ibbi-zikir</td><td>v3–dn</td><td></td></tr>
<tr><td>ir$_3$-kab</td><td>ar</td><td></td><td></td><td></td><td></td><td></td><td>irkab-ar</td><td>v3–dn</td><td></td></tr>
<tr><td>ir$_3$-kab</td><td>da-mu</td><td></td><td></td><td></td><td></td><td></td><td>irkab-damu</td><td>v3–dn</td><td></td></tr>
<tr><td>ir$_3$-kab-b|</td><td></td><td></td><td>|u$_3$</td><td></td><td></td><td></td><td>irkab-u</td><td>v3–HY</td><td></td></tr>
<tr><td>iš-ma$_2$</td><td>da-mu</td><td></td><td></td><td></td><td></td><td></td><td>išma^c-damu</td><td>v3–dn</td><td></td></tr>
<tr><td>iš-ma$_2$</td><td>gar$_3$-du</td><td></td><td></td><td></td><td></td><td></td><td>išma^c-qardu</td><td>v3–dn</td><td></td></tr>
<tr><td>iš-ma$_2$</td><td>il</td><td></td><td></td><td></td><td></td><td></td><td>išma^c-il</td><td>v3–dn</td><td></td></tr>
<tr><td>iš-ma$_2$</td><td>li-im</td><td></td><td></td><td></td><td></td><td></td><td>išma^c-lim</td><td>v3–dn</td><td></td></tr>
<tr><td>PUZUR$_4$-RA</td><td>^{d}ma-lik</td><td></td><td></td><td></td><td></td><td></td><td>ṣilli-malik</td><td>n–n</td><td></td></tr>
<tr><td>ra-i-z|</td><td></td><td></td><td>|u</td><td>1</td><td></td><td></td><td>rāʾiṣ-u</td><td>n–HY</td><td>Krebernik 1988: 6</td></tr>
<tr><td>ra-i-z|</td><td></td><td></td><td>|u$_2$</td><td>2</td><td></td><td></td><td>rāʾiṣ-u</td><td></td><td></td></tr>
<tr><td>ra-i$_3$-z|</td><td></td><td></td><td>|u$_2$</td><td>3</td><td></td><td></td><td>rāʾiṣ-u</td><td></td><td></td></tr>
</table>

TABLE 2. *Notes*

a. The transliteration template is identical to the one found in the Documentary Data Base (table 1), except that the elements are split and placed in different columns. Where the boundary between elements does not match graphemic boundary, then the divider | is used. For example, $r||um_2$ is to be read as a single sign rum_2. Small capitals in transliteration preceded by an asterisk are used to identify readings with unknown or alternative graphemic values. They are thus to be distinguished from the small capitals used for logograms. All the conventions used to render as closely as possible the graphemic structure of the data are fully discussed in the user's manual.

b. Db = doublet: double (or multiple) writing of the same name, with sequential numbering. Gr/Mr = graphemic/morphemic alternate interpretation: different readings of the same name occurrence, yielding different name items (lettered sequentially in upper case for graphemic, and lower case for morphemic variants).

c. The elements are here given in phonemic transcription, identical to that found in the Element Data Base (table 3), where one will find full lexical and grammatical information about each individual element.

d. Name Structure: v1/2/3 = finite verbal form, 1st/2d/3d person; dn = divine name; n = noun; pp = preposition; HY = hypochoristicon. The final version will contain a full typology of name formation, and the codes will be fully explained.

e. In the final version of the *Repertory*, notes will contain full discursive information about treatments of the names in secondary literature, comparative data, and the like. They will be placed at the bottom of the page.

f. The second occurrence of a doublet may be traced back to the first occurrence (where not in immediate proximity, as is the case here) through the transcribed form of the name. The name structure, however, is not repeated.

g. The *Repertory* will contain readings which are not considered plausible, such as this one, whenever it is deemed that they deserve special mention. The footnotes will indicate in some detail what the various degrees of probability are, and will refer to pertinent discussions.

TABLE 3. *Onomastic Data Base: Elements*

ElTemplate[a]	Gr	Lx	Mr[b]	NmStr[c]	Pos[d]	Transcr[e]	Translation	LPT[f]	Root/Base	Meaning[g]	St[h]	T[i]	P	N	G	C[j]	Notes[k]
								Internal Inflection				External Inflection					
a-mu-r|			a	v1–HY	1	*ʾāmur*	I see	s v *	*ʾmr*	to see	b	2	1	s	c		
a-mu-r|			b	v2–HY	1	*ʾamur*	see!	s v 1	*ʾmr*	to see	b	1	2	s	m		
da-mu		1		v3–dn	2	*damu*	clan	s n p	*dam*	blood	1a	n		s	m	n	Krebernik 1988: 80
da-mu		2		v3–dn	2	*damu*	Dumu	? n 1	*dumu*	Dumuzi		n		s	m		Krebernik 1988: 80
i-bi$_2$				v3–dn	1	*ibbi*	he called	s v d	*nb:*	to call	b	2	3	s	m		
ir$_3$*-kab*				v3–dn	1	*irkab*	he rode	s v *	*rkb*	to ride	b	2	3	s	m		
iš-ma$_2$				v3–dn	1	*išmaᶜ*	he heard	s v *	*šmᶜ*	to hear	b	2	3	s	m		
ra-i-z|				n–HY	1	*rāʾiṣ*	helper	s n *	*rʾṣ*	to help	pa	n		s	m		
*ZI-*KIR	A	1		v3–dn	2	*zikir*	name	s n *	*zkr*	to name	4i	a		s	m		
*ZI-*KIR	A	2		v3–dn	2	*zikir*	male	s n p	*zikar*	male	4ia	a		s	m		
*ZI-*KIR	B	3		v3–dn	2	*sipiš*	sun	w n p	*sipiš*	sun	4i	a		s	m		

The layout given here, as with that of the other two data bases, reflects as much the structure of the data base in its current formulation, as a preliminary draft for the final publication in book format. The element data base presented on this table is more indicative of the data-base format than of its published version counterpart. In particular, there are too many codes which cannot be resolved without taking up too much space. A more proper use of these codes is illustrated below in the tables which present the different possibilities of data-base utilization in computer format. Once the data base is completed, and after it has been used on an in-house basis while preparing the data base itself, we will be in a better position to make a decision as to the proper selection of information to be retained for presentation in the published version of the data base. It must also be borne in mind that a proper utilization of the vast amount of information provided in the data base can only be had with reference to the user's manual, where the codes (and their underlying logic) are fully explained. These tables must be viewed only as indicative of method. In this respect it may further be noted that the few examples shown are meant to reflect the variety of different cases which the data-base system is set up to handle, and do not have any particular substantive value.

TABLE 3. *Notes (cont'd.)*

a. The transliteration template is identical to that found in tables 1–2. As in table 2, in those cases where the boundary between elements does not match graphemic boundary, the divider | is used. For instance, the full grapheme is *rum*$_2$ or *ru*$_{12}$-*um*; the graphemic readings may be obtained from the name data base (table 2).

b. Gr/Mr = graphemic/morphemic alternate interpretation (see table 2 note b). Lx = lexical alternate interpretation: this includes alternate interpretations of the root or base, and as such it is found only here at the level of the element, and not in the name data base.

c. Name Structure: see table 2 note d.

d. Position of the element in question within the name structure given in the preceding column: thus for instance *da-mu* is the second element (position 2) in a name of the structural type v3–dn.

e. This transcription matches the one given in the name data base (where elements are combined to form a whole name).

f. L stands for linguistic affiliation of the element in question: s = Semitic, w = West Semitic, ? = unknown. P refers to the part of speech: v = verb, n = noun, p = pronoun, x = preposition. T stands for the type of word within the part of speech: p = primary (unmotivated) noun, l = loanword, * = strong root, 1/2/3 = 1st/2d/3d weak root, d = double weak root.

g. This column gives the meaning of the lexeme, which is occasionally different from the meaning of the element occurring in the name. This may result from the fact that a root is inflected in the name, or that the meaning of a word within a name is assumed to differ from the meaning of the lexeme as reconstructed through etymology (e.g., *damu* 'blood' as an etymon, but 'clan' within the context of a theophoric name).

h. Stem/pattern: with verbal forms, this column contains codes for the stem, i.e., the verbal conjugations (e.g., b = Basic or G stem). With nominal forms, this column identifies the pattern for nouns derived from roots (e.g., 1 refers to the pattern *pVr*, and 1a indicates vocalism a, hence *par*); it also identifies the shape for unmotivated primary nouns (other than loanwords), e.g., 4i refers to the shape *piris* for *sipiš*.

i. T refers to the tense (for a verb) or state (for a noun). Thus, e.g., 1 = imperative, 2 = preterite, n = normal, a = absolute.

j. P = person (for verbs and pronouns), N = number, G = gender, C = case (for nouns and pronouns only).

k. As with the other data bases, notes will be extensive and will include, especially, references to secondary literature, comparative material, and argumentation. They will be at the bottom of the page.

Next follows a reference to the structural type of name within which the element is attested. This information qualifies each morpho-lexical element in terms of its "syntactical" environment, as it were, by reference to the type of name formation within which it occurs. The full list of actual names which match this structural definition and which contain that particular element is to be found in the name data base described above (see table 2).

The next column gives the phonemic transcription and the translation of the element in question. Where alternate interpretations are possible, these are numbered sequentially within each template. For example, two different transcriptions and translations are registered for *a-mu-r|um*$_2$ and two different translations are registered for *da-mu*.

The next column identifies the linguistic affiliation of the element in question. While in most cases this might be "Semitic" at best or "unknown" at worst, it will be of interest to note here incidences of West Semitic or Sumerian presence, or the like.

The next six columns deal with the element viewed as a word (internal inflection): part of speech, type of word, root or base, pattern (stem for the verb, noun formation for the noun), and state (for the noun) or mood/tense (for the verb).

Finally, details of external inflection are tabulated in the last four columns (extending notes in the last column): person, number, gender, case. As with the previous two data bases, discursive notes will be appended at the bottom of the page as needed. The footnotes for this concordance will be especially important because they will contain comparative references to other Semitic languages.

2.6. General Indexes (Tables 4–5)

Different types of indexes complete the utilization of the data base. General indexes provide a sort of certain types of information in such a way as to make the published data bases more useful. For instance, an index to the name data base will list all name transcriptions in alphabetical order, with a reference to their respective name templates. Similarly, there will be indexes for elements in their phonemic transcription (see a minimal sample in table 4) and for roots (see a minimal sample in table 5), bases of unmotivated nouns, patterns, structural types of name formation, and the like.

Selected tabulations will also be provided (not illustrated in this article). They will contain, for example, computations about frequencies of phonemes (such as are given in Gelb's *Computer-Aided Analysis of Amorite*), morphemes, and lexemes.

3. Onomastic Analysis of Ebla Personal Names: Data-Processing Considerations

Both the *Ebla Electronic Corpus* and *Cybernetica Mesopotamica* (the former is a part of the latter) are obviously heavily committed to a computer-oriented

TABLE 4. *Index by Elements*

Element	Pos[a]	NmStr[b]	Template
aḫa	1	n–pp–dn	*a-ḫa-ka-il*
ʾamur	1	v2–dn	*a-mur-da-mu*
	1	v2–HY	*a-mu-rum*$_2$
	1	v2–HY	*a-mu-ru*$_{12}$*-um*
ʾāmur	1	v1–dn	*a-mur-da-mu*
	1	v1–HY	*a-mu-rum*$_2$
	1	v1–HY	*a-mu-ru*$_{12}$*-um*
ʾar	2	v3–dn	*ir*$_3$*-kab-ar*
damu	2	v1–dn	*a-mur-da-mu*
	2	v3–dn	*dar-kab-da-mu*
	2	v3–dn	*i-bi*$_2$*-da-mu*
	2	v3–dn	*ir*$_3$*-am*$_6$*-da-mu*
	2	v3–dn	*iš-ma*$_2$*-da-mu*
ibbi	1	v3–dn	*i-bi*$_2$*-da-mu*
	1	v3–dn	*i-bi*$_2$*-ku-ra*
	1	v3–dn	*i-bi*$_2$-*ZI-*KIR
il	2	v3–dn	*iš-ma*$_2$*-il*
	3	n–pp–dn	*a-ha-ka-il*
irʾam	1	v3–dn	*ir*$_3$*-am*$_6$*-da-mu*
irkab	1	v3–dn	*ir*$_3$*-kab-ar*
	1	v3–dn	*ir*$_3$*-kab-bu*$_3$
	1	v3–dn	*ir*$_3$*-kab-da-mu*
išmaʿ	1	v3–dn	*iš-ma*$_2$*-da-mu*
	1	v3–dn	*iš-ma*$_2$*-gar*$_3$*-du*
	1	v3–dn	*iš-ma*$_2$*-il*
	1	v3–dn	*iš-ma*$_2$*-lim*
ka	2	n–pp–dn	*a-ha-ka-il*
kura	2	v3–dn	*i-bi*$_2$*-ku-ra*
lim	2	v3–dn	*iš-ma*$_2$*-lim*
malik	2	n–dn	PUZUR$_4$-RA-^{d}*ma-lik*
qardu	2	v3–dn	*iš-ma*$_2$*-gar*$_3$*-du*
rāʾiṣu	1	n–HY	*ra-i-zu*
	1	n–HY	*ra-i-zu*$_2$
	1	n–HY	*ra-i*$_3$*-zu*$_2$
sipiš	2	v3–dn	*i-bi*$_2$-*ZI-*KIR
ṣilli	1	n–dn	PUZUR$_4$-RA-^{d}*ma-lik*
tarkab	1	v3–dn	*dar-kab-da-mu*
ṭūbi	1	n–dn	*du-bi*$_2$-*ZI-*KIR
zikir	2	n–dn	*du-bi*$_2$-*ZI-*KIR
	2	v3–dn	*i-bi*$_2$-*ZI-*KIR
zikar	2	n–dn	*du-bi*$_2$-*ZI-*KIR
	2	v3–dn	*i-bi*$_2$-*ZI-*KIR

a. position of the element within the name.

b. Structure of the name. The sort is by position and name structure first, and then by name.

TABLE 5. *Index by Roots*

Root	Type[a]	Element
ʾmr	1	*ʾamur*
		ʾāmur
nb:	d	*ibbi*
rʾm	*	*irʾam*
rkb	*	*irkab*
		tarkab
šmᶜ	*	*išmaᶜ*
ṭ:b	2	*ṭūbī*
zkr	*	*zikir*

a. Type of root: * = strong; 1/2/3 = 1st/2d/3d weak; d= double weak.

approach, but with the following provisos. In the first place, our commitment is, if anything, even greater with regard to the substantive aspect of the data. Linguistic considerations set the rules for coding and analysis, and embodiment of these in an electronic format is done simply in order to make use of a better tool, certainly not as an end in itself. Where the tool affects the scholarship is in certain intellectual aspects which are often not sufficiently appreciated when dealing with electronic data processing. At the level of analysis, the rigor of formal correlations, which the electronic medium encourages, calls for greater lucidity in the articulation of grammatical structure. At the level of documentation, we can reach through a vast capillary system to the most-minute bit of information while retaining at the same time a full view of the whole. At the level of the utilization of the data, scholars will find an immensely wider range of opportunities for personal inquiry by pursuing interactive searches with the electronic data bases. Much as a microscope leads to a refinement of any theory based on empirical observation, so the computer leads to a much-heightened ability to correlate data and thereby to a dramatic refinement of our analytical powers. This all goes to say that the intellectual impact of the computer is not so much in the technique itself, but rather in the way in which it leads to a substantial restructuring of our scholarly mental categories.

A second proviso which derives naturally from the first is my concern not so much with state-of-the-art software or hardware, but rather with the most broadly based common denominator in the way of both equipment and programming.[10]

[10] At an earlier stage of the onomastic project we had envisaged a more ambitious system of programming support, which O. Rouault was going to develop and which he has described in 1988. For a number of reasons we have fallen back to a simpler set of programs, which will serve some basic research needs, in the expectation that the highly structured configuration of the data will lead others to develop their own programs.

TABLE 6. *Analytical Elaboration: Reflex.RXD Files*

(Sample elaboration performed on data files provided on computer disks; not intended for publication)

Sort by Part of Speech and Pattern

PrtSp	Ptrn	Root/Base	Meaning	NmStrct
i		ka	like	np–pr–dn
total: 1				
n	2a	aḫ	brother	np–pr–dn
	2i	il	god	np–pr–dn
	4a	qrd	to be heroic	v3–dn
	4a:i	rʾẓ	to help	n–hy
	4ai	mlk	to counsel	v3–dn
	4i	zkr	to name	v3–dn
total: 6				
u	2a	dam	blood	v3–dn
	4i	spš	sun	v3–dn
	4ia	zikar	male	v3–dn
	?	Dumu	Dumu(zi)	v3–dn
	?	kura	?	v3–dn
total: 5				
v	b	ʾmr	to see	v3–hy
	b	ʾmr	to see	v1–hy
	b	nb:	to call	v3–dn
	b	rkb	to mount	v3–dn
	b	rkb	to mount	v3–dn
	b	ryb	to replace	v3–dn
	b	šmʿ	to hear	v3–dn
total: 7				
total words:19				

Sort by Part of Speech and Root/Base

PrtSp	Root/Base	Meaning	NmStrct	Element
i	ka	like	np–pr–dn	ka
total: 1				
n	aḫ	brother	np–pr–dn	aḫa
	il	god	np–pr–dn	il
	mlk	to counsel	v3–dn	Malik
	qrd	to be heroic	v3–dn	qardu
	rʾẓ	to help	n–hy	ra:ʾiẓ
	zkr	to name	v3–dn	zikir
total: 6				
u	dam	blood	v3–dn	damu
	Dumu	Dumu(zi)	v3–dn	Dumu
	kura	?	v3–dn	Kura
	spš	sun	v3–dn	sipiš
	zikar	male	v3–dn	zikir
total:	5			
v	ʾmr	to see	v3–hy	amur
	ʾmr	to see	v1–hy	a:mur
	nb:	to call	v3–dn	ibbi:
	rkb	to mount	v3–dn	tarkab
	rkb	to mount	v3–dn	irkab
	ryb	to replace	v3–dn	iri:b
	šmʿ	to hear	v3–dn	yišmaʿ
total:	7			
total words:19				

TABLE 7. *Statistical Elaboration: Reflex.RXR and .RXP Files*

(Sample elaboration performed on data files provided on computer disks; not intended for publication)

Distribution of names according to archive

Name	e1 (main)	e2 (small)	Notes
a-a-du	0	6	
ab-NE	1	6	
da-da-NI	4	16	
da-dub-si-nu	0	6	
ga-du-wa-du	1	9	
ha-na-ba-du	2	7	
ha-za-ri_2	1	8	
ib-dur-iš-lu	2	20	
ig-da-BE	1	12	text from e1 is a ration text
iš-lu-du	1	12	
lu-du-u_3-na	0	20	
ma-kum-D=-ku-r	1	5	
ma-li-i_3-lu	1	5	written ma-li-i_3-a in e1
NAM-ša-ha-lu	0	7	
NE-ra	0	12	
NI-ba	0	10	
za-li	1	8	
zu-ma-NE	1	11	

The real quantum leap vis-à-vis traditional scholarship, it seems to me, is in the restructuring of the data for electronic data processing. Even a simple computer utilization of the data so structured is superior by an order of magnitude to standard (non-electronic) data processing. Hence it seems more useful to aim our system to computer configurations and users' skills at the low end of the spectrum, so as to serve the widest possible range of scholars. The printed output that will be part of our publications especially in the early stages will hopefully be viewed as an inducement toward a more-aggressive exploitation of the data than any merely printed version could ever make possible, however large in size and internally differentiated in structure.

With this in mind, I will describe briefly the nature of the data as distributed on disk. The three data bases described above will be made available on computer disks. The fields for these data bases correspond essentially to the columns as found in the paper edition described above, with the notes appended in separate text files, keyed to the individual entries in the data bases. The obvious difference between the electronic and the printed editions is that the electronic edition will be susceptible to a practically infinite number of correlations that can be established dynamically within the data base itself and, eventually, with other data bases to which it can be related. Two minimal examples of such cor-

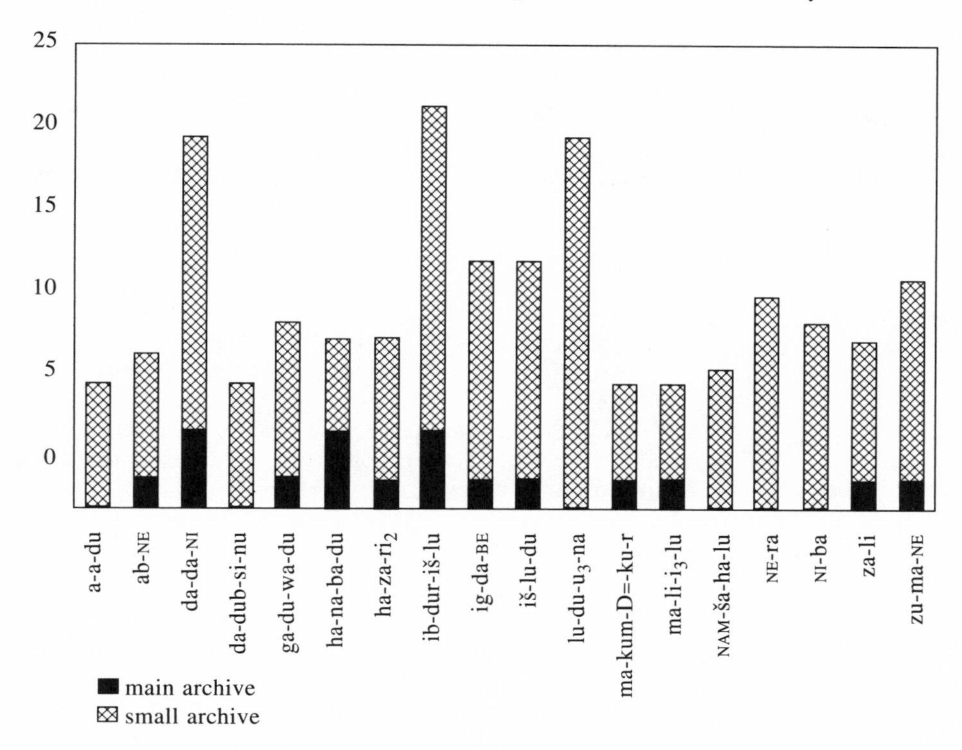

relations are offered in tables 6 and 7: in a purely indicative manner, these two tables show how special sorts and special statistical tabulations may be created, by using a very simple (and inexpensive) commercial program (Reflex).

The user's manual, which will accompany the disk edition, will not only explain details of the format and of the encoding, but will also show how to prepare the data for their utilization with commercial programs, as just mentioned. The manual will be written in such a way as to assist colleagues who are even minimally acquainted with established data base management systems to concretely make use of the data as proposed in the exemplifications provided.

Explicit statements will be provided about the data structure of the data bases (both for the ASCII and the DBMS versions), so that full independent manipulation of the data will be possible by the users.

Some of the simple programs included will perform a few formatting and indexing operations of the type we are currently using for in-house processing of the data. This includes, for instance, utilities to perform the following tasks: convert double, low ASCII characters to single, high ASCII characters for letters with diacritical marks (e.g., to convert s^ to *š*); convert numeric sign indexes to subscripts (e.g., rum12 to rum_{12}); sort on files with special characters; download special character fonts for dot matrix and laser printers.

Since the disk edition will also include all subsidiary materials given in the printed edition, such as introductions and descriptive chapters, it is apparent that any user with a laser printer will be able to reproduce exactly the text of the printed volume as published separately. Obviously, this will deal a major blow to the commercial chances of the printed edition—which is precisely why it is expected that we will not be publishing paper editions for very long. After all, no one better than an Assyriologist ought to know that, if we have come a long way from using clay, we can go an equally long way in trading paper for disks!

References

Buccellati, G.

1990a "*Cybernetica Mesopotamica.*" Pp. 23–32 in *Sopher Mahir: Northwest Semitic Studies Presented to Stanislav Segert.* Edited by E. M. Cook. Winona Lake, IN (= *MAARAV* 5–6).

1990b "The Ebla Electronic Corpus: Graphemic Analysis." In *Proceedings of the International Idlib Conference.* Edited by K. Touer. *Annales Archéologiques Arabes Syriennes* 40:8–26.

Buccellati, G., A. H. Podany, and O. Roualt

1987 *Terqa Data Bases 1. Cybernetica Mesopotamica: Texts* (disk 1A). Malibu.

Fronzaroli, P.

1979 "The Concord and Gender in Eblaite Personal Names." *UF* 11:275–81.

Gelb, I. J.

1981 "Ebla and the Kish Civilization." Pp. 9–73 in *Lingua.*

Krebernik, Manfred

1988 *Die Personnennamen der Ebla-Texte: Eine Zwischenbilanz.* Berliner Beiträge zum Vordern Orient 7. Berlin.

Milano, L.

1990 *Testi amministrativi: Assegnazioni di prodotti alimentari (Archivio L. 2712–Parte I).* ARET 9. Rome.

Platt, J. H.

1988 "Notes on Ebla Graphemics." *Vicino Oriente* 7:245–48.

forthcoming *Comprehensive Ebla Bibliography.* In *Cybernetica Mesopotamica: Bibliographies* (disk B1A and volume M1A).

Platt, J. H., and J. M. Pagan

1990 "Orthography and Onomastics: Computer Applications in Ebla Language Studies." In *Proceedings of the International Idlib Conference.* Edited by K. Touer. *Annales Archéologiques Arabes Syriennes* 40:27–38.

Platt, J. H., J. M. Pagan, and M. A. Arrington (with the collaboration of A. Archi and L. Milano)

forthcoming *The Ebla Electronic Corpus: ARET 1–4.* In *Cybernetica Mesopotamica: Manuals.*

Rouault, O.

1988 "Le traitement informatisé des données onomastiques assyriologiques." ARES 1:191–203.

Saporetti, C., J. H. Platt, and J. M. Pagan

1987 *The Middle Assyrian Laws. Cybernetica Mesopotamica: Texts* (disk 2A). Malibu.

The Ebla Exorcisms

CYRUS H. GORDON

Magic has played a prominent role largely because it claims to do what science has not yet succeeded in doing. Thus in Mesopotamia, which early on was watered by a network of canals between the Tigris and Euphrates, there was little need to resort to spells or prayers for rain. But in Canaan—which depends precariously on seasonal rain and dew—rituals, prayers for rain and dew, and incantations were a major aspect of the important fertility cult. Some of the woes of life have always lent themselves to dependence on magic: incurable diseases, pain, enemies, and (from whatever cause) fears.

There are five interconnected Eblaite incantations published by D. O. Edzard in ARET 5 (incorporating observations of M. Krebernik). The translatable parts of these incantations are of interest philologically at two levels: linguistically and as regards magical praxis. At the same time, these texts are still full of difficult passages that defy interpretation. To set forth my findings without wasting space, I present in full only text 1, giving wherever possible the transliteration, normalization, and translation, followed by a philological commentary that includes parallel passages in the other four texts. Comments on texts 2–5 are then added to cover the remaining items of interest in those tablets.

Text 1 (ARET 5: #1)

	Transliteration	*Normalization*	*Translation*
i:1	*a-za-me-du*	*ˀaṣmidu*	I have bound
	ḫa-ba-ḫa-bí	*ḥabḥabī*	Ḥabḥaby.
	a-za-me-du	*ˀaṣmidu*	I have bound
	KA-ME		(his) tongue
5	*a-za-me-du*	*ˀaṣmidu*	I have bound
	du-ḫu-rí si-ne-mu	*šinnêmō*	the barrier (?) of his teeth
	[a-z]a-me-du	*ˀaṣmidu*	I have bound
	[ ]	[ ]	[ ]
ii:1	*mu-za-da*		
	a-za-me-ga	*ˀaṣmikka*	I have bound you
	al₆	*ˁal*	on
	1 NA₄	*ˀabni*	a black

5	MI		stone
	dag-x		
	tal-da-an	*daltān*	the double doors
	ma-za-gi-lu		
	1 KA-NU	*qanû*(?)	a reed(?)
10	*ti-*É-⟨*ma*⟩*-tim*	*tihâ*⟨*ma*⟩*tim*	the sea(?)
	a-za-me-ga	*ʾaṣmikka*	I have bound you
	al$_6$	*ʿal*	by
	7 ^{GIŠ}AL$_6$		seven mighty
iii:1	*du-na-an*	*dunnân*	contraptions.
	a-za-me-ga	*ʾaṣmikka*	I have bound you
	al$_6$	*ʿal*	by
	zi-da-nu		
5	*a-ma-na-a*		
	a-za-me-ga	*ʾaṣmikka*	I have bound you
	al$_6$	*ʿal*	by
	zi-na-ba-t[i]	*ḏinabâti*	the tails
	^{d}UT[U]		of the Sun
10	*al*$_6$	*ʿal*	(and) by
	su-lu-la-a		the horns
	1 ITI		of the Moon.
	7 GURUŠ	7 *ḫardū*(?)	seven youths
iv:1	7 SIKIL	7 *ḫardâtu*	(and) seven maidens
	na-zi-a-du	*naśîʾâtu*(?)	exalted(?) (f. pl.)
	MÍ		(and) female
	1 SUD	*kabkabu*	the Star
5	*mi-nu*		
	*ti-na-*NI*-si-du*		
	a-bi-nu-um	*ʾâbinu*(*m*)	The bricklayer(s)
	i-a-ba-nu	*ʾiʾabanu*	will lay
	SIG$_4$-GAR	*libitta*	the brick(s)
10	*al*$_6$	*ʿal*	by
v:1	2 KÁ	*daltā*(*n*)	the double doors
	I-li-lu	*ʾilîlu*	of Elil
	A-MU	*ʾabî*	father
	DINGIR-DINGIR DINGIR	*ʾilī*	of the gods
5	*wa*	*wa*	and
	iš$_{11}$*-da-ga-sù*	*ištakassu*(?)	the Star
	1 SUD	*kabkabu*	has established(?) him
	MAŠKIM-E-GI$_4$-*ma*		as representative
	si-in	*sin*	to
vi:1	*i-li-lu*	*ʾilîlu*	Elil
	A-MU	*ʾabî*	father
	DINGIR-DINGIR DINGIR	*ʾilī*	of the gods

	TÚG *gi-da-du-wa*		
5	*ša-gi-du-ma*		
	a-gu-du		
	TÚG *gi-tum*		
	i-na-É-*áš*	*inaḫḫaš*	Elil, the
	na-É-*su*	*naḫâšu*	father of
10	*i-li-lu*	*ʾilîlu*	the gods
	A-MU	*ʾabî*	performs
	DINGIR-DINGIR DINGIR	*ʾilī*	the magic.
vii	(uninscribed)		
viii:1	UD-DU_{11}-GA		Spell of
	1 SUD	*kabkabu*	the Star.

ARET 5: #1 is designed to foil the mischief of a much-feared demon called Ḥabḥaby. The magician starts with the declaration that he has silenced the demon by tying his tongue and other organs of speech. He then addresses the demon directly to inform him that he (the magician) has invoked cosmic forces and performed various rituals to make doubly sure that Ḥabḥaby is rendered helpless to resist the supreme reduction to total and enduring impotence through the spell performed by the god Elil, who heads the pantheon as "father of the gods." The text ends with the grand climax: Elil himself works the magic.

i:1, 3, 5, 7. *a-za-me-du* = *ʾaṣmidu*, the preterite indicative of the simple conjugation (I or G). This tense covers the instantaneous present as well as the past, as in both Akkadian and Hebrew. Thus Akkadian 'I herewith give' is *inanna addin*; compare Hebrew *hinnê natattī* 'behold I now give'. Note that the final *-u* indicates the indicative as in Arabic and Ugaritic (and not the subjunctive as in Akkadian). Also observe that *z* and *ṣ* fall together in the orthography. The open-syllable orthography conceals the existence of closed syllables; thus *ʾaṣ* is written as though that closed syllable were two open syllables. This type of syllabary is perhaps best known from Japanese. It also happens to characterize the Aegean syllabary (Linear A, Linear B, and also the Cypriote syllabaries). Eblaite shows that it was known in the Near East since the Early Bronze Age. In such systems the zero vowel appears as though it were the same as the vowel in the adjacent syllable. Thus *a-za* is written for *ʾaṣ*. Accordingly since the vowels of *me* and *du* do not agree with the vowels in the adjacent syllables, they reflect the real vowels in the pronunciation.

i:2. Ḥabḥaby is written *ḫa-ba-ḫa-bí* in accordance with open-syllable orthography. Demonic names are often reduplicated in the Babylonian Talmud and the Aramaic magic bowls.[1] The unreduplicated form of this demon's name appears at Ugarit as *Ḥby* and in Isa 26:20 as *Ḥăbī*.

[1] Such details are discussed in C. H. Gordon, "Ḥby, Possessor of Horns and Tail," *UF* 18 (1986) 129–32.

i:4. KA-ME means 'tongue'. In normal Sumerian ME is written inside KA 'mouth' and the compounded sign is pronounced eme 'tongue'. In Aramaic the word for 'tongue' is *liššân*; in Hebrew it is *lāšôn*; in Arabic it is *lisân*; in Akkadian it is *lišân*. We may assume that the Eblaite for 'tongue' is of the same root (*lšn*) but I forbear to assign any particular vocalization because that would imply a specific classification of Eblaite, which this source leaves completely open.

i:6. The second word is 'teeth' (*šinn*) with the suffix *-êmō* 'thereof' (in this context 'his'). The first word (*du-ḫu-rí*) is elusive as to etymology. Other ancient literatures suggest that it refers to the parting of the two rows of teeth. Ugaritic *lṣb* (through which words are uttered) means the space between the two rows of teeth (*UT* §19.1393).

ii:1. *mu-za-du* possibly means '(the) exit', that is, where a word leaves the mouth of the speaker to enter the atmosphere. In which case, we suggest *môṣaʾtu* (cf. Hebrew *môṣâʾ* 'exit' + f. *-tu*), and the shift of *aʾ* > *eʾ* (*UT* §5.16) does not take place.

ii:2, 11; iii:2, 6. *a-za-me-ga* = *ʾaṣmikka* < **ʾaṣmid* + *ka* 'I have bound you'. The assimilation of *dk* to *kk* was unexpected, like so many features of Eblaite. Note also that *g* covers also *k* and *q* in the orthography, as in the Minoan syllabaries.

ii:5–6. Black stones have a special power. The Black Stone (in the Kaʿba) at Mecca is the holiest cultic object in Islam. I do not normalize MI 'black' (e.g., from the root *ṣlm* as in Akkadian, or from *šḥr* as in Hebrew), because that would imply an East or Northwest Semitic classification, respectively, for which there is no evidence in the case of this word, which is indicated by a Sumerogram that provides the meaning but not the pronunciation.

ii:7. Krebernik's suggestion that *tal-da-an* = *daltān* 'double doors' is borne out in Isa 26:20 where the *ktîb dltyk* 'your double doors' appears in a context dealing with Ḥăbī (= Ḥabḥaby). Here, *daltān* is not the dual *casus rectus* but the dual *casus obliquus*: *daltān* < **daltayn*, with the shift of the diphthong *ay* > *ā*.[2]

ii:9–10. The suggestion that KA-NU = *qa-nu* 'reed' is tentative, as is also the addition of *-ma-* in *ti-É-⟨ma⟩-tim* 'sea'. This reading has been prompted by references to *tihâmat-* 'Sea' in these texts (#4:i:6).

iii:6–12. Binding the demon by the "tails of the Sun and the horns of the Moon" invokes the totality of cosmic power because the expression is a double merism expressing totality. The sun and moon convey the notion of universality since they are the two great luminaries. The horns are in front while the tail is in the rear, thereby constituting another merism. Note that *z* covers also the Semitic phoneme **ḏ* in Eblaite orthography. The meaning of *zi-na-ba-ti* is strongly suggested by the Sumerogram KUN 'tail' that occurs in another Ebla incantation (#5:i:3, iii:3), but it is proved by Ḥaby's description in Ugaritic as *bʿl qrnm w ḏnb*

[2] See G. A. Rendsburg, "Monophthongization of *aw/ay* > *ā* in Eblaite and in Northwest Semitic," in *Eblaitica* 2:91–126.

'possessor of horns and tail' (see n. 1 above). The plain meaning of *za-na-ba-ti* renders invalid the assertion of Krebernik (followed by Edzard) that initial *ḏ cannot appear as *z* in Eblaite. (They insist that initial *ḏ- must appear as *š* in Eblaite because of *ša-*, *šè-*, *šu-*.) The bottom line in philology and linguistics is meaning. Once the meaning is established, no amount of technical hyperfinesse or inference can change it.

We do not yet know the Eblaite equivalent of ᵈUTU 'the Sun-god'. Nor has the last word been said about the derivation of *su-lu-la-a* 'the two horns'. The meaning of the latter is fixed by the ideographic writing of *su-lu-la-a*; to wit, 2 SI (#4:iii:5) 'the two horns'.

Since *su-lu-la-a* properly means 'the two horns of the crescent moon', the form is dual and might be related to Arabic *hilâl* 'the new or crescent moon'. The *h/s* correspondence is attested (albeit sporadically) in Semitic; for example, causative *h-/š-* (*hifᶜil/šafᶜel*), the pronoun *hū/šū*, the directive postposition *-h* in Northwest Semitic (see *UT* §11.1) vs. *-š* in Akkadian (*ᵓárṣah kənáᶜan* 'toward the land of Canaan' vs. *qirbiš-bâbili* 'in the midst of Babylon'), and Ugaritic *hm* vs. Akkadian *šumma* 'if'.

iii:13–iv:1. The Sumerograms GURUŠ and SIKIL mean 'young men' and 'young women' respectively. The ritual mock-battle of 'seven youths and seven girls' has a magical significance and will be discussed below. That 'young women' was to be pronounced *ḫardâtu* is established in another incantation (#3:v:1). That the masculine plural (7) GURUŠ was *ḫardū* in Eblaite may be less certain, though it is favored by Ugaritic *ḫrd*, which seems to mean 'a youth' (*UT* §19.1002). I shall also discuss *ḫardâtu* below.

iv:4. 1 SUD is to be read *kabkabu* 'the Star', probably referring to a particular star like *Kôkāb* among the Phoenicians (also in Amos 5:26). This reading is based on the variant *ga:ga:ba:bu* = *kabkabu*. The invocation of the Star is one of the means by which the magician achieves the cooperation of the head of the Pantheon. The importance of the Star is reflected in the colophon, which labels this text "Spell (of) the Star" (viii:1–2).

iv:7–v:4. This section has to do with a brick structure built by the double-door entrance of the shrine (actually = the entire temple) of Elil, the Father of the Gods. Such structures are instruments used by the magician. The spell is recited, but the praxis also calls for acts that accompany the spoken word. When the magician says "I have bound you" to Ḥabḥaby, we may assume that he actually ties a puppet representing Ḥabḥaby, and that here a *(*l*)*âbinum* 'brick-mason' is actually to lay bricks (**ilabanu* > *iᵓabanu*). The loss of the consonantal quality of *l* is to be compared with Aramaic *yəhâk* 'he will go', *limhâk* 'to go' from the root *hlk*.[3] Geez *hôka* 'to go' is the same verb. Mehri *kôb-* 'dog' (from *klb*) should also be compared.

v:6. $iš_{11}$*-da-ga-su* is very problematic. I suggest (but only as a *pis aller*) that it contains the root *škn* 'to place, establish', as in Akkadian *šakânu*. The

[3] Ezra 5:5, 7:13.

conjugation would be Gt (I_2). The meaning would be that the Star (7) is assigned an official status (such as emissary) vis-à-vis Elil.

vi:4–7. The garments actually were used in such spells. For example, in the cuneiform Aramaic incantation from Uruk,[4] the magician strips the garment of rage off his client and then dresses him in the garb of well being. In Zech 3:4–5 a change of clothes marks the transition from an impure to a pure state. Here I would suggest that the Star is clad in his regalia of authority so that he has the influence to induce Elil to perform the supreme magical act that will undo Ḥabḫaby and put a permanent end to his evil machinations.

vi:8–12. The spell ends with the almighty Father of the Gods himself performing the magic. Compare the Ugaritic Epic of Kret where, after all the gods refuse to work the magic that will cure King Kret of his life-threatening disease, El himself performs the magic (*UT* #126:v:10–28) so that Kret is brought back to health. The verb is the imperfect D (= II or *pi*ᶜᶜ*el*) of the root *nḫš* followed by the infinitive absolute. This is the verb applied to the divination practiced by Joseph by means of his special cup (Gen 44:5, 15). É never stands for the simple vowel *e* in Eblaite (or in any cuneiform text that I can recall). It always represents a syllable beginning with a laryngeal followed by an original *a*-vowel. Note that the vocalic ending of the infinitive absolute is *-u*, as in Ugaritic and Akkadian (*UT* §9.27). We are to normalize the verbal combination *inaḫḫaš naḫâšu*. Note that the vowel of the prefix is not *u* (in the II conjugation = *pi*ᶜᶜ*el*) as in Arabic and Akkadian but *i* (from *a as in Ugaritic and Hebrew; cf. *UT* §9.35).

viii:1–2. UD-DU$_{11}$-GA 1 SUD 'a spell (by) the Star' is the colophon, labeling the text. It is not a part of the incantation, as indicated by the blank column vii that separates text from colophon.

Text 2 (ARET 5: #2)

ARET 5: #2 is larger than the other Ebla incantation texts; the opening lines are broken away and much of the surface is uninscribed. It may be a practice tablet of a sorcerer's apprentice. Such a text does not lend itself to complete interpretation and yet there are parts that are very instructive.

a-zi-mi-ga (i:8, 12; ii:3, 8) = *a-za-me-ga* of text 1 and is to be normalized *ˀaṣmikka* 'I have bound you'. Note that *me* and *mi* are interchangeable orthographically. Also, note that the zero vowel can be represented in the orthography as the preceding or following vowel in the word. Thus *ˀaṣmi-* can be spelled either with *a-za* or with *-zi-mi.*

The demon is tied by 7 ^{GIŠ}AL$_6$ ^{d}É-*da* (= Hadda) 'the seven contraptions of Hadd (= Baal)'.

a-zi-mi-ga a za-za-um la-da-bu (ii:1–5) 'I have bound you on Z., O no-good-one!' Note that *a* is used instead of *ᶜal* 'on, by'. The substitution of *ˀa* for *ᶜal* is familiar in Babylonian Aramaic: from Mandaic, the Babylonian Talmud,

[4] See C. H. Gordon, "The Aramaic Incantation in Cuneiform," *AfO* 12 (1938) 105–17.

and the cuneiform Aramaic incantation from Uruk. With *la-da-bu*, compare the technical term *lâṭâbā* 'a no-good-one', and plural *lâṭâbê*, referring to demons in the Aramaic incantation bowls.[5]

Text 3 (ARET 5: #3)

Sections of ARET 5: #3, an (incomplete?) incantation, parallel, though with significant variants, sections of text 1.

Text 3 starts with ^{d}UTU *ti-a-ba-an* SIG$_4$-GAR Ì-DÍM É ^{d}*I-li-lu* A-MU DINGIR-DINGIR-DINGIR (i:1–ii:2) 'O Sun-god! May you lay the bricks (and) build the house of Elil the Father of the Gods!' (cf. #1:iv:6–v:5). Because the bricklayer (*a-bi-nu-um*) is masculine in #1, it is somewhat more likely that the Sun-god is masculine rather than feminine. However #2 by itself (with *ti-a-ba-an*) could equally well imply that the solar deity was feminine (as at Ugarit and among the Hittites). Text 3 shows that Elil is being won over by the construction of his whole temple/palace (É) and not simply its portals (as *daltān* in #1 might be construed). Compare the Ottoman title "the Sublime Porte," whereby the gate stands for the Royal Palace which indicates the sultan (even as "the White House" can man the president or his authority in expressions such as, "The White House announces that ———"). For the building of the house/palace for a god, compare the construction of Baal's palace in the Ugaritic texts. El assigns the laying of the bricks to a lesser deity (*UT* #51:iv–58:v:63).

The next section of #3 is *wa iš*$_{11}$*-da-ga-su ga:ga:ba:bu dag-da-su si-in* ^{d}*I-li-lu* A-MU DINGIR-DINGIR-DINGIR (ii:3–iii:2) 'the Star is appointed as the emissary to Elil the Father of the gods' (see the parallel passage in #1:v:5–vi:3). My suggested analysis and interpretation of the verb are conjectural. The variant for SUD 'far, distant' (#1) is here *ga:ga:ba:bu* (= *kabkabu*): a cryptic writing for the Star. The function of the Star is here called *dag-da-su* = MAŠKIM-E-GI-*ma* in #1. The meaning is provided by the service he is to render; namely, as intermediary between the magician and the supreme god Elil. Intercession is a common motif in ancient Near Eastern as well as modern religions. Specifically, in Ugaritic mythology, ᶜAnat intercedes with Asherah, who in turn intercedes with the supreme god El, who alone can authorize the construction of the palace for Baal.[6]

Immediately following is TÚG *gi-da-du-wa ša-gi-tum la-mu-gu-du ša-gi-tum* (iii:3–6); compare the parallel (with variants) in #1:vi:4–7. This section deals with a ritual performed with garments. While the Ebla incantations do not describe the praxis, ancient Near East magical usage indicates that the change of garments induces the transition from a wrong state to the right one.

The next section specifies NAG (written KA-A) A *bù-la-na-tim* DU$_{10}$ (iv:1–4) 'drink(ing) good water of the Euphrates', reflecting the Mesopotamian factor in

[5] See, e.g., bowl 13:5–6 in J. Naveh and S. Shaked, *Amulets and Magic Bowls* (Leiden, 1985).

[6] For the fragments of Ugaritic literature arranged in a proper order, translated, and interpreted, see C. H. Gordon, "Poetic Legends and Myths from Ugarit," *Berytus* 25 (1977) 5–133 (pp. 92–96, for the account of the intercession).

these incantations. The exchange of *l* for *r* (in the river name) is a common sound shift in Eblaite, where *l* can replace an original *r* (though an original *l* never shifts to *r*). This phenomenon is to be compared with the falling together of *l* and *r* in the orthography of Egyptian, Linear A, and Linear B. In dealing with those three scripts it is important to bear in mind that when Egyptian and the two Cretan languages were eventually written alphabetically (i.e., as Coptic, Eteocretan, and Greek) the distinction between *r* and *l* reappears (because of the emergence of different dialects of the same respective languages).

Very instructive is the next section: 7 GURUŠ NI/*ʾ*a_x*-bù-ḫu da-nu-nu* 7 *ḫar-da-tù* NI/*ʾ*a_x*-bù-ḫa da-nu-na* (iv:1–v:3) 'seven young men—they are girded (and) strong—(and) seven young women—they are girded and strong'. The parallel (in #1:iii:13–iv:1) 7 GURUŠ 7 SIKIL 'seven lads (and) seven girls' provides the meaning, while *ḫardâtu* (in #3) supplies the Eblaite pronunciation. In Egyptian, *ẖrd* 'child' is common. For its attestation in Ugaritic, see *UT* §19.1002. And now its appearance in Eblaite carries it back to the Pyramid Age in Semitic. In the Fourth Dynasty, *ẖrd.t* already appears in the sense of grown young women, exactly as in this incantation. Erman and Grapow (*Wörterbuch der ägyptischen Sprache* 3:398 and *Belegstellen* 3:81) list *ẖrd.t* 'child woman woman woman'. *ẖrd.t* = the consonantal skeleton of *ḫardâtu* 'young women'; the determinatives indicate youth (child) and female maturity (woman). The triple repetition of 'woman' indicates plurality.[7] That SIKIL can be read *ḫardat-* in Eblaite is certain; slightly less certain is the inference that GURUŠ = Eblaite *ḫard-*. This brings up an Egypto-Semitic problem. Although *ẖrd* has been regarded as purely Egyptian, should we regard *ḫrd* in Ugaritic and Eblaite as a loan into Semitic? Its appearance in the Early and Late Bronze Ages in Semitic Eblaite and Semitic Ugaritic make this hard to accept. We should also bring into the discussion the fact that Ugaritic *mṯ* 'child, son' and Eblaite *maš* 'child, son'[8] cannot be unrelated to Egyptian *ms* 'child, son'. The simplest explanation is that *ẖrd* and *ms* are Egypto-Semitic but that they were replaced by other Semitic words in the Iron Age, leaving the impression that they were exclusively Egyptian. There is an apt parallel to such a replacement: the common Semitic noun for 'son' is *bn* (as in Hebrew *bēn* and Arabic *ibnu*); yet the normal word for son in Akkadian is *mâru*, derived from the root *mhr*, which in Arabic refers to the young of an animal (specifically, *muhr* 'colt'). Sumerian MÁŠ designates a young goat but it comes into Eblaite as *maš-* meaning 'child, son'. Comparably, 'kid' in colloquial English is frequently used in the sense of 'child'.

[7] Note that this is attested in the Pyramid Age, specifically in the Fourth Dynasty. Hieroglyphic inscriptions bearing the names and/or titles of two pharaohs, namely Chefren (Fourth Dynasty) and Pepi I (Sixth Dynasty), have been found in the archeological context of the Ebla archives.

[8] The PN (meaning literally 'Son of the King') is written either *ma-aš-ma-lik* or *mas-ma-lik* (ARET 8:30). If my explanation of *máš*-É (as equivalent to בן־בית 'one born in the house', meaning a home-born slave as distinct from a bought slave) is correct, the origin of *máš/mṯ* 'child, son' from Sumerian MÁŠ 'young goat, kid' is accounted for.

The description of the young men and women as girded and strong suggests that they engage in ritual (= mock) combat. 'Girded' may mean 'equipped with battle gear'. The use of the wrestling belt is well attested in the ancient texts and especially in the glyptic art of Mesopotamia—notably during the Akkad period. Bellicose women are a persistent theme in antiquity; for example, the blood-thirsty ᶜAnat of Ugarit, the Egyptian goddess Sekhmet, and the Greek tradition of the Amazons who are "the peers of men in battle." The opposition of seven heroic males and seven heroic females employs the special number 7 and the merism of men and women. Note that the masculine plural suffix is -û while -â marks the feminine plural; this is common Semitic; for example, Akkadian masculine *ṭâbû*, feminine *ṭâbâ* 'they are good', and Aramaic masculine *qṭîlû*, feminine *qṭîlâ* 'they are/were killed'.

Text 4 (ARET 5: #4)

ARET 5: #4 overlaps with the preceding texts in that it evokes the tail(s) of the Sun and the horns of the Moon. As for the remainder of #4, it goes its own way.

The opening section is KI ŠU-DU$_8$ *ba-ša-nu ba-ša-nu ba ti-É-ma-du* [ ] (i:1–8) 'The earth has confined(?) the serpent; O serpent in the sea!' Compare *UT* #1003, where we find *b-arṣ* 'in the earth' corresponding to KI, and then *ym* 'sea' corresponding to *ba-tihâmat* 'in the sea'. Note that #4 uses West Semitic *ba* 'in' instead of *in* 'in', which is far more frequent in Eblaite and goes with Akkadian *in*(*a*) 'in'. The word for 'serpent' is *bašan-* (root *bṯn*) and is applied to the dragon of evil, *Lôtân* (Leviathan) in Ugaritic.[9] The repeated *ba-ša-nu ba-ša-nu* has hitherto been taken (I think mistakenly, as explained below) to indicate plurality, as is common in Sumerian but only occasionally in Semitic. (The function of the opening of #4 is, in any event, to curb the forces of evil.)

The second section reads: *en-ma da-ga-ma an-na i-za-ba-de-ga* (ii:1–4) 'so says Dagama: "I have smitten thee." This is declared by the magician (Dagama) to the dragon. Since the accusative pronoun is singular (*-ka* and *kuwâtika*), *bašanu* 'dragon', though repeated, is singular.

The next two lines, 2 *ba-li-ḫa wa-ti-a* 'the two Baliḫs———', refer to two deified rivers ending in dual *-â*. Can *wa-ti-a* be cognate with Arab *wâdi*(*n*) 'wady'? In any event the invocation of the two holy rivers reflects a northwest Mesopotamian variant of a widespread theme that the supreme god dwells at the source of "the Two Rivers." One may think of the Twin Rivers of Mesopotamia as inspiring the motif; and of the representation of the Mesopotamian goddess with the flowing vase, whence emerge the two streams. But the clearest formulation of this theme does not come from Mesopotamia, but from Ugarit on the shores of the Mediterranean. Ugaritic mythology describes El's abode as at the sources of the two rivers or two deeps (*UT* §19.1623).

[9] See *UT* #67:i:1–3 and Isa 27:1.

There are two magicians who form a team to carry out this incantation and its praxis. They both have speaking parts. We have already heard from Dagama, now we hear from his colleague: *en-ma ti-gi si-in zi-ne-éb-ti* ^{d}UTU *si-in* 2 SI ^{d}*sa-nu-ga-ru*$_{12}$ *na*-AN NU-ḪI-MU-DU (ii:7–iv:2) 'so says Tigi to the tail of the Sun (and) to the two horns of San-Ugaru (= Moon-of-the-Field): "——— let (him?) not bring!"' Here we find the singular *zinebt-* (instead of the plural *zi-na-ba-ti*), as in Ugaritic *ḥby b*^{c}*l qrnm w d̲nb* 'Ḥaby possessor of two horns and a tail'.

Instead of *su-lu-la-a* ITI we read in #4:iii:5–6, 2 SI ^{d}*sa-nu-ga-ru*$_{12}$ 'the two horns of San-Ugaru (= Moon-of-the-Field)'. The old form of the Moon-god's name is *Su-en.* The familiar form of the name is *Sin.* Note however that here in #4 the diphthong has been reduced to *a*, so that the name is pronounced *San.* This form of the Moon's name appears in the Bible in the PNs *San-ḥêrîb* (Sennacherib) and *San-ballaṭ* (= Sin-uballiṭ). R. Stieglitz has shown that the PN Beth-shan means 'House of the Moon-god', written either *Byt-šn* or *Byt-š*$^{\supset}$*n.*[10] The latter spelling reflects the full original *u+e* of *Su*$^{\supset}$*en.* The divine Ugar is attested in the GN Ugarit, whose patron deities are the paired *Gpn-w-Ugr* 'Vine-and-Field'. The name *San-Ugaru* is treated indeclinably, retaining the nominal *-u.*

The entire section we have been discussing reads: *en-ma ti-gi si-in zi-ne-éb-ti* ^{d}UTU *si-in* 2 SI ^{d}*sa-nu-ga-ru*$_{12}$ *na*-AN^{ki} NU-ḪI-MU-DU (ii:7–iv:2) 'so says Tigi to the tail/ray of the Sun (and) to the two horns of the Moon-of-the-Field: "——— do not bring"'. After the latter prohibition, comes the contrasting command: ḪI-MU-DU ^{d}*ha-da* NA$_4$ *na-mur-ra-tum* ÍB+3 TÚG SUD (iv:3–7) 'may Hadda fetch the dazzling stone (and) the triple-garment of the Star(?)'. The meaning is far from clear. My conjectural suggestion is that the god Hadd (= Baal) is to fetch the special garment for the Star (SUD = Kabkabu) (who, as we know, is appointed to induce Elil to perform the requisite magic).

Directly afterward comes the following parallel climactic section: ḪI-MU-DU NA$_4$ *gi-gi-za-nu* NA$_4$ *ba-ra-du* LÚ-ŠÀ *wa-mu-mu mu-ra-du du-na*-NE LÚ *a-a-ti-mi* (v:1–iv:1) 'may the man of the ——— (and) the man of the ——— fetch the *gigizanu*-stone and the "hail"-stone ———'. Note that *mu-ra-du*, orthographically and phonetically, could be the masculine singular participle meaning '(he who) bestows gifts' (the root is **wrd*); the conjugation is causative ($^{\supset}$*af*^{c}*al* in Arabic and *šaf*^{c}*el* in Ugaritic; see *UT* §19.1150). But this analysis of *mu-ra-du* will stand or fall depending on the correct interpretation, which has not yet been established. LÚ *a-a-ti-mi* could mean 'the man of the falcon'. A bilingual defines a certain MUŠEN ('bird') as Eblaite *a-a-tum* (= Hebrew ^{c}*ayya*(*t*-) 'a certain bird of prey' (such as the "falcon").[11] The genitive suffix (attached to the feminine *-t*) *-tim* is written in open-syllable orthography *-ti-mi*. Note the reference to MUŠEN 'bird' in the sequel.

Immediately following is the final section: ḪI-MU-DU (erasure) AN N[I]N-UŠ-MUŠEN-ŠEŠ-2-IB DUL-DUL *ma-ša-gi* ÍB-2 TÚG SA (vi:2–8), which orders a divine bird to fetch a garment. The reference to the garment parallels (with obvious

[10] R. Stieglitz, "Ebla and the Gods of Canaan," in *Eblaitica* 2:78–89, especially 87.

[11] MEE 4:352 #049.

variants) a passage already covered in an earlier incantation (#3:iii:3–6). Possibly this text is to be concluded on another tablet.

Text 5 (ARET 5: #5)

ARET 5: #5 is an incantation which ties in unmistakably with the preceding texts, but it is full of exegetical difficulties.

KUN 'tail' (i:3, iii:3), though in obscure contexts, recalls *zinebtu* and *zinabâti* 'tail(s) = ray(s)' of the Sun in the preceding texts.

AN NIN-UŠ-MUŠEN-ŠEŠ-2-IB DUL-DUL *ma-šè-gi* ÍB-2 TÚG *ir-ga-tum* ŠU AB-SI-GA *a*-NE [———] (ii:3–iii:2). This parallels, with notable variants, #4:vi:3–9. See the notes to #4 above.

There are a number of *figurae etymologicae*: *bu-ru*$_{12}$ *ba-ra-ru*$_{12}$ (iii:10–11), *ḫu-mu-zu ḫa-ma-zi* (iv:9–10), and *gu-lu ga-wa-lu* (v:2–3). The final *-u* (specifically in *ba-ra-ru*$_{12}$, *ḫu-mu-zu*, and *ga-wa-lu*) may be the *-u* ending of the infinitive absolute that goes with this construction in East as well as Northwest Semitic (see *UT* §9:27).

The cryptic writing *ga:ga:li:la* (v:6) may stand for *galgal* 'wheel', with *-li-* to represent vowelless *l*.

DNs include ^{d}UTU (iv:5) 'Sun', ^{d}NI-LAM (vi:8), and 2 ^{d}*ba-li-ḫa* (vii:7). ^{d}UTU occurs repeatedly in connection with the 'tail(s) of the Sun' and 'the Two Baliḫ Rivers' which have been discussed under #4:ii:5 above.

7 TUN GAL 7 TUN TUR (v:7–8) 'seven large TUNS (and) seven small TUNS' indicate a ritual involving 7 + 7 objects totaling 14. When Utnapishtim's ark lands after the Deluge, he sets up twice seven (= fourteen) cultic vessels. In the preceding incantations, 'seven young men (and) seven young women' illustrate the widespread predilection for seven and for its double.

This text too may not have been completed. The final columns (viii–xiii), lined off by the scribe, are uninscribed.

Ebrium at Ebla

WILLIAM W. HALLO

In November 1976, Paolo Matthiae, the excavator of Ebla, and Giovanni Pettinato, the (then) epigrapher of the expedition, landed in New York for their first and highly publicized lecture tour of the United States. Their initial stop was at New York University, where they, and all who came to hear them, were besieged by the media. I myself consented to answer the persistent questions of a reporter from *Newsweek*, though I should have known better. Of an interview that probably lasted an hour, only two sentences survived into print, but they were zingers: "It's debatable, but it is possible that Ebla's Ebrium is the link in genealogy between Noah and Abraham. These tablets reopen the whole question of the historical authority of the Book of Genesis."[1]

Contrast this maximalist pronunciamento, stripped bare of all the usual scholarly hedges, with an equally extreme illustration of the minimalist position, of more recent vintage: "There is no strictly philological evidence for the tenure of Ebrium as en [king]." "The burden of proof is in fact upon those who would prefer to view the extant texts as the royal archives and to posit that Ebrium and Ibbi-Zikir, not to mention other persons, were the rulers of the whole city-state." Piotr Michalowski, to whom we owe these revisionist views, proposes, as an alternative, that "it is conceivable that we are dealing with the fragmentary documentation of but one of many major organizations in the city, whose chief administrator was designated en."[2]

Thus the battle-lines are drawn with respect to Ebrium—or should we say Ebrum or even Ibrum since, to quote Edmond Sollberger, "the etymology of the name is uncertain, but a connexion with Akkadian *ibrum* 'friend' is by no means ruled out."[3] On one view, he was a great king, not only of the city of Ebla but of

Author's note: Lecture delivered to the Center for Ebla Research, New York University, May 21, 1989. The written version was submitted to the editors shortly thereafter; no attempt has been made to update this essay by reference to materials published in the last several years.

[1] *Newsweek*, November 15, 1976, as quoted by H. Shanks, *The American Zionist* 49:5 (June–July 1979) 23.

[2] P. Michalowski, "Third Millennium Contacts: Observations on the Relationships between Mari and Ebla," *JAOS* 105 (1985) 293–302; quotations from 295 n. 18 and 297. Cf. also M. J. Geller, "The Lugal of Mari at Ebla and the Sumerian King List," in *Eblaitica* 1:145: "The idea of the en at Ebla representing kingship . . . must be subject to serious doubt."

[3] ARET 8:25. But cf. M. Krebernik, "Zu Syllabar und Orthographie der lexikalischen Texte aus Ebla," *ZA* 72 (1982) 178–236; 73 (1983) 1–47, esp. pp. 205 and 210–11.

an entire empire—an empire inscribed in clay, as Pettinato entitled his book on the archives of Ebla[4] —whose memory may still reverberate in the Hebrew Bible; on the other, he may have been little more than the chief administrator of one of many organizations in the city of Ebla. How are we to choose between these alternatives, between these two extremes of credulity and skepticism? For, as I put it in my 1989 presidential address to the American Oriental Society, we must set limits both to our credulity and to our skepticism.[5] The truth, as so often, probably lies somewhere in between.

Fortunately, a tool lies at hand, thanks to the rapid pace at which the Ebla texts are being published—a tool that Michalowski himself proposed,[6] namely prosopography, or the study of individuals identified by their personal names. This technique needs to be distinguished from onomastics, the study of names from the linguistic point of view. Much good work has already been done on the onomastics of Ebla; a bibliography on the subject recently compiled by Giorgio Buccellati lists over fifty items, and Buccellati himself has launched a project for an "Onomastic Repertory of Ebla," which will employ all the resources of computer technology and will devote considerable attention to the prosopographic component.[7] But the published literature has, until very recently, included only two tentative efforts in the area of systematic prosopography, by Pettinato himself and by F. Pomponio.[8] Now, however, a major stride has been taken in this direction by the publication, in 1988, of a symposium held three years earlier in Rome. Dealing with both the onomastics *and* the prosopography of Ebla, the volume is entitled *Eblaite Personal Names and Semitic Name-Giving* (it is edited by Alfonso Archi, the current epigrapher of the expedition).[9] It is Archi's own contribution to the volume (together with Maria Biga and Lucio Milano) that enables me to corroborate my own perusal of the published texts in search of Ebrium.[10]

Before attempting a thumbnail sketch of Ebrium (or Ibrium as I should call him in keeping with current convention), and deciding whether he was king or commoner, we need to consider the nature of the evidence. Abundant as they are, the third-millennium texts from Ebla are limited as to their genres. They include no monumental texts at all—normally the best source for names, titles, filiation, and realm of rulers. In the canonical category, they feature no epics, king lists, omens, or chronicles—which are the stuff of which Mesopotamian historiography is made. They do include important lexical texts, which provide

[4] G. Pettinato, *The Archives of Ebla: An Empire Inscribed in Clay* (Garden City, NY, 1981).

[5] W. W. Hallo, "The Limits of Skepticism," *JAOS* 110 (1990) 187–99.

[6] Michalowski, "Third Millennium Contacts," 295–96.

[7] National Endowment for the Humanities Grant Application RT 21111 (11–22–88); see above, pp. 107–28.

[8] Pettinato, *Archives of Ebla*, 123–33; F. Pomponio, "La datazione interna dei testi economico-amministrativi di Ebla," in *Ebla 1975–85*, 249–62.

[9] A. Archi (ed.), *Eblaite Personal Names and Semitic Name-Giving: Papers of a Symposium Held in Rome July 15–17, 1985* (ARES 1; Rome, 1988) (henceforth cited as ARES 1).

[10] A. Archi, M. G. Biga, and L. Milano, "Studies in Eblaite Prosopography," in ARES 1:205–306 (henceforth cited as "Studies").

some useful data, and, of course, there are the thousands of archival texts. But even these archival texts, extensive and numerous though they are, rarely have date formulas, and those that exist lack the explicit allusions to the reigning king in the form then evolving in Mesopotamia—and with them the readiest clue to the identity of successive rulers.

To begin with the lexical evidence, the great bilingual Sumero-Eblaite vocabulary published by Pettinato equates Sumerian nam-en with Eblaite *malīkum*,[11] and nam-nam-en with *tumtallikum*[12]—both derived from West Semitic *mlk* 'to rule', not from Akkadian *malāku* 'to counsel, to advise',[13] let alone from the Amorite *malku, māliku* 'chthonic demon, dead king' (though that may indeed be the source of the numerous Eblaite theophoric names in Malik).[14] An equation is also alleged between Sumerian NIN and Eblaite *maliktum* 'queen', but I have not been able to verify this.[15] I note only the "sign-name" *urusum* for NIN (ereš) in the text published by Pettinato as the "Syllabary of Ebla" and by Archi as "The 'Sign-list' from Ebla."[16]

The more common Sumerian word for king, lugal, appears in the "Vocabulary of Ebla," but, unfortunately, without an Eblaite equivalent.[17] From Mesopotamian lexical texts, we know that it was equated with Akkadian *šarru*, and this in turn with West Semitic *malku*, but we cannot always be sure whether the Sumerogram LUGAL is used in the Eblaite archival texts in the sense of 'king' (*šarru* = *malku*) or of 'prince, high official' (West Semitic *śar*).

A third candidate for the royal title at Ebla is Akkadian *bēlum*, feminine *bēltum*, or their Eblaite cognates *baᶜalum*, *baᶜaltum*, construct state *baᶜal*, *baᶜlat*. In Mesopotamia, the masculine term is equated with both lugal and en (Emesal umun), the feminine with ereš and nin (Emesal gašan), but at Ebla they are equated with BE (or BAD) and BE.MÍ, respectively—generally interpreted as abbreviated writings of the Akkadian (or Eblaite) forms.[18] But this title appears to be restricted to deities, notably but not exclusively Dagan, who may be

[11] *ma-li-gú-um*: MEE 4:318, VE 1088. Cf. on this form P. Fronzaroli, "Un atto reale di donazione dagli Archivi di Ebla (TM.75.G.1766)," *SEb* 1 (1979) 6.

[12] *tù-tá-(li)-gú-um*: MEE 4:318, VE 1089. Cf. on these forms M. Civil, "Bilingualism in Logographically Written Languages: Sumerian in Ebla," in *Bilinguismo*, 83; Fronzaroli, "Un atto reale," 6; and Archi, "Les textes lexicaux bilingues d'Ebla," *SEb* 2 (1980) 86.

[13] J. Renger, "Zur Wurzel MLK in akkadischen Texten aus Syria und Palästina," in ARES 1:165–72.

[14] Note that *ma-lik* occurs *only* in personal names, and *only* in syllabic spelling, and never with the divine determinative, but this is true of many other divine names as well. Cf. A. Archi, "Cult of the Ancestors and Tutelary God at Ebla," in *Fucus: A Semitic/Afrasian Gathering in Remembrance of Albert Ehrman* (ed. Y. L. Arbeitman; Current Issues in Linguistic Theory 58; Amsterdam, 1988) 103–12, esp. 110.

[15] E. Sollberger, ARET 8:62 s.v. *ma-lik-tum*. I note only the equation nin-ni = *a-ḫa-tum* 'sister' in MEE 4:326, VE 1183.

[16] Pettinato, MEE 3:187–205, #30; Archi, "The 'Sign-List' from Ebla," in *Eblaitica* 1:91–113.

[17] MEE 4:339, VE 1402′.

[18] Archi, "Les titres de en et lugal à Ebla et des cadeaux pour le roi de Kish," *MARI* 5 (1987) 37–52, esp. 38 and nn. 14–15.

the "lord of the land" that appears both in a literary text[19] and in the Vocabulary of Ebla.[20]

When we turn, then, to the archival texts, we find a curious imbalance. While the word for 'queen' is always written syllabically (*ma-lik-tum*), the words for king are invariably written logographically (lugal or en), the single published exception being the case of a certain *I-mi-ir*-NI, *ma-lik* of *I-za-rí*-LUM^{ki},[21] to which Archi adds an unpublished instance, an unnamed *ma-lik* of *I-ni-bu*$_4$^{ki}.[22]

When these words are reduplicated, representing the plural, they cannot well refer to a multiplicity of reigning or at least living kings of Ebla. In the case of lugal-lugal, the plural may well allude to men of slightly lesser status such as princes or high officials.[23] In the case of en-en, Pettinato's proposal to understand them as 'former rulers'—especially in the sense of former but still living—needs to be modified.[24] In some cases they may be deceased rulers, as in the contemporary texts from Lagash,[25] where 'spirits' (gídim) could even be substituted for en-en.[26] This is demonstrably the case in "a list of offerings to dead kings."[27] In others, as Archi has shown, they are the contemporary rulers of cities other than Ebla.[28]

To return to the list of dead kings for a moment: these are, to date, the best source for the names and order of the Eblaite rulers. They are of two kinds. One is attested so far by only a single example, a sort of school-text[29] with personal names, beginning with what looks like a "genealogy of the Ebla Dynasty."[30] This "genealogy" begins with *Iš*$_{11}$*-ar-Da-mu* who, while unknown as king (en),

[19] D. O. Edzard, ARET 5:31: *be-al*$_6$ KALAM-*tim*.

[20] MEE 4:289, VE 795a and 795b. Cf. Krebernik, "Zu Syllabar und Orthographie," 183.

[21] ARET 4: #24:17. Cf. Michalowski, "Third Millennium Contacts," 294 n. 6.

[22] Archi, "Les titres," 37: TM.75.G.2241. For an unnamed en of *I-ni-bu*^{ki} see, e.g., ARET 8: #531:13.

[23] F. Pomponio, "I lugal dell'amministrazione di Ebla," *Aula Orientalis* 2 (1984) 127–31. Cf. Archi, "Les titres," 37; and W. Heimpel, "Review of G. Pettinato, *Ebla: Nuovi orizzonti della storia*," *JAOS* 109 (1989) 123.

[24] Pettinato, *Archives of Ebla*, 78–79.

[25] A. Deimel, "Die Listen über den Ahnenkult aus der Zeit Lugalandas und Urukaginas," *Orientalia* 2 (1920) 32–51; Y. Rosengarten, *Le régime des offrandes dans la société sumérienne d'après les textes présargoniques de Lagaš* (Paris, 1960), chap. 2; and eadem, *Le concept sumérien de consommation dans la vie économique et religieuse* (Paris, 1960), chap. 7.

[26] P. Talon, "A propos d'une graphie présargonique de ŠL 577 (Gídim)," *RA* 68 (1974) 167–68. Cf. also the writing en-en-durun$_x$ (TUŠ.TUŠ)-ne and simply durun$_x$-ne (cf. J. Bauer, *Altsumerische Wirtschaftstexte aus Lagasch* [Studia Pohl 9; Rome, 1972] 474).

[27] ARET 7:150, as described by Archi, "Studies," ARES 1:212. Cf. his earlier edition of the text in "Die ersten zehn Könige von Ebla," *ZA* 76 (1986) 213–17; and his remarks in "Cult of the Ancestors," 105–6.

[28] Archi, "Studies," ARES 1:217–18.

[29] If so, it is "the only school-text found outside the main archive L.2769" (thus Archi, "Studies," ARES 1:214 n. 30).

[30] Archi, "Studies," ARES 1:213; copy of obverse in Pettinato, *Archives of Ebla*, 43; partial transliteration by Pettinato, "Testi cuneiformi del 3. millennio in paleo-cananeo rinvenuti nella

occurs once as 'son of the king' (dumu-nita en).[31] It continues with [*Ìr*]-*kab*-[*Da*]-*mu* and [*I*]*g-rí-*[*iš-Ḫ*]*a-lam*[32] who have been regarded, hitherto, as successive kings of Ebla—but in the opposite order.[33] This suggests that the entire list must be read backward, like the "Ahnentafel" of Shamshi-Adad contained within the Assyrian King List,[34] and also like the Ugaritic King List.[35] Like the Assyrian King List and the "Genealogy of the Hammurapi Dynasty," it may have included nonroyal ancestors. In any case it takes matters all the way back to the eponym of the dynasty whose name, like that of their city itself, is *Eb-la* (written without the geographical determinative). What follows in this text are six obscure entries and then personal names arranged, as in later Mesopotamian school-texts,[36] by their first component.

A second type of text listing the dead kings of Ebla consists of offering lists. Here the kings again appear in reverse order, as in the school-text. The most complete example, already mentioned (above, n. 27), gives ten names, beginning with [*Ìr*]-*kab-Da-mu* and *Ig-rí-iš-*⟨*Ḫa*⟩*-lam*; the remaining eight names are identical with names 4–11 in the school-text. As in the Ugaritic King List, each is preceded by the word 'deity' or 'deified' (dingir). Each is (apparently) provided with one sacrificial sheep. The fifth and sixth names in the list recur in a similar context but in the opposite (i.e., chronological) order in another offering list, and the sixth in still another list.[37] Still earlier royal names occur, one or more at a time, in the coronation texts for the new king (en-gibil), recently studied by P. Fronzaroli.[38]

---

campagna 1974 a Tell Mardikh = Ebla," *Or* 44 (1975) 369–71; English translation in Pettinato, "Old Canaanite Cuneiform Texts of the Third Millennium," *Monographs on the Ancient Near East* 1 (1979) 152–54.

[31] MEE 2: #30 = ARET 2: #14:41. Cf. Archi, "Studies," ARES 1:215, for another possible mention of the same prince. Cf. also the more frequent princely name NE-*ar-Da-mu* (ibid.).

[32] Or read *Ḫa-iš*$_{11}$ (with Edzard, ARET 2:113), rather than *Ḫa-lam* (with Archi, "Studies," ARES 1:208), which is a geographical rather than a divine name. At Ebla, geographical names functioning as theophoric elements in personal names usually add the geographic determinative; cf. Archi, "Die ersten zehn Könige," 217 n. 21. Cf. perhaps Haniš, but note also Halum (ARET 8:10).

[33] Pettinato, *Archives of Ebla*, 70; and Archi, "Studies," ARES 1:207–8.

[34] First recognized as such by B. Landsberger, "Assyrische Königsliste und 'Dunkles Zeitalter,'" *JCS* 8 (1954) 33. Cf. W. W. Hallo, "Zāriqum," *JNES* 15 (1956) 221 n. 9.

[35] *KTU* 1.113. Cf. K. A. Kitchen, "The King List of Ugarit," *UF* 9 (1977) 131–42, who also cites Egyptian parallels (p. 135).

[36] E. Chiera, *Lists of Personal Names from the Temple School of Nippur* (Publications of the Babylonian Section 11; Philadelphia, 1916–19); and W. G. Lambert, "An Old Akkadian List of Sumerian Personal Names," in *A Scientific Humanist: Studies in Memory of Abraham Sachs* (ed. E. Leichty, M. deJ. Ellis, and P. Gerardi; Philadelphia, 1988) 251–60.

[37] Archi, "Studies," ARES 1:212 n. 24; and idem, "Die ersten zehn Könige," 215.

[38] P. Fronzaroli, "Il culto dei re defunti in ARET 3.178," in *Miscellanea Eblaitica* (ed. P. Fronzaroli; Quaderni di Semitistica 15; Florence, 1988), 1:1–33; and idem, "A proposito del culto dei re defunti a Ebla," *NABU* (1989) 1–2. Cf. also Archi, "Studies," ARES 1:214.

Of all these names, however, only Igrish-Halam and Irkab-Damu are attested in other texts with the full title 'king of Ebla' (en *Eb-la*^{ki}). The former occurs thus in a list of assignments of gold and other metals, the latter in the much-debated "Hamazi letter" and one other document.[39]

Some names *not* included in the lists of dead kings but thought to belong to kings of Ebla allegedly occur, very occasionally, with the abbreviated title 'king' (en) but without the addition of Ebla. They are Arrurum (Ar-ennum),[40] Ebrium,[41] and especially Ibbi-Zikir.[42]

Several reasons can be suggested why so few explicit references to the full royal title are found in the texts. One would be the nature of the documentation, already discussed above. In the case of the earlier names of the dead rulers, it could be argued that their archives did not survive, if indeed they ever existed. In the case of the latest name on the school-text, Iš'ar-Damu, Archi suggests that he may have died shortly after, or even before, succeeding to the kingship.[43] In the case of Arrurum, it could be argued that the lists of dead kings were composed in his reign, and therefore did not include his name. But in the case of Ebrium and his son Ibbi-Zikir, who are generally agreed to have followed Arrurum, we must now ask whether they were in fact kings of Ebla at all.

Since the search for references to Ebrium (and Ibbi-Zikir) as "king of Ebla" or even simply as "king" has proved unproductive and inconclusive, I now turn to the innumerable references to an unnamed king (en) to see if any of them can be assigned to Ebrium. (Ibbi-Zikir must be left for another occasion.) This approach was first tried by Pomponio, who compared the names of persons identified as children of the king with those identified as children of Ebrium and found only one clear case of convergence.[44] That case is significant, since it is Ibbi-Zikir, Ebrium's presumed successor, who occurs frequently as son of Ebrium, and once as "son of the king" in a text which, unfortunately,

[39] The three texts are (1) MEE 2: #45 (for which see Pettinato, *Archives of Ebla*, 69 and 109 n. 5; and Archi, "Studies," ARES 1:215), (2) TM.75.G.2342 (for which see Pettinato, *Archives of Ebla*, 97–98; and Pettinato, "Gli archivi reali di Tell Mardikh-Ebla," *Rivista Biblica* 25 [1977] 238–42), and (3) TM.75.G.1536 (for which see A. Archi, "Berechnungen von Zuwendungen an Personengruppen in Ebla," *Altorientalische Forschungen* 13 [1986] 197). Pettinato, *Archives of Ebla*, 69 and 109 n. 7, cites this last text as calling Irkab-Damu simply 'king' (en).

[40] MEE 2: #37:rev.xi:5–6. Pettinato, *Archives of Ebla*, 109 n. 8, also cites TM.75.G.1881 (unpublished). Archi, "Studies," ARES 1:208 n. 16, disputes both these instances.

[41] ARET 3: #274. For the alleged case of TM.75.G.1444 (Pettinato, *Archives of Ebla*, 109 n. 9), see Michalowski, "Third Millennium Contacts," 295 n. 18.

[42] ARET 1: #3:49, ARET 1: #8:41, ARET 4: #18:3, ARET 7: #23, Archi, "Reflections on the System of Weights from Ebla," in *Eblaitica* 1:72 n. 29. Archi, "Studies," ARES 1:208 n. 16, now disputes all these instances.

[43] Archi, "Studies," ARES 1:215. Cf. M. G. Biga and F. Pomponio, "Iš'ar-Damu, roi d'Ebla," *NABU* (1987) 60–61. Identity with the Iš'ar-Damu of TM.75.G.1444:34 (D. O. Edzard, "Der Text TM.75.G.1444 aus Ebla," *SEb* 4 [1981] 35–59) seems unlikely.

[44] Pomponio, "Datazione."

is as yet unpublished.[45] (It is useful in this connection to recall that the Sumerian terms *son/daughter of the king* imply *prince* or *princess* [in general], rather than specifically son or daughter of the reigning king, a principle recently invoked also for the Ebla texts.)[46]

But these sparse indications can now be augmented by the more systematic prosopographic studies of Archi. He has provided many more references to the families of the kings and of Ebrium respectively, and added some of their principal officials as well. And here there is a conspicuous lack of convergence. Archi does not record the unpublished reference to Ibbi-Zikir as son of the king, and among the fifty names he *does* so record, not one corresponds to the twenty-five sons of Ebrium.[47] The same situation is true of the names identified as 'man' or 'the one' (lú̩) of the king or Ebrium, respectively, which Archi takes (at least sometimes) as equivalent to 'son'.[48] Though it is not entirely clear whether, therefore, both mean 'son' or both mean 'man', his examples of known sons of Ebrium described as 'man of Ebrium' can already be augmented, especially by reference to archive L. 2752.[49] Archi's list of the sons of the king can also be expanded, but the additions provide no new equations with the sons of Ebrium.[50]

Turning next to daughters of the king, Pomponio lists ten of these, and ten daughters of Ebrium—all with different names.[51] But in at least one case, one is tempted to equate *Ṭá-bi* or *Ṭù-bí*, the daughter of the king, with *Ṭù-bí-Ma-lik*, the daughter of Ebrium.[52] The latter is identified as a priestess (dam-dingir) in common with a number of other princesses.[53] It may also be worth noting another daughter of Ebrium, *Kir-su-ud.*[54]

Pomponio's list is considerably expanded by Archi, who registers thirty-one daughters of the king and twelve daughters of Ebrium, still without a clear overlap.[55] But again there is one tempting equation, namely between *Ar-za-du*,[56] daughter of the king (and also—in other texts—sister of a king, implying that

[45] MEE 1: #1179 (TM.75.G.1741).

[46] Cf. already W. W. Hallo, "Review of M. Çığ, H. Kızılyay, and A. Salonen, *Die Puzriš-Dagan-Texte der Istanbuler Archäologischen Museen: Teil I*," *BiOr* 14 (1957) 232 s.v. dumu-lugal; and idem, "Review of D. O. Edzard, *Die 'zweite Zwischenzeit' Babyloniens*," *BiOr* 16 (1959) 236–37. For the Ebla texts, see Archi, "Gifts for a Princess," in *Eblaitica* 1:117.

[47] Archi, "Studies," ARES 1:222–35.

[48] Ibid., 222, 233–34, 305 n. 4.

[49] For example, *I-rí-ik-Da-mu* [lú *Ib-rí-um*]: ARET 3: #458; *A-ba-ga*: ARET 8: #525:18, ARET 8: #541:10; *Gi-rí*: ARET 8: #534:24; *In-ma-lik*: ARET 8: #534:56, ARET 8: #540:10. For archive L. 2752, see E. Sollberger, ARET 8:6–9; and Biga, "Studies," ARES 1:305–6.

[50] *A-ti*, *I-ku*-NI, *Ig-rí-iš-Da-mu*, KA.DU, *Ṭù-bi-Da-mu*, *Ù-ti*; cf. Pomponio, "Datazione," 258–59.

[51] Ibid., 260.

[52] MEE 1: #831 (where, however, the name is transliterated *Ṭa-bí*, which is also the reading of Archi, "Studies," ARES 1:239 s.v. *Da-bí*) and ARET 1: #3:54″ respectively.

[53] Cf. Archi, "Studies," ARES 1:248.

[54] For the reading *kir* of the sign PEŠ, see Edzard, ARET 2:15; and Krebernik, "Zu Syllabar und Orthographie," 193.

[55] Archi, "Studies," ARES 1:238–42.

[56] Sollberger, ARET 8:17, reads "*ar-ṣa-tù*: 'earth'(?)."

her brother had succeeded her father),[57] and *Bar-za-du*, daughter of Ebrium. I note here the garments issued to a certain girl for anointing the head of *Tá-ḫir-Ma-lik*, daughter of Ebrium, on the occasion of her (Tahir-Malik's) wedding (*in* u_4 níg-mu-sá), along with garments for the "bridesmaid's" father, his brothers, and his wife.[58]

When we turn to the other "women" of the king, we face the problem that Sumerian dam, literally 'spouse' is used at Ebla not only as a logogram for 'wife', but also for 'servant-girl'.[59] In fact, polygamy is well attested, at least in courtly circles,[60] and a whole hierarchy can be reconstructed for the harem, so that the distinction between wife and servant-girl may have faded in the lower ranks.[61] With these reservations in mind, we may note that Pomponio counted twenty-six wives of the king, and four wives of Ebrium. One name recurs in both lists, namely *Kir-su-ud*, whom we have already met as *daughter* of Ebrium. We meet her now as his woman or wife in one text[62] and as the wife of the king in another, where she heads a list of six such wives.[63]

Archi distinguishes no less than sixty of these royal women (of whom some forty-five functioned at any one time) and sixteen women of Ebrium, including the mother of Ibbi-Zikir (Azimu).[64] This time there is considerable convergence between the names on these expanded lists. In addition to many new attestations of *Kir-su-ud*, both as dam-en and as dam Eb-rí-um, a certain *Nu-*ru_{11}*-ud* (once: *Nu-lu-ud*) occurs many times as dam-en and once as dam of Ebrium; the *Ḫa-su* (variant *Ḫa-sum*) who occurs as wife of Ebrium bears comparison with the *Ḫa-su-ud* (variant: *Ḫi-su-ud*) who is wife of the king; and the frequently mentioned *Ma-ga-ra-du* wife of the king (dam-en) resembles the unique *Ma-ga-na-a-du* wife of Ebrium (dam Ebrium). Note also the *Zi-gi-*ru_{11}*-du* (variant: *zi-kir-*ru_{11}*-du*), omitted by Archi, who occurs as wife of Ebrium in connection with the city of *A-te-na-at*^{ki},[65] which is frequently associated with Ebrium.[66]

But perhaps the most interesting text in this connection is one which D. O. Edzard characterized as the record of four speeches of Ebrium (or Jabrium in his transcription) to the king on behalf of three of his sons and on related mat-

[57] Archi, "Studies," ARES 1:247–48; for the implications, cf. pp. 220, 248 (with reference to Sabib-Dulum).

[58] ARET 1: #11:41. Cf. Archi, "Ancora su Ebla e la Bibbia," *SEb* 2 (1980) 20 = A. Archi, "Further concerning Ebla and the Bible," *BA* 44 (1981) 146, who cites unpublished parallels.

[59] H. Waetzoldt, "Frauen (dam) in Ebla," in *Ebla 1975–1985*, 365–77. Cf. also Archi, "Studies," ARES 1:245; and idem, "About the Organization of the Eblaite State," *SEb* 5 (1982) 207.

[60] Archi, "Studies," ARES 1:249, based on wool for "the mothers of the sons of the king of Mannuwad and for his wife."

[61] Ibid.

[62] ARET 3: #877; for the reading, see above n. 54. Note that the reading *Ib*-[*rí-um*] is partly restored.

[63] MEE 2: #19:rev.x:18 = ARET 1: #11:55.

[64] Archi, "Studies," ARES 1:250–59, 245.

[65] ARET 3: #468:obv.viii; ARET 3: #732:iv.

[66] Cf., e.g., ARET 3: #458:rev.ii, ARET 3: #628:ii, ARET 3: #672, and perhaps TM.75.G.1669 obv.viii:7, for which see Archi, "Notes on Eblaite Geography," *SEb* 2 (1980) 12.

ters.[67] The repeated introductory clause of these speeches (or letters?),[68] 'Thus (spoke) Ebrium to the king' (*en-ma Eb-rí-um sí-in* en), leaves no doubt that Ebrium was not, or at least not yet, king. But what Edzard did not realize is that the "related matters" in this text *also* concern the family of Ebrium, for the *Ti-lu-du* who acts for her sons in paragraphs 3 and 15 is herself known as a wife of Ebrium! She occurs in three administrative texts near the head of a list of wives of Ebrium (dam-dam *Eb-rí-um*, respectively dam-*sú*), preceded only by the sisters of the king Sabib-Dulum and Tarᵓib-Damu, and by Azimu, the mother of Ibbi-Zikir.[69] And her name is followed in these same lists by, among others, five of the names that follow hers in paragraphs 17–18 of Edzard's text, namely *Ti-a-Da-mu* and the familiar *Kir-su-ud*, Tamur-Damu, Halud and Hasum. Hence the entire text can be seen to involve negotiations between Ebrium and the king regarding his own family.

Speaking of family, we may pass over here other members such as brothers, sisters, fathers, and mothers, all ignored by Pomponio and dealt with briefly, or in other connections, by Archi.[70] The status of 'elder brother' (šeš-pa$_4$) suggested by Sollberger may be rather the anointed (or anointing) priest (pa$_4$:šeš);[71] in any case there are no coincidences between the names identified as such with Ebrium and the king respectively.

I will also refrain from considering here the officials serving the king and Ebrium and move on instead to some tentative conclusions.

Archi himself came to the conclusion that Ebrium, his son Ibbi-Zikir, and his grandson Ṭubuhu-Hadda were not kings, but held a position second in importance to the king's, which, provisionally, he would like to call vizier.[72] Such a high position would be one reason for the prominence of their names in the archives of Ebla; another would be the assumption that most of the archives come from that part of the administration of Ebla which they headed. Archi's new interpretation represents a major contribution to the reconstruction of Ebla's history. In articles which appeared as recently as 1987[73] and 1988,[74] he still refers to Ebrium as *king* of Ebla. His insightful new study (which arrived as I was finishing a first draft of this paper) will thus need to be weighed carefully and dispassionately by other scholars, even if they lack his firsthand acquaintance with the published texts and his access to the yet unpublished ones. I will content myself here with subjecting the theory to four brief questions that it raises in my mind: (1) What was the name of the office held by Ebrium and his descendants? (2) How did it become hereditary? (3) What functions did it involve? (4) With

[67] Edzard, "Der Text TM.75.G.1444 aus Ebla," 35–59.

[68] So Michalowski, "Third Millennium Contacts," 297.

[69] Archi, "Studies," ARES 1:248, 257 (19), 260–61 (2–3).

[70] Cf. especially ibid., 244 (brothers of Ibrium).

[71] ARET 8:66 s.v. šeš-kúr.

[72] Archi, "Studies," ARES 1:220.

[73] Archi, "Gifts for a Princess," 115–24 (e.g., p. 117: "the time when Ibrium was king").

[74] Archi, "Cult of the Ancestors," 108: "king Ibrium."

what rulers, foreign or domestic, can it be correlated? These questions must be raised even if they cannot all be answered satisfactorily here and now.

Let us look, first, for a possible title—other than 'king'—for Ebrium, his son Ibbi-Zikir, and his grandson Ṭubuhu-Hadda. We may rule out 'lord of the treasury' or 'lord of the palace' (lugal SA.ZA$_x$^{ki})[75] since the only attested incumbent of this office is a certain *A-ḫa-ar*,[76] conspicuous by his obscurity. But the Sumerian title for 'vizier', or at any rate for the official ranking immediately after the king, is sukkal-maḫ, literally 'chief messenger', more freely 'prime minister'.[77] While this exact term is unknown at Ebla, the term sukkal (literally 'messenger') is attested both in the "sign-list" from Ebla[78] and in the archival texts.[79] And one of these texts actually lists the son of a sukkal-gal 'a great sukkal' between those of an 'elder' and of the 'king'.[80] If the reference here is to the Eblaite hierarchy and not, as Archi thinks,[81] to that of Mari, it may just possibly answer our first question.

As to the hereditary character of the office, we may compare the situation in neo-Sumerian Lagash, where Lani, his son Ur-Shulpaʾe, and his grandson Ir-Nanna functioned successively as sukkal-maḫ of the Ur III Empire.[82] But it must be admitted at once that the analogy is a tenuous one, if only because the hereditary principle in the royal house itself was far more securely established (and documented) in Ur III times than at Ebla.

Let me turn then to the functions of the presumed office, confining myself for the most part to Ebrium himself, and even in his case only to some of his multifarious activities. First, and perhaps most disconcertingly, Ebrium functions twice in what is generally taken to be a date formula, '1 year, finished(?) / Ebrium' (DIŠ MU TIL/*Eb-rí-um*), once at the end of a very large account tablet (MEE 2: #1) and once in a small fragmentary one (ARET 3: #436). Similarly, we find the notation '1 / year / new one / Ibbi-Zikir' (DIŠ MU GIBIL I.) at the end of an as yet unpublished text belonging to one of the smaller archives excavated in 1976.[83] In

[75] Archi, "Studies," ARES 1:219 n. 42.

[76] MEE 2: #42, where he occurs in the "day-date" at the end of the text. Cf. in a similar role at the end of MEE 2: #43 a certain NI-*zi* lugal. Geller, "The Lugal of Mari," 142–43, considers him the king of Mari. So also A. Archi, "Le synchronisme entre les rois de Mari et les rois d'Ebla au IIIe millénaire," *MARI* 4 (1985) 48–49.

[77] W. W. Hallo, *Early Mesopotamian Royal Titles* (American Oriental Series 53; New Haven, 1957) 92–121, 128, where it is translated as 'prime minister'. For a different view, see D. M. Scharaschenidze, "Die sukkal-mah des alten Zweistromland in der Zeit der 3. Dyn. von Ur," *Acta Orientalia* 22 (1974) 103–12.

[78] MEE 3: #199:90 = Archi, " 'Sign-list' from Ebla," 97 (90).

[79] Cf., e.g., ARET 3: #749:i and ARET 3: #798:iii.

[80] ARET 7: #6:4. The writing gal-sukkal reflects the Mesopotamian preference for putting gal ahead of signs with which it forms a kind of ligature.

[81] ARET 7:14, 233.

[82] See above, n. 77.

[83] Biga, "Studies," ARES 1:302. With the notation MU/GIBIL, cf. the occasional Old Babylonian year-dates of the form mu-gibil-egir . . . —such as Samsu-ditana 2,19 and 21, for which

the present state of our knowledge, we cannot really assess the significance of these formulas.[84]

Second, Ebrium (or his agents) traveled widely—to *A-la-ga*^{ki} (ARET 1: #18:3 and *passim* in this text), *Ḫa-ra-bí-ig* (ARET 4: #11:24), Tuttul ([*Du*]$^{?}$-*du-la*^{ki}) (ARET 4: #15:8),[85] *La-ru*$_{12}$*-ga-du*^{ki} (ARET 1: #11:18),[86] *Ma-nu-wa-at*^{ki} (ARET 3: #657), even Kish (ARET 8: #540:28—a subordinate is involved). He or his son Ibbi-Zikir were briefly resident (lú : tuš) in *Ḫal-sum*^{ki} (ARET 3: #868), and *Su-ra-an*^{ki} (ARET 3: #807).

Third, Ebrium and his son made votive and other offerings to the deities and their temples in the company of the king, the queen, and other royalty, or received gifts from them. So, for example, a pound of silver formed an offering (nídba) of the king and Ebrium to the god Resheph (^{d}*Ra-sa-ap*) (ARET 3: #635).[87] The queen-mother made several gifts (níg-ba) to Ibbi-Zikir son of Ebrium (ARET 3: #380), including one on the occasion of the marriage of Ebrium's daughter (ARET 4: #30). The king himself made a present or votive offering when the wife of Ibbi-Zikir gave birth to a son.[88] Ibbi-Zikir in turn was heavily involved in the "official cult at Ebla," as Pettinato has shown.[89]

There is no time here to go into the numerous economic and administrative activities of Ebrium and his descendants. Suffice it to say that they receive and deliver, buy and deposit enormous quantities of metals and clothing,[90] and dispose of sizable amounts of livestock and agricultural products.[91] They command the loyalties of numerous officials and functionaries in much the same manner as the king himself. In short, while they are often clearly distinguished from the king in any given text, the overall picture that emerges is of a family at or near the pinnacle of authority and the center of activity.

Finally, if they are not successors to the known kings of Ebla, can we say that they were contemporary with them? Archi has provided the makings of a relative chronology, involving the entire family of the king, certain officials (notably the judges), and even contemporary kings of Mari.[92] In the Appendix, I have tried to

---

see S. I. Feigin and B. Landsberger, "The Date List of the Babylonian King Samsu-Ditana," *JNES* 14 (1955) 144; and J. J. Finkelstein, "The Year Dates of Samsuditana," *JCS* 13 (1959) 41, 44.

[84] For lists of Ebla "date-formulas," see Pettinato, MEE 1:xxxii–xxxiii; idem, *Archives of Ebla*, 145–47; and idem, "Relations entre les royaumes d'Ebla et de Mari au troisième millénaire, d'après les archives royales de Tell Mardikh-Ebla," *Akkadica* 2 (1977) 22–23.

[85] Here apparently offering votive gifts in the company of the queen(-mother) *Du-si-gu*.

[86] If du$_{11}$-ga here means 'order or make (an offering)'. For the place-name, see F. M. Fales, "*(L)Arugatu*^{ki} in a Ugaritic Text?" *SEb* 7 (1984) 83–85.

[87] Cf. also above, n. 85.

[88] ARET 3: #801; cf. Pomponio, "Datazione," 252.

[89] G. Pettinato, "Culto ufficiale ad Ebla durante il regno di Ibbi-Sipiš," *OA* 18 (1979) 85–215 and plates 1–12. See especially the tabulations on pp. 188–93.

[90] Cf. Archi, "Studies," ARES 1:210.

[91] Ibid., 209; cf. also above, n. 89, for offerings of small cattle by Ibbi-Zikir and others.

[92] For the family of the king, see Archi, "Studies," ARES 1:222–62; for judges, see pp. 263–65; for kings of Mari, see idem, "Le synchronisme," 47–51.

represent some of these proposals graphically. Unfortunately it is precisely the identity of the *kings* of Ebla that remains uncertain, and has perforce to be represented by X, Y, and Z. Perhaps X is Igrish-Halam, Y is Irkab-Damu, and Z, for all we know, the hapless Išʾar-Damu. In fact, in their short note on Išʾar-Damu, Biga and Pomponio have proposed still another solution to this problem. In their opinion, "Ebrium and his descendants are part of the royal family" and they even add a fourth generation ruler (Irhak-Damu) after Z.[93] While they themselves furnish no proof for this assertion, I call attention to the fact that an Išʾar-Damu appears in the "deposition" of Ebrium discussed earlier. If he is, as Edzard, suggests, the son of Tulidu, and if she is, as I have noted, a wife of Ebrium, then Ebrium is husband to the mother of the king of Ebla!

Obviously, much remains tantalizingly elusive about Ebla and about Ebrium at Ebla. Whether he was king or vizier or something else (a sort of Lord Mountbatten to the royal family?) may never be known for sure. But the concentrated documentation, now estimated to cover no more than thirty-odd years, is gradually yielding to analysis, made possible by the speedy publication of the texts and the wide interest they have generated. The Center for Ebla Research at New York University has contributed to this interest both through its symposiums and through its publications. I am glad to have taken a part in its ongoing efforts.

[93] See above, n. 43.

Appendix: Relative Chronology of Ebla

King (en) of Ebla	Queen	"Vizier"	Judges	King (lugal) of Mari
X	Dusigu	Arrurum	Lada + Ennanil Ennanil + Iptur-Išar Ennanil + Irʾam-Dar	Iplul-Il, NI-zi Enna-Dagan
Y	Tabur-Damu	Ebrium	Ennanil + Iš-Damu Iš-Damu + Ilʾe-Išar	Ikun-Išar
Z		Ibbi-Zikir	Iš-Damu + Ganunum Iš-Damu + Ennani	Hidaʾar
?		Ṭubuhu-Hadda		

Eblaite *sa-su-ga-lum* = Hebrew *ssᶜgr*

GARY A. RENDSBURG

The Eblaite lexical texts, as with all such texts from the cuneiform world, abound with information on the flora and fauna of the Near East. In particular, there are numerous birds listed in these documents.[1] The identification of these birds can be a difficult matter, but the task is made simpler when collateral evidence is available. The Sumerian terms often can be linked with the same or similar terms appearing in other Sumerian texts,[2] while the Eblaite terms sometimes have cognates in the other Semitic languages.[3]

In MEE 4: #9–11:xi:28–29 appears the bilingual equation Sumerian nam-dar-mušen = Eblaite *sa-su-ga-lum* (=VE 1097). The Sumerian equivalent would suggest a colored bird of some sort (dar = "color").[4] While the exact form does not appear in previously attested Sumerian texts, about a dozen other terms for bird include the element dar (a-dar-dar-mušen, da-dar-mušen, dar-mušen, dar-gi-zi-mušen, etc.).[5]

The Eblaite form is no doubt the cognate of later Northwest Semitic *ssᶜgr*, attested in Deir ᶜAlla and in Hebrew. It appears in the former in Combination I, line 7, written consonantally *ssᶜgr*.[6]

The context at this point in the inscription is the reversal of natural happenings, and in this particular case we read *ssᶜgr ḥrpt nšr* 'the *ssᶜgr*-bird reproaches the eagle'. Accordingly, we may conclude from the Deir ᶜAlla text that *ssᶜgr* refers to a small bird, one that normally would not be a threat to the eagle.

Author's note: For assistance on Assyriological matters in the preparation of this brief article, I am indebted to my colleague David I. Owen.

[1] The standard work, though published before the Ebla texts came to light, is A. Salonen, *Vögel und Vogelfang im alten Mesopotamien* (Helsinki, 1973). For the bird list from Ebla, see G. Pettinato, "Liste presargoniche di uccelli nella documentazione di Fara ed Ebla," *OA* 17 (1978) 165–78.

[2] See, e.g., D. I. Owen, "Of Birds, Eggs and Turtles," *ZA* 71 (1981) 29–47; and idem, "Observations on the Ebla Bird Lists and the Ur III Summary Account FLP 145," in MEE 3:277–78.

[3] E.g., MEE 4: #89–90:iii:1–2 $buru_4$-mušen = *a-a-tum* (=VE 1370′) with the latter equaling Hebrew *ʾayyâ*, a forbidden bird mentioned in Lev 11:14, Deut 14:13, and Job 28:7. See C. H. Gordon, "Eblaitica," in *Eblaitica* 1:22.

[4] R. Labat, *Manuel d'épigraphie akkadienne* (Paris, 1976) 91.

[5] Salonen, *Vögel und Vogelfang*, 101, 151–56; Owen, "Of Birds, Eggs and Turtles," 36–37; Pettinato, "Liste presargoniche di uccelli," 167–68.

[6] J. A. Hackett, *The Balaam Text from Deir ᶜAllā* (Chico, CA, 1980) 47.

The word appears in Biblical Hebrew in two places. In Isa 38:14 the name of the bird is written as two words *sûs ʿāgûr*, and in Jer 8:7 the text actually treats the form as two separate terms *sûs* (Qere *sîs*) *wĕʿāgûr*. Early translators and commentators were split as to whether these words refer to one bird or to two separate birds.[7] The LXX at Isa 38:14, for example, translates simply *chelidon* 'swallow', implying that *sûs ʿāgûr* is but one species.[8] Similarly, the Vulgate at Isa 38:14 translates *pullus hirundinis* 'young swallow', apparently understanding the word *ʿāgûr* as an adjective following the noun *sûs*.

Other traditional sources, on the other hand, understood the Hebrew expression as referring to two separate birds, not only in Jer 8:7 where the word *and* is specifically included, but also in Isa 38:14 where the conjunction is lacking.[9] The form *sûs* typically has been translated 'swallow' or 'swift',[10] and the form *ʿāgûr* generally has been rendered 'crane'.[11]

The evidence of both the Deir ʿAlla inscription and the Eblaite bilingual suggests now that the latter interpretation of these words as two birds should be discontinued. Instead, we most probably are dealing with only one bird, as sensed by such early sources as the LXX and the Vulgate in their renderings of Isa 38:14.[12] To assist us in further identifying this species, note that Jer 8:7 refers to migration and that Isa 38:14 refers to the chirping (*ṣpṣp*) of this bird. It is more than likely, therefore, that the *ssʿgr* was a migratory songbird.

For the identification of Eblaite *sa-su-ga-lum* and Hebrew and Deir ʿAlla *ssʿgr* to be correct, we must assume that in this instance the consonant *s* is represented in the Eblaite syllabary by the S-signs. This would run contrary to the normal use of the Z-signs to signify *s*.[13] But occasionally, other examples of

[7] For much of what follows I am indebted to two unsigned entries in the *ʾEnṣiqlopediya Miqraʾit*: 5 (1968) 1008–9, and 6 (1971) 73–74. See also E. Ben-Yehuda, *Millon ha-Lashon ha-ʿIvrit* (Jerusalem, n.d.), 8:3988–89, 9:4305–6.

[8] The Revised English Bible (Oxford and Cambridge, 1989) 622 also translates 'swallow', but then adds a marginal note "*so Gk; Heb. adds* a wryneck." Apparently, the scholars who produced the REB believed that the *Vorlage* of the LXX had only *ss*, without the *ʿgr* of the MT. But this remains an unproved assumption, and it is just as likely that the *Vorlage* of the LXX read *ssʿgr* (either as one word or as two), which the translators correctly understood as the name of a single bird. On the specific choice of 'wryneck' to render *ʿāgûr*, see G. R. Driver, "Birds in the Old Testament, II: Birds in Life," *Palestine Exploration Quarterly* 86 (1955) 132.

[9] Note the comment of I. W. Slotki, *Isaiah* (London, 1949) 180: "The word *or* is implied."

[10] F. Brown, S. R. Driver, and C. A. Briggs, *A Hebrew and English Lexicon of the Old Testament* (Oxford, 1906) 692; L. Koehler and W. Baumgartner, *Lexicon in Veteris Testamenti libros* (Leiden, 1953) 656; and Driver, "Birds in the Old Testament," 131.

[11] Thus already Saadia Gaon on his comment to Isa 38:14, and the Jewish Publication Society versions of both 1916 and 1978. See the discussion in Driver, "Birds in the Old Testament," 131–32.

[12] The presumed Hebrew original *ssʿgr* may have split into two words due to the attraction of the first syllable to the word *sûs* 'horse', with *ʿāgûr* developing into an independent vocable. Or, there may have been a bird name *sîs*, as actually exists in Arabic, meaning 'swift', and this may have led to splitting *ssʿgr* into two terms.

[13] M. Krebernik, "Zu Syllabar und Orthographie der lexikalischen Texte aus Ebla, Teil I," *ZA* 72 (1982) 214.

S-signs to represent *s* have been posited, for example, Eblaite *sà-la-tum*, *sà-a-tum* ‘farina’, cognate with Akkadian *siltu*, Hebrew *sōlet*, Aramaic *sōlĕtā*;[14] Eblaite *sa-ʾà-bù* ‘drag away’, cognate with Hebrew, Arabic, and Ethiopic *sḥb*;[15] Eblaite *ra-sa-um* ‘wet, damp’, cognate with Akkadian *russû* ‘bathe’, Ethiopic *rasḥa* ‘damp’;[16] and perhaps Eblaite *su-bù-lu* ‘fastening stone’ (?), cognate with Mari Akkadian *sablum*, Hebrew *sēbel* ‘burden’.[17]

In light of these examples of S-signs used to represent *s*—three sure and one possible—there can be little doubt that Eblaite *sa-su-ga-lum* is a third-millennium etymon of Hebrew and Deir ʿAlla *ssʿgr*.

The exact identification of this bird still cannot be determined with certainty, but the clues from Ebla, Deir ʿAlla, and the Bible allow us to conclude that it was a small, colored, migratory songbird. My tentative suggestion is the golden oriole.[18] This species is common throughout the Near East (including northern Syria and Israel), it migrates to Africa in the winter, it is “colourful and quite unmistakable,” and it is well known for “the flutish and distinctive song of the male.”[19] In short, it meets all the requirements of the *ssʿgr*, at least as far as can be determined from the references to this bird in ancient Near Eastern texts.

[14] See F. Pomponio, “‘Peculiarita’ della grafia dei termini semitici nei testi amministrativi eblaiti,” in *Bilinguismo*, 315.

[15] G. Conti, *Il sillabario della quarta fonte della lista lessicale bilingue eblaita* (Quaderni di Semitistica 17 = Miscellanea Eblaitica 3; Florence, 1990) 73.

[16] Ibid., 82–83.

[17] See K. Butz, “Bilinguismus als Katalysator,” in *Bilinguismo*, 132.

[18] Other possibilities are several species of warblers and wagtails, but the golden oriole is the most likely candidate.

[19] U. Paz, *The Birds of Israel* (Lexington, MA, 1987) 228. See also F. S. Bodenheimer, *Animal Life in Palestine* (Jerusalem, 1935) 140, 155; E. Smolly, *Ṣipporim be-Yiśraʾel* (Ramat-Gan, 1968) 64–65; R. Inbar, *Ṣippore ʾEreṣ Yiśraʾel* (Tel Aviv, 1971) 50–51; and B. E. Allouse, *Birds of Iraq* (Baghdad, 1962), 3:39–40 and plate XIII (this plate also appears in Salonen, *Vögel und Vogelfang*, Tafel XIII).

Index

Ebla Texts

Biblical References